8311

McNEE'S LAW

Sir David McNee

McNEE'S LAW

COLLINS
8 Grafton Street, London W1
1983

William Collins Sons & Co. Ltd
London · Glasgow · Sydney · Auckland
Toronto · Johannesburg

First published 1983
Copyright © Sir David McNee 1983

ISBN 0 00 217007 8

Photoset in Linotron Sabon by
Rowland Phototypesetting Ltd
Bury St Edmunds, Suffolk
Made and printed in Great Britain by
William Collins Sons & Co. Ltd, Glasgow

*To my wife Isabel,
and daughter Heather*

CONTENTS

ILLUSTRATIONS

ACKNOWLEDGEMENTS

As I have discovered, writing a book calls for a great deal of patience and support from those nearest to you. As she has done throughout my career, in this task also my wife Isabel has given me all that and more. I am indebted to my erstwhile colleague and close friend Jimmy James who has discussed the book with me in detail and given me, as usual, good and sound advice – not all of which I have taken. My thanks go also to Barbara Bell, my former typist at the Yard, who in her retirement has tackled the thankless task of typing and retyping endless drafts, and to my two former staff officers John Newing and Bill Taylor who have read successive drafts and checked them for factual accuracy; any errors are mine not theirs.

IN PERSPECTIVE

I SET OUT to write the story of my life. I suppose I have done that, but in looking at the end result I must admit that it is less an autobiography and more an account of the years I spent as Commissioner of the Metropolitan Police. Those were turbulent years for Britain. In politics a Labour Government fell and the Conservative Government elected in its place pursued policies which aroused considerable controversy; the Labour Party moved further to the Left, and a new political party, the Social Democrats, was born. Fringe political parties, like the National Front and the Socialist Workers, took to the streets to pursue their aims. It was a period of severe economic depression. Unemployment rose to over three million with major casualties being young people. Racial issues came to the fore, sharpened by the recession and fuelled by extremists of the right and left.

Internationally the years were no quieter. Afghanistan was invaded and occupied; Poland was in turmoil; the Middle East – Iran, Iraq, Israel, Lebanon, Syria, Egypt – was rarely at peace. Zimbabwe became a nation by a painful process of birth. The frontiers of South Africa saw ceaseless border warfare. The location of nuclear missiles was the centre of protest and the neutron bomb was born. The tragedies of Ireland – north and south – dominated the news. Acts of terrorism were commonplace at home and abroad. And all this was reflected in one way or another on the streets of London.

When my appointment as Commissioner was first announced I immediately came under the spotlight of television. One interviewer asked what difference I expected to find between being Chief Constable of Strathclyde and being Commissioner of the Metropolitan Police. On television you have little time to consider your answers and the best I could do was to reply that I thought the principles of good policing tend to be the same everywhere and that perhaps the policing of London would be like policing Strathclyde with a multiplier. John Timpson was in charge of the programme and he ended with the words, 'A multiplier indeed!' He spoke with more truth than he knew, as I was to learn by hard experience.

First, there are features and responsibilities of the Metropolitan Police which distinguish it from any other police force. The relationship between the Metropolitan Police and other police forces in the United Kingdom is not always correctly understood. The Metropolitan Police provides certain national services like the availability of central criminal records and fingerprints at New Scotland Yard, and is always ready to help with expert and other assistance if asked. But this is as far as it goes for each police force is autonomous, and the Metropolitan Police has no brief, sometimes contrary to what is supposed, to investigate serious crimes committed outside the Metropolitan Police District. In early years some police forces asked for experienced senior detectives from London to help investigate murders etc. in their areas, but this ceased following the amalgamation of small police forces into much larger units. There are, of course, close working relationships at all levels and at all times between officers of provincial forces and Metropolitan Police officers, and much mutual assistance.

The Metropolitan Police District comprises the whole of Greater London, exclusive of the City of London, and includes thirty-two London Boroughs together with parts of Essex, Hertfordshire and Surrey. Unlike any other police force in Britain, the Metropolitan Police has a direct and continuous responsibility for protection of the Queen and the Royal Family. Not only are their officers on duty at Buckingham Palace, Windsor Castle and other royal residences, but all the protection officers for Her Majesty and her family are Metropolitan Police officers. The whole force is involved on royal occasions like the Prince of Wales's wedding, and each year there are more than 300 occasions on which members of the Royal Family travel to official functions in London.

Similar special responsibilities fall to the Metropolitan Police for the protection of heads of state and other VIPs who come to London, and for the security and protection of major conferences, like the Commonwealth Conference.

All embassies and the premises of High Commissioners – nearly 250 buildings in all – are in London, and all are possible targets for acts of terrorism, demonstrations or abuse.

The Government and Parliament are located in London and this means that special protection has to be provided for the Prime Minister, other ministers, the Houses of Parliament and for government buildings. The constitutional rights of Members of Parliament have to be safeguarded and mass lobbies around Parliament have to be policed. It is not unusual these days to have more than fifty such lobbies of Parliament annually, each involving thousands of demonstrators.

All police forces have problems with crime, public order and so on, but the commitments in London are exceptionally heavy. Nearly 50% of robberies recorded in England and Wales, and about 70% of all those where firearms are used, take place in the Metropolitan Police district. Around 55% of all registered drug addicts in England and Wales are registered in London. More than half of the terrorist bombings and shootings in Britain have occurred in London. Over 25 million people pass through London Airport in any one year. In addition to a resident population of around seven million, hundreds of thousands of people commute in and out of the capital each day and around eight million foreign tourists visit London each year. Over 600 demonstrations, more than 300 Football League matches and many other sporting occasions have to be policed each year.

To cope with this and much more, as well to meet the demands of ordinary policing and the control of traffic, the strength of the Metropolitan Police now stands at 26,500 officers. It is these men and women who had to face up to the many major and more ordinary events which characterized the years of my Commissionership.

The prolonged and sometimes violent industrial dispute at the Grunwick factory in Cricklewood.

The National Front marches in Lewisham and Southall which led to street violence, injury to hundreds of police officers and civilians, and to the tragic death of Blair Peach.

A major increase in acts of terrorism by Arabs and the IRA, which included the murder of Airey Neave MP and the six day siege of the Iranian Embassy.

Riots at Brixton and Southall.

The annual Carnival at Notting Hill.

The funeral service of Lord Mountbatten at Westminster Abbey.

The major processions and celebrations of the Silver Jubilee of Her Majesty the Queen.

The 150th Anniversary of the Metropolitan Police.

The celebrations of the eightieth birthday of Her Majesty the Queen Mother.

The wedding of His Royal Highness the Prince of Wales.

Major events such as these make heavy demands on the men and women of the force, but it is doubtful whether they are any more difficult and complex than the day to day policing of London. As London's chief police officer it is easy to become preoccupied with the policing of major events and exceptional incidents to the detriment of routine operational policing. I had continually to remind myself that there was a police force to run and that I had a constant responsibility for the welfare of all the police officers, special constables, civil staff and cadets in the force. Above all, it was necessary to consider the ever present and pressing needs of London's citizens.

Giving attention to day to day requirements is not always easy. It is also a much more difficult task to keep one's finger on the pulse of policing in a force of over 40,000 persons (26,500 police officers,

15,000 civil staff, 2000 special constables, and 600 police cadets) than in a force of less than 10,000 officers. In addition to co-ordinating the work of four Assistant Commissioners and maintaining a working relationship with all police Commanders and heads of civil departments – all undertaking work of a widely different character – it is crucial to get through to the policeman and woman on the ground to ensure that he or she understands what you are seeking to achieve and what needs to be done.

I take comfort at least from certain facts which are not in dispute. During the time I was Commissioner, police pay, and especially the pay of London police officers, was substantially increased in recognition of the importance of their role and special responsibilities. Second, thousands more officers were made available for policing the streets of London.

To make best use of this additional manpower, I looked initially – as I have always done throughout my police service – at the organization of which I was head. By the end of 1979 the police organization in districts and at headquarters had been substantially revised; by 1981 all the departments of the large civil support staff had been totally reviewed – for the first time since 1829 – and the consequent reorganization put in hand. Provision of a comprehensive computerized system of command and control to cover the whole force was launched in 1978. By the end of 1980 the methods of recruitment and training, at all levels, had been comprehensively reviewed with outside assistance and most of the recommendations which followed put into effect. Perhaps most important of all, more frequent meetings and a closer friendship had been established, at the top of the force and locally, with representatives of the London boroughs, with heads of Churches, with community leaders, and with many others.

At an early stage I introduced a Five Year Plan which set out objectives for the heads of all police and civil departments. This was related to the period which even then I expected to be my allotted span. Meeting these objectives involved a series of major undertakings and careful fiscal management, and progress was secured only by constant oversight from the top.

It is certainly not for me to judge whether what was done was worthwhile and how far this or that succeeded or failed. I am content to let the record stand and readers can judge for themselves.

What follows must perforce be part only of my story, for to tell fully some of the events, like the siege of the Iranian Embassy or the riots, would make books in themselves. Without more ado then, let me start with my beginnings.

I

Early Life

AN ONLY CHILD, I was born in a typical Glasgow tenement of the
1920s.

Made up of a number of 'closes', comprising three floors with
three two-roomed apartments on each floor, by comparison with
today it was very primitive accommodation. The two rooms in
which my parents lived had an inside water closet, which by local
standards put us among the more well-to-do. On rising in the
morning washing was done under a single tap – with cold water
only, of course – in the kitchen sink. Friday night was not music
night but time for the weekly ritual of bathing in a zinc tub in front
of the kitchen fire, and it was only when I was older that I went to the
Glasgow Corporation public baths to stand in a queue waiting my
turn for use of a so-called modern bath.

The 1920s were difficult times. Money was short, and what
there was had to be spent on the necessities of life. Pennies had to be
counted. Glasgow's tenement dwellers, including my family, knew
more than a little of what deprivation meant. Such experience is
never forgotten and its recollection has come back to me over and
over again throughout my life when meeting men, women and
children facing poverty and hardship. The rough and tumble of life
in central Glasgow during the years of the Depression left indelible
impressions on all who lived through it, and I am no exception.

During my time as a chief police officer, but particularly when I
was Commissioner of Police, I had to deal with many demonstrations connected with industrial disputes or with controversial issues

like picketing during strikes, and I was not infrequently told by people who claimed without much justification to represent the working class, that I was acting unreasonably and that I knew nothing of industrial troubles and trade union affairs. The truth of the matter is that as the son of a railway worker who was a member of a railway union throughout his working life, trade union activities and the interests of industrial workers were always part and parcel of my early family life.

My father, John, who is happily very much alive today, was the eldest of a very large family and at fourteen he knew what it was to work for a living. He was running errands for a Glasgow grocer. At eighteen he joined the London, Midland and Scottish Railway (the LMS) at the lowest grade on the locomotive side. He advanced through a variety of jobs to be driver of many famous trains, including the 'Royal Scot', and finally to hold a senior position in the locomotive sheds in Glasgow. A hard worker himself, he has always had strong views about people's duties and responsibilities, firmly believing, as I do, that if you want to get anywhere in this world and make any contribution you have to work for it.

To give one example, when my father was working as a fireman on a train travelling from Edinburgh to Glasgow, he had to climb to the top of the tender to pull back the coal. He was so preoccupied with what he was doing that he failed to notice a low overhead bridge and as the train passed beneath it, my father was knocked heavily by the brickwork and fell back into the tender. The whole of his body was badly bruised but he finished the journey to Glasgow before retiring in much pain to his bed at home. I can remember to this day that he regarded his recovery as a regrettable enforced absence from work and his only wish was to get back to his job as quickly as possible.

My mother, Mary Blackstock, was the daughter of a railwayman – a telegraph line worker, who was one of the same kind as my father. When my grandfather died in his ninetieth year the doctor commented, 'Mrs McNee, they're not making them in this mould any more.'

The eldest of a family of three, my mother had lived through a hard upbringing. Her mother had died when she was very young and her married life was not much easier, for she often rose at all hours of the night to get my father to work on time, which very often involved him in a five mile walk (not something which many workers would contemplate today). She was born and brought up in Glasgow, but her family roots were in Dumfriesshire – Lockerbie in particular – and as a boy Dumfriesshire was for me the greatest place in the world.

Why? Because I would leave the grey, hard confined streets of central Glasgow and travel by train with my mother to stay with her aunt and cousins in the country. It was another world. During these visits I learnt to love the countryside and the activities to be found there. I was taught by my mother's cousins to fish in the River Milk, a tributary of the River Annan. This sport has remained an interest and relaxation for me throughout my life, although only too rarely enjoyed.

The visits to Dumfriesshire were not rare, as my mother sought to take me there every holiday from school as a way of escape from Glasgow and its tenements. She was able to do so because of the allocation of free travel tickets available to railway workers like my father.

The pleasure I took in the countryside did not mean that I was unhappy in Glasgow. On the contrary, the street in front of the tenements was our playground and it was there that I would play football with other boys – and girls – until chased off by the local policeman. In summer a wicket would be drawn in chalk on a wall for a game of cricket or rounders. And there were other games like 'kick the can' or 'hopscotch' with a peever, which is how we Scots refer to a stone puck, or 'spin the peerie', which was a kind of whipping toy, or skipping with odd bits of rope (for buying a proper skipping rope was beyond our means). It was all rough and ready stuff. It taught me how to survive. It taught me how to give and take. I value my childhood for the lessons learned in Glasgow's streets and tenements. It taught me about human nature which a more affluent and protected childhood might not have done.

My parents had first met in an evangelical mission hall – the Grove Street Institute – and it was this mission hall which was to be a predominant influence over my early life. Mission halls were established on nonconformist principles in many parts of Scotland by Christian businessmen at the end of the nineteenth century following the evangelical mission of two Americans, D. L. Moody and Ira D. Sankey, and they made a great contribution to the life of the Church and people in Glasgow.

Among the earliest recollections of my boyhood are of going with my mother and father to services in our mission hall, sometimes on three or four occasions on a Sunday and as many times during the week. Each Sunday there was a service at 11 a.m., Sunday School at 2 p.m., Bible class at 5 p.m. and an evening service at 7 p.m. If frequent attendance at church was all that was needed to make me good, I would never have been in any difficulty!

Such attendance at church services may seem burdensome today, when going even once to church on a Sunday is sometimes regarded as an unwelcome interruption, but I did not find it a matter for complaint; it was wholly part of my life, week in and week out, and accepted as such. This pattern of regular attendance at mission hall services continued for eighteen years until I was called up for service in the Royal Navy, and if nothing else it gave me a knowledge of that great book, the Bible. The teaching of the scriptures to those coming to the mission halls was not by highly educated men but, by heavens, they were enthusiastic, and capable of bringing out the meaning of a biblical passage so that this raw young Glaswegian and others could understand it.

The pastors at the mission halls – each maintained financially by the congregations – were fine men. George Hood was the Pastor at Grove Street Institute and as you listened to him speak or watched him go about his work, you could but say, as many did, 'There goes a truly Christian man – a man of God.' The help which such men provided in Glasgow during the years of the great Depression before World War II was immeasurable. They supported and guided, spiritually amd materially, the many unemployed of those most terrible years, including holding special meetings at which food would be distributed to hungry men and women and words of comfort spoken.

Men like George Hood made a great contribution to their fellow men and women but they did not seek political involvement. Their aim was to make every effort to bring men, women and children into the Church to live the spiritual life which Christianity offered them. I wish that some ministers of the Church today would have this aim more in mind in their work rather than get bogged down in politics. After all, if they aimed more to 'make all things new' in the spiritual man, and if they were active and successful in this, policemen might become unnecessary!

Both my parents were strongly committed Christians. For them the Christian faith was not only recognized but honoured, and under their care and influence I committed my life at an early age to Jesus Christ. I have tried ever since to fulfil this commitment although I have too often failed to do so.

Hundreds of youngsters used the mission hall at Grove Street as the focal point of the community in which we lived, for in addition to the religious services, there were choral singing, talks and magic lantern shows. The nearest we ever got to a 'movie' film was when a still picture was put in front of a bright lantern light and a device inserted to make it wiggle. What a contrast to today with all its sophisticated viewing and gadgetry.

In my eighteen years at the hall I was taught to read music and to sing, and the love of music and singing has remained with me. Indeed, those who came many years later to spend an evening in my home in London were sometimes surprised to find the Commissioner going to the piano after dinner and singing a song or two to entertain his guests. William Carlyle, who had been a miner, was my teacher and brass band music was the love of his life. He was totally committed outside his work to arranging, playing and conducting music at the mission hall, and his band included my father playing the largest instrument, a double bass, which appeared to me to weigh a ton.

The mission hall was thus at the very centre of my life for virtually the whole of my youth, and it is perhaps not surprising that this influence was to affect me profoundly throughout the years that followed. Some may say that such circumstances were too narrowly oppressive and restrictive and that they did not allow me enough scope to express myself and act as freely as a young man should. I understand the claim but all I can say is that I did not feel it to be so at the time, and in retrospect I have not changed my mind. Although I would not have put it in quite such a way as a young man, the Collect for Peace in the Book of Common Prayer – which is not a bad quotation for a Presbyterian Scot – contains the words: 'The author of peace and lover of concord . . . whose service is perfect freedom,' and these words express my thoughts more closely than I could ever write. My parents and the Church instilled in me during these years the fundamentals of Christian belief, which in later years I accepted quite freely of my own accord. They set standards for living based on truth, integrity and compassion.

Above all, the early education by the Church and my parents was to teach me the difference between right and wrong. My mother's approach was simple and easily understood: she made plain to me that an imaginary line divided what was right from what was wrong and that you stepped over that line at your peril. Once or twice, of course, you suffered the painful consequences of any such transgression, but it was plain as plain that she loved me so much that she did not want me to do wrong. I have missed her greatly ever since her death in 1970.

My parents never abdicated their responsibilities. They understood that the influence of the home is the keystone to the growth and development of youngsters. They knew how confusion can be caused in the minds of children if the distinction between right and wrong becomes blurred.

Beyond the immediate family circle, good neighbourliness was the order of the day for those who lived in the tenements of Glasgow. We lived close by each other, we knew each other, and we helped each other. If anyone was sick, or in difficulty or need, the families in the neighbourhood would come to each other's aid without expecting anything in return. All were familiar with whatever can befall one, and in the tenements were those who could act as nurses, who knew how to deliver babies or care for the old. There were virtually no social services and I sometimes wonder whether we have gone too far today in providing welfare services and thereby undermining neighbourhood self-sufficiency.

I remember this coming to mind when I was attending, as Commissioner of Police, a weekend seminar at the Ditchley Conference Centre to discuss problems of juvenile delinquency. I learnt that very substantial sums of money were being paid by a major local authority in the south to neighbours to care for the elderly and infirm. Not for a moment am I criticizing the excellent work now undertaken by the social services, nor am I questioning the obligation to care for those in need. But I cannot think that there is a substitute for spontaneous good neighbourliness. It is certainly not nostalgia for earlier times that makes me think that we have lost in recent years some of the art of helping each other; that we are not the caring society that we should be; that we are selfish and self-centred to an extent that imperils our ability even to get along with each other.

When I came of school age, I went to Dundas Vale Primary School. In the neighbourhood this school was described as 'the normal school' and it is good to know that, at least at the beginning of my life, I was normal enough to go to such a school. There we were taught the 'four Rs' — reading, writing, arithmetic and religious knowledge.

Discipline was strict but, contrary to what is often alleged, I do not recall the strap being used frequently or being abused. Many of us did not like going to school, but we were respectful when we got there and the teachers, men and women, had few problems of control. Their authority in class was never in dispute.

The school was at the heart of the area in which I lived in central Glasgow, and one of my strongest memories is that of mothers coming in mid-winter in the morning to put cups of hot tea through the railings for their children. There were no school canteens of any sort in those days.

All parents sought if they could to ensure that their children were well turned out for school, if only 'to keep up appearances'.

But there were families who could not afford to buy clothes and their children were provided by the local authority with 'Parish clothing'. It was a very hard thing to happen to any child. The clothes were stiff and uncomfortable and the boots were awful. They were fitted with big metal toe and heel plates, hob-nailed and too heavy to wear. Above all, the outfits identified a child as coming from a very poor home and in need of public assistance, and this made him or her a target for taunts and unkindness from other children.

When I was eleven I successfully passed a competitive examination which gained me entry to Woodside Senior Secondary School, the equivalent I think of an English grammar school of the time. We wore uniform at this school and I recall that the school motto on the badge of our maroon blazers was 'Fortitudine' – 'With Courage'.

My academic career was neither long nor distinguished for I left school at the age of fifteen. My parents earnestly urged me to continue with my school studies but that was not my wish. I was a headstrong youngster who was seeking only to get out of school as quickly as possible into the outside world where I thought 'real things' were to be found. The life around me was also very unsettling at the time. It was 1940 and World War II had begun in earnest; the whole country was in turmoil and our schooling, because of the shortage of teachers, had been reduced to half a week. I know now that I should have accepted the guidance of my parents and stayed longer at school, but in the event the course I took brought me into a different form of schooling, that of man dealing with man, and maybe in the long run things turned out better than I deserved.

As Commissioner I have heard it suggested that I was unfavourably disposed towards people with academic qualifications. This is quite untrue. I have worked in close, harmonious and profitable partnership with men who had distinguished academic records. What I have said, and said consistently, is that it is not enough for a man to join the police service having obtained a university degree and to think that this is all he needs to be a competent policeman, let alone achieve a Chief Constable's baton or senior post in the service. It does not necessarily lead to anything of the sort. The police service is first and last a practical service dealing with all classes of people and their problems. To be effective, police officers need in their make-up a large measure of humanity, practicality and common-sense. The very best type of police officer in my experience is one who remembers what he or she has been taught at school or university, who uses his or her intelligence to the utmost, and at the same time retains the common touch. The need is for the man or woman to learn every day from their policing experience on the streets and to seek to exercise good sense, professionalism and compassion in all that he or she does. The old lady in the Gorbals or in Brixton who has been attacked, robbed or had her home broken into is not concerned with the academic record of the police officer who comes to her aid. She is concerned only with how he treats her, how he helps her with her problems and distress, and how he gets on with his job. If his academic degree contributes to his effectiveness as a police officer, that is good; if it does not, it counts for nothing in the officer's work and relations with the public.

My wife Isabel was also a pupil at Woodside but she reminds me often that I had left school before she started there. When we returned together to the school during my time as Chief Constable of Glasgow following an invitation for Isabel to present the prizes and for me to speak, it was an emotional experience for both of us. In particular, I saw tears coming to Isabel's eyes when she handed the sports cup to a young girl who was captain of Woodlands House, of which Isabel herself had been a prefect in her time. Our times at school cannot have been all that unhappy if, years later, we could feel like this.

There were other influences at work by the time I was fifteen. Football has always been of absorbing interest to me and to my wife, who is an enthusiastic supporter of the game. I began, as I have said, playing football on the streets, I played throughout my time at school, and I played in later years for the Marine Division of the Glasgow Police. A determined right half, some extravagantly minded Scottish journalist dubbed me 'Clogger McNee', but for my part I am sure that I was far more scientific and skilful in my play than that. Association football throughout my life has remained for me a great sport, and in addition I have been responsible in my time for the policing of some of the most important matches in Scotland and England. It saddens me much that this fine game, with its great tradition and history, should be spoilt so often by mindless misconduct both on and off the field.

Outside my family and school, the Boys' Brigade made a major contribution to my early life. The object of the Boys' Brigade is: 'The advancement of Christ's kingdom among boys and the promotion of habits of obedience, reverence, discipline, self-respect and all that tend towards a true Christian manliness.' The Brigade was founded in Glasgow in 1883 by William A. Smith, later Sir William, who incidentally had close links with the Grove Street Institute. Of him, it is truly said:

> He led his boys by living
>> The life he'd have them live;
> He sought to search by giving
>> The whole he had to give.

It is not the purpose of this book to write a history of the Boys' Brigade and it is sufficient to say that several millions of boys of all colours have served in the Brigade with benefit to themselves and others.

I was one of them. I joined the Boys' Brigade as a 'Life Boy' at the age of nine (today it would be joining the Junior Boys' Brigade) and I 'graduated' to the Brigade proper at the age of twelve and remained there until I was eighteen when I was called up for service in the armed forces. The years with the Boys' Brigade did much for me, not least in teaching me further how to associate with my fellows.

Each week I would go down to a meeting of my local company at a church hall and there we would be taught all sorts of skills, including playing in a brass or pipe band, singing, physical training and drill. We also had some wonderful camps in the summer on Naomi Mitchison's estate at Carradale in the Mull of Kintyre. After some years I was promoted to Staff Sergeant of my company and awarded the King's badge.

I owe much to the Brigade and I have never lost touch with them over the years. I have visited various companies, carried out inspections (including inspecting the London Battalion of the Brigade in 1977 when I was Commissioner of Police) and presented what is now the Queen's Badge to boys of the Brigade. I count my election as Vice President of the Brigade in 1980 as one of the greatest honours I have ever received.

I have already made it plain that music became a major influence early in my life and that it has remained so. The instruments I usually played in the mission band or in the Boys' Brigade band were the trombone and euphonium. My other great musical love is singing. When I came back to Glasgow after the war I spent three years as a tenor, studying voice production. This led to a continuing involvement in singing, and in particular singing in churches.

The church in which I used to sing most often was the parish church of St George's Tron which is right in the centre of Glasgow. This led me to know well a wonderful man, the Reverend Tom Allan, a minister of the Church of Scotland. After noble work elsewhere, Tom Allan had become in September 1955 Minister of St George's Tron. From that day St George's Tron was committed to a ministry never known before in the area. Tom Allan sought to reach out to everyone, and the poor, the maimed and the blind in spirit as well as in body were brought in. St George's Tron became known as 'the church at the heart of the city, with the city at its heart'. People queued in the rain and overflowed into other churches when evangelistic rallies were held at St George's Tron, and these rallies led to a major rehabilitation centre and hostel being set up.

I first met Tom Allan by arrangement at Renfrew Airport on a very cold, foggy morning in the early 1950s. We were to travel to Inverness where I was to sing at an evangelistic meeting. He greeted me and spoke as if we had known each other for years. This meeting and my singing at the Inverness rally was the beginning of a very close association.

Tom asked if I would sing at his church and this led to my almost being the resident soloist there. Later he was to take me with him on his evangelistic rallies, including visits, or rather crusades, to America and Canada. When Tom Allan died in 1964 after a series of heart attacks many people including the then Secretary of State for

29

Scotland and the Lord Provost of Glasgow, wrote tributes about him which were collated together in a pamphlet called 'A Fraction of His Image'. This is part of what I wrote (at the time I was a Detective Inspector in the Glasgow Police):

> Tom Allan's greatness was not that he was a brilliant graduate of Glasgow University or a great preacher or a great evangelist, much as he was indeed those. His greatness lay in his ability to get alongside his fellows and speak to them about Christ and His claim on their lives in a language which they could easily understand. In other words, Tom was very much a man's man and sought at all times to make the Gospel pertinent to a person's everyday affairs.
>
> Tom Allan made a tremendous impact on my own life and thinking. One cannot work and live with such a person without a little bit of him rubbing off. I thank God for him and for the privilege which was mine to meet such a man and work so closely with him.

I remain of the opinion today that he was the most outstanding Scottish churchman of his time and I grieve that he died so soon. Like many others, I owe a great deal to him.

Back to business. When I left school I joined Clydesdale Bank to earn the lordly sum of fifteen shillings a week for acting as a general 'dogsbody' who ran errands, licked stamps and did any other job which came my way. They were happy days. Alas, I remained within the banking system for only just over two years, for on 23 March 1943, when I was eighteen, I received instructions calling me to service in the forces of our country. I never in fact returned to the bank until I became a director shortly after my retirement from being Commissioner of Police. It must have been one of the biggest promotion leaps in the history of the bank.

The instructions I received from HM Government were to report to *HMS Royal Arthur*, a training establishment at Skegness in Lincolnshire; the instructions were accompanied by a postal order and a single railway ticket (perhaps the Government thought I was going on a journey of no return). In any event, this journey was to be the first time, as for many other youngsters, that I was to leave home.

It was a sight to be seen. McNee as a naval rating – bell-bottom trousers and all. I have no intention of writing a history of how McNee helped to win World War II so let me confine myself to a few memories which still remain with me.

One is of the very first breakfast at Skegness. Most of us had joined the Navy only a few hours previously, and how polite and courteous we were to each other at table. 'Would you pass the bread please?' . . . 'Can I get you another cup of tea?' . . . and so on.

What a change had come about after a few hours, by which time we were all in uniform and met again for lunch. We were back, as in the streets of Glasgow, to the survival of the fittest and the devil take the hindmost. Certainly if you did not look after Number One you risked getting almost nothing to eat. Nor was it profitable to complain about the food. I did so once when I found a cockroach in my soup only to be told sharply by the Petty Officer of the day: 'McNee, hush your mouth. You have more meat in your soup than anyone else.' I finished the soup and never complained again!

On a more serious note, I recall how comprehensive was the medical care given to new recruits – contrary to what is often alleged. I still remember the medical examination at Skegness, at which any physical defect would be found and remedied. I recall in particular one unfortunate youngster who within hours of arrival had every tooth removed; perhaps to make sure that he did not prejudice the war effort in his subsequent service by getting tooth-ache!

Lastly, Skegness seemed to be in the direct line not only of a continuous east wind but also of every German bomber on its way to attack Britain. There were nights when we seemed to spend, under orders, more hours in cold, crude shelters than in bed. Later on, I was to find the accommodation of these shelters luxurious in comparison with other naval quarters to which I was allocated.

Six months saw the end of my time at Skegness and I was posted as a fully qualified telegraphist to the Portsmouth Division of the Royal Navy and assigned to Combined Operations. I also joined my first ship, which was lying at anchor off Portland; she was *HMS Empire Mace*, a landing craft headquarters ship built in the United States of America.

For months after I joined this ship – towards the end of 1943 – our training was wholly in preparation for the landing of the Allied armies on the Continent. On 6 June 1944 – 'D' Day – *HMS Empire Mace* was one of the first ships to stand off Gold Beach in Normandy as the landing commenced. After the operation was over, I served in several ships, the last being the fleet aircraft carrier *HMS Theseus* which was built and commissioned on the Clyde. After trials this ship went south to be provisioned for service in the Pacific. In the Solent off Portsmouth, however, she collided with a floating dock, and this accident led to my obtaining early release from the Navy to join the police service.

This broadly covers my career in the Royal Navy, a great service in which I am proud to have played a part and which I remember with affection and high regard.

Many years after I had left the Royal Navy and when I was first designated as the next Metropolitan Police Commissioner, my predecessor, Sir Robert Mark, and the then most senior officers of the force held a small 'in house' reception at New Scotland Yard to enable me to meet in advance those in command positions with whom I would be working. No outside guests had been invited and it was therefore somewhat surprising to find that among those present was one who I am reliably informed was self-invited – Earl Mountbatten of Burma.

When Lord Mountbatten and I were introduced he said, 'McNee, you were in the Royal Navy.'

'Yes,' I said, 'but lower deck.'

'That's where all the bloody work is done,' was his reply, to which I answered,

'Lord Louis, in my experience that is right.'

'What discipline were you in?'

'I was a communicator.'

'I wrote the Communications Handbook for the Royal Navy.'

'Lord Louis, I followed it to the letter.'

Lord Mountbatten then looked across at Robert Mark and said, 'I got him his job, you know.' True or false, this was the kind of extravagance in which the great man delighted.

The story does not end there. At the end of the same year I was knighted by Her Majesty the Queen and I received a letter from Lord Mountbatten in his own handwriting which read as follows:

> My dear David
> Although your selection to succeed Bob meant in due course the knighthood which goes with the job it is all the same gratifying to your many friends and admirers to be able to address you as 'Sir David' – though I'm not sure that I do not feel emotionally stronger about PO Tel McNee!
> Please accept my heartfelt congratulations, David, and all best wishes for the future.
> Yours ever,
> Mountbatten of Burma

We remained friendly until Lord Mountbatten's tragic death in Ireland. His letter to me, and other subsequent acts of kindness, are but further examples of the personal attention he gave to small acts of courtesy as well as to great issues of State.

Just prior to leaving the Navy I applied to join both the City of Glasgow Police and the Metropolitan Police. Only Glasgow replied and accepted me. (After becoming Commissioner I gave instructions that replies should be sent to all applicants.) Little did I know that I would be taking up my second choice later in life. Clad in my demob suit, about which it would be kind to make no comment, and armed with a ticket to Glasgow provided by the Government – that return ticket which had previously been denied me – I returned to the city of my birth to start my new career.

From what I have already written, you will not be surprised to learn that I first met my wife, Isabel, at a church meeting in Glasgow. She was the daughter of a grocer whose shop was in the centre of the city. Both her parents were very devout Christians and wonderful people. Right from the first time I met them, they were kind and loving to me, as indeed they were to all who came their way.

Isabel and I were married on 25 March 1952 in Anniesland Hall, which is a Christian Brethren church, and the reception was held at the Grand Hotel, Charing Cross, Glasgow. It was a beautiful building, full of character, and a landmark of the city centre but alas it was demolished to make way for a new inner city ring road. Our daughter Heather was born four years later.

Throughout a most busy life, at all levels of responsibility, I have never been in any doubt that the bedrock to all that I have tried to do, and to anything that I may have achieved, has been the companionship and comfort my wife has given me. Being the wife or child of a police officer is never an easy lot – I can in fact think of no other form of employment, including service in the armed forces, where year in, year out the burden is more consistently onerous. A police officer can be away from home for long hours, with his return often seriously delayed for some unexpected reason; he can be called out for duty at very short notice for what often appears to the family to be unreasonable cause; he can be called away for service at weekends, and sometimes weekend after weekend, or at other times which much disrupt family and social life; his safety can be under threat. All this is part of the life of a policeman's wife and children.

During our marriage Isabel always put my needs as a police officer first. She has never failed me; this is perhaps because at the very beginning of our life Isabel and I determined together that come what may and whatever our circumstances, our life together would be a Christian life and our home a Christian home. So it has remained, and it is this which has given me courage and consolation to face whatever has come my way in the form of responsibilities and dangers and whatever setbacks have had to be met, whether as Police Constable or as Police Commissioner.

2

From Coppering to Command

IF BOOKS, FILMS and television programmes are anything to go by, police work has unmatched glamour and drama. The image of solitary or outnumbered law officers facing up to danger and violence as they bring offenders to justice has an age-old appeal. It fulfils a sense of adventure which every applicant for the police service shares. I was certainly no exception when, on 29 April 1946, I joined Glasgow's police force.

Any romantic notions I held about police work were quickly dispelled. It did not take long to find out that the reality of policing was very different from its fictional image. Police training was fairly rudimentary in those days and the austerity of post-war Scotland did little to enhance life at Glasgow's Police Training School in Oxford Street in the heart of the Gorbals. I have always felt that the siting of the training centre was a superb piece of planning – putting policemen where they were most needed. Police training closely replicated my early naval training; dormitories and drill. With twenty of us to a dormitory (all ex-servicemen) our daily routine consisted of foot drill, physical training, unarmed combat, learning the basics of the job and how to write reports, and being introduced to the essential elements of the Scottish criminal law.

Although my parents lived in Glasgow I was not allowed to live at home during my initial training. The Training School was kept full of recruits and a sum was deducted from pay for our board and lodgings. Life was spartan and discipline strict. I remember clearly walking back to Oxford Street on my first night there, after a quick evening visit home, and passing a police sergeant 'belling' off a constable whom he had caught smoking. It led me to wonder whether I had made the right decision. When, a month later, I left the Training School for the Marine Division, that question was still uppermost in my mind.

I reported for duty on 24 May. The practice then was for new recruits to work on the night shift until they were used to wearing their uniform on the streets. Glasgow's Marine Division, as you will have gathered from its name, bordered the Clyde, from Pitt Street to the city boundary with Dunbartonshire. Its northern boundary ran from the Great Western Road to Sauchiehall Street. Six of us were posted there together and interviewed by the Divisional Commander, Superintendent Macdonald. A big man physically, Superintendent Macdonald was a 'doonhammer'* and a sportsman interested in tug-of-war and wrestling, so when he heard my Glaswegian accent and found out that I was a footballer, it was the end of his interest in PC 249 McNee.

Night shift introduced me to that sense of apprehensive solitude that is unique to policing a large city beat. The silence of the small hours filled only by the empty echo of your own footsteps, never quite sure what the next alleyway and corner holds for you is an abiding memory that a policeman never entirely loses – no matter how senior he becomes.

Newcomers to a division had to wait before being given their own beat. In the interim they worked relieving duties, filling in for regular beat officers during their absence. The Glasgow police force, unlike others, did not have fixed routes for its beat officers to follow. The beats were small; and you soon got to know the people living and working there. After some two years I got a beat of my own in Partick. Constables paraded at the divisional station and went to their beats on foot or by public transport. If you had an outlying beat you did not return to your police station but took your half-hour meal break in a police box. Supervision was very strict. To be found off one's beat was almost a capital offence. Failure to

* a person coming from Southwest Scotland

discover a 'break-in' on the night shift would inevitably lead to an officer being summoned from his bed at home to explain why it was undiscovered; punishment frequently followed. Such discipline certainly concentrated the mind, but it had one unfortunate and unforeseen effect. The old sweats knew that to keep out of trouble with the sergeant it was best to find out and report 'break-ins' already committed rather than to concentrate on preventing them. Prevention meant being round the streets for the whole of your duty in all kinds of weather. In consequence they tended to put most effort into the last three hours of the night shifts, making sure that they did not miss any break-ins which had happened.

Police officers were well known to their local communities and many were given nicknames by the public, which were individually most descriptive: 'The Hinges', 'Twinkletoes', 'Greetin Peter', 'Tom Mix', 'The Wolf', 'Cheerful'. I remember the last one walking me round my beat one night. He was never a great talker but suddenly he piped up.

'McNee, can you type?'

'No.'

'Can you speak Gaelic?'

'No.'

'Can you play the bagpipes?'

'No.'

At this he threw his arms up and said, 'McNee, you should pack up now. You've no . . . chance.'

It was a tough, hard physical life for a policeman, particularly around closing time at the public houses. Glaswegians full of cheap wine have traditionally regarded policemen as legitimate targets. But tough as it was I only once had occasion to draw and use my truncheon, and that was during a Friday night brawl outside a public house in Partick.

Crime and deprivation on my Partick beat were rife. Tenement areas with four storeys, sometimes with eight homes on each level and one WC on the half landing serving eight families were commonplace. Living conditions in these areas were deplorable and it was little wonder that there were epidemics. Life however had its lighter moments, thank goodness.

I recall one Sunday morning at 4 a.m. coming upon a game of football in the street – sixteen players, eight-a-side, with their jackets on the ground for goals. Conscious that one of the city's more important bye-laws was being broken and, more relevantly, that those living nearby might want to sleep, I grabbed the players' coats, put a stop to the game, and with strict professional impartiality booked both teams.

One youth ran off, presumably because he had no jacket. It had only been my possession of their jackets that had kept the other players there whilst I administered due justice. Unluckily for the young man (as I thought then – unlucky for me as it turned out) I recognized him and decided it was hardly fair that he should escape the full majesty of the law. He lived with his mother and sister close by, and I decided to tie up the one remaining loose end and call on him before my night shift ended.

I found the house door open; mother and sister were asleep in bed. Of son there was no sign. A noise from the outside WC, however, revealed a shivering figure in shirt and braces sitting in hiding. I took him back indoors and, apart from reporting him, that would have been the end of it. But his mother and sister woke up and I suddenly found myself under attack from all three. The two women were still in their night clothes but that did not stop them. Clad only in a short shirt, the mother was as awesome as any mother bear defending her cubs. And Constable McNee was the sole object of her wrath.

I have made my share of mistakes during my lifetime but it was now I made one of my greatest. Faced by this maternal amazon, I decided to arrest the son for breach of the peace. The next few minutes saw bedlam in the household. As I grabbed the son and pulled one way, his mother pulled him from the other, whilst his sister pulled and pushed me from every direction – or so it seemed. Out of the house and into the street we struggled, me determined to keep hold of my prisoner and the mother, baring all (or nearly all) to the early morning air, equally determined that I should not. The youth was in the middle waking up the neighbourhood and drawing attention to all that he wanted kept private by shouting, 'Mr McNee, look what you've done to my mam' as the lady exposed all to the neighbourhood and finally collapsed.

Justice finally triumphed, or my version of it; I got the son to the police station and the womenfolk retreated to the privacy of their home. Believe me, when, over thirty years later, Lord Scarman drew attention to the need on occasions for police to defer law enforcement in favour of preserving public tranquillity, I knew exactly what he meant.

It pays for police officers to have a sense of humour, and a well-developed one at that. But it is just as important to know when to exercise it. A humorous remark or inadvertent laughter at the wrong time can cause all manner of difficulties. It was just as well I had learned that particular lesson when, one quiet Sunday afternoon, I was called to a disturbance at a house where a pitched battle was taking place between the men who lived there and their next door neighbours.

In I went to calm things down which, with the exercise of a little tact and diplomacy and a fair measure of dire threats about the future, I managed to do. As I separated the main protagonists, the kitchen door was pushed open to reveal the grown up sister of the owner of the house taking her Sunday afternoon bath. As she stood stark naked staring towards the door, her brother snapped, 'For God's sake, girl, cover your nakedness.' Instantly she reached out, picked up her bra and held it in front of her. It struck me as funny then and even now when I look back, it still causes me to smile. Had I smiled then or made the wrong remark, however, hostilities would have been resumed, and this time almost certainly directed against me.

Time passed quickly as a beat officer. The demands and challenge of the daily routine added to my experience until I was ready for plain clothes duty. In Glasgow then it was the custom (as it still is in most forces) to employ police officers in plain clothes to deal with infringements of the licensing, betting, gaming and vice laws. As a Glasgow boy familiar with life on the streets of the city, street bookmakers were nothing new to me. I had seen them operating all my life and almost instinctively found it easy to enforce the law against them.

Enforcement was generally tempered with discretion. Gambling was an integral part of Glasgow working-class life and the street bookmakers catered to a pretty wide social demand. Even to a man who did not bet, nor saw the need for it, it would plainly be only a matter of time before the law was changed; and enforcement of the gambling laws was rarely oppressive. Manpower resources, neither then nor now, are sufficient to prosecute all observed infringements against the licensing, gaming and vice laws. Even if they were, I doubt whether individual police discretion, shaped as it is by social pressures, would permit it. Exposure to the iniquities of gambling, vice and drink was seen as a corrupting influence on police officers. Because of this, officers were allowed to work on these duties alone for a maximum of twelve months.

I served my time in plain clothes in the West End of Glasgow, including the Charing Cross area. In this area in the centre of the city there was a coffee stall which was a favourite place for prostitutes to gather. It was here that we too would spend part of the time – getting to know the 'girls' (indeed many of them were not much more than girls), listening to their gossip, exchanging pleasantries. They showed little or no antagonism towards the police and we in turn rarely judged them in moral terms. They knew the rules of the 'game' and there was a spirit of friendly competition between us. Compassion and fairness on the part of the police were often rewarded by useful criminal information.

One night, not far from the coffee stall, two of us came across an Irishman, slumped back in a doorway; he was obviously the worse for drink and was singing at the top of his voice a version of Galway Bay. I can remember some of it now –

> Have you ever been across the sea to Belfast?
> To land there on the 12th day of July.
> To see the banners waving with King William.
> And to watch the Orange men go marching by.

Religious differences between Catholics and Protestants are never far below the surface of life in Glasgow. He was in quite the wrong part of the world to be singing such a song, and we decided we had best stop him whilst he was still in one piece. In response to our words of advice, which seemed to have little effect – given his condition this was hardly surprising – he told us he was a visitor from Northern Ireland, that he knew another dozen verses and did we want him to sing them for us? No, we did not, and for his safety it seemed sensible to keep him engaged in conversation and move him on. Asked whether the Catholics would ever take over Ulster, his fervent reply was to the effect that not whilst there was a drop of good Protestant blood in his veins would they do so. That kind of bigotry was and still is commonplace in parts of Glasgow in which religious divisions are just as strongly formed and held as they are in Northern Ireland.

The Celtic-Rangers football matches were described by one of my senior officers as 'the biggest outdoor religious festival held anywhere in the world'. Perhaps the ritual of these events has been instrumental in providing an outlet for the differences between the two communities.

The Irish influence in Glasgow is a strong one and it was at an unlicensed Irish dance hall in a basement in Stobcross Street that I had a most hair-raising experience. Two of us in plain clothes were first sent in to get the necessary evidence to establish if entry was dependent upon the purchase of a ticket and whether it was operating as a dance hall. The place was packed so tight that there was hardly room for the proverbial cat let alone room to swing it around. I was dancing with an Irish girl, who was propositioning me, when our Sergeant and a dozen men charged in. What we had not realized was that the purpose of the dance was to raise money to bail a well-known Glasgow-Irish criminal who was then in custody on criminal charges, and the reaction to the arrival of the police was such that I thought for a moment that World War III had started! So fierce was the opposition that I was never more glad to get out of anywhere once our job was done.

Twelve months' plain clothes duty over, it was back into

uniform – back to the beat. After five years' service I applied to join the CID and was admitted to the Department in December 1951. The flair I had shown for catching criminals – 'thief-taking' – stood me in good stead and I was selected. Good detectives have to have a nose and an eye for the job. You have to be something of a 'nosey parker', naturally inquisitive without inhibitions about 'poking your nose' into things. Assertiveness and self-confidence are essential.

As a Detective Constable I remained in the Marine Division where I was to serve for the next eleven and a half years before being promoted to Detective Sergeant. More than sixteen years as a Constable both in uniform and CID may seem a long time by present standards, but it meant that I learnt my craft by hard experience and later on, when in command of men, those years enabled me to know the problems encountered by serving officers and how they should be dealing with them.

A glut of American and British television series has done a disservice to criminal investigation work. There is nothing glamorous about being a good detective. Effective detection is a hard, painstaking, time-consuming process, which demands attention to detail. It is about knowing when to pursue a certain inquiry or line of inquiry, and having the ability to determine which line of inquiry is the most likely to bear fruit. Practical experience is the greatest teacher of these things. It is about getting to know people, about cultivating informants, and that takes time. Information and intelligence are the life blood of CID work. Television, books, magazines, newspapers rarely convey the routine of policing. They show it in a glamorous light when in fact it merits nothing of the kind. And the real problem is that too many young officers see it in those terms and try to make the job live up to their image of it. Too often they lack the persistence and dedication that the job requires. I know of nothing which provides the same sense of fulfilment and satisfaction as a successful end to a complicated and comprehensive investigation.

Whilst the daily routine of detective work demands patience and application and is not at all glamorous, if the cases hit the headlines, then the detectives too are thrust into the public eye. Success as a detective in a criminal *cause célèbre* inevitably attracts publicity and captures the public imagination. It was not unusual in the past for detectives in charge of major inquiries – men for example such as Bob Fabian in the 1950s – to be more of a household name than their chief officers. That in part reflected the nature of public concern at that time, when people were more interested in reading about police work than indulging in critical debates about the structure and philosophy of policing.

The emphasis of press and television coverage has certainly undergone a change since the mid-1960s. The media are now much more critical and inquiring about our social institutions, including the police service, than in the past. And the politically conscious have learned how to use the media to their own particular advantage. Television is tailor-made for militant pressure group politics, feeding as it does upon the very essence of controversy and conflict. Police reporting was once almost exclusively about personalities, today it is as much if not more about issues.

The Marine Division of Glasgow City dominated my operational police career both as a detective and beat policeman. Transferred to Govan on promotion to Detective Sergeant in 1962, I was back in the Marine Division within the year. Twelve months later I was promoted to Detective Inspector and transferred to the Flying Squad. In 1966 I was transferred again and served a year in Glasgow's Special Branch, before becoming the first Glasgow police officer to be selected for the Senior Command Course at the National Police College in Hampshire.

As a detective I had a fair share of publicity, particularly when in charge of a section of the Flying Squad. This was largely because of close involvement with some notorious cases.

One of these was that of John Duddy. On 12 August 1966, the whole country had been deeply shocked by the murder of three Metropolitan Police officers at Shepherds Bush. After extensive inquiries, the criminals were identified; one of them was a Scotsman, John Duddy, who had relations and associates in Glasgow, and it was thought that he could well have come back to the city for refuge. Large numbers of police were mustered at Glasgow Central police station, and formed into squads to seek out Duddy. For obvious reasons, selected officers in each squad carried guns. We had successfully traced Duddy's brother Charles and he told us that John Duddy was hiding in a single apartment in Stevenson Street, Bridgeton. The squad of which I was a member went with Charles Duddy to the premises and he let us into the apartment. There we found Duddy, fortunately unarmed and ready to surrender.

Another very dangerous man was Walter Scott Ellis. In the years after World War II safe blowing was virtually a daily occurrence. Later, bank robberies became the fashion. One of the first of such robberies took place in Greenview Street in Pollokshaws in April 1966 at a branch of the National Commercial Bank. Three masked men armed with a shotgun broke into the bank, shot and wounded the manager and the accountant and stole nearly £20,000 before making off in their getaway car. A massive police investigation followed, led by my very good friend Elphinstone Dalglish. One by one the criminals were identified. The leader was Ellis, who had a reputation for violence and a readiness for being armed. I was in charge of the squad sent in the early hours of one morning to arrest Ellis in a cottage a few miles from Newton Mearns, a suburb of Glasgow. We were told that he was armed and we were ready for shots to be fired. He gave us no problems – or perhaps more accurately we gave him no chance to give us any; no gun was found on him. But he carried a ticket which led us to a left luggage office in the bus station at Buchanan Street, and there we found his gun and ammunition. Ellis was convicted and sentenced to twenty-one years' imprisonment. As he was taken away to serve his sentence, he was heard to say that he would have got less for killing the bank officials. Such attitudes by dangerous men have played a part in the rise in violent crime. Soon after being released from serving such a long sentence, Ellis was again back in custody.

The Gorbals in Glasgow harboured a number of vicious men who lived by use of the razor and the knife. In the 1960s one such character sought to 'rule the roost' at the head of a string of followers. This was James Boyle, who had links with criminals throughout Glasgow and beyond. It was believed that the network with which he was associated went as far south as London and the Kray twins. In 1967 Boyle was acquitted of a murder charge. His reputation and that of his associates for instant and vicious violence did nothing to help encourage witnesses to come forward to give evidence against him. On 14 July 1967, Boyle went with another man to a house at 45 Cornwall Street, the home of one William Rooney, affectionately known in criminal circles as 'Babs'. Rooney was murdered in the presence of his common law wife. Among other criminal activities, Boyle used to exact retribution on persons who failed to repay borrowed money, and Rooney owed money at the time. I was closely involved in directing the investigation of the case, and we learnt that Boyle had fled to London. Still later we heard that some of his associates were travelling by car to meet him there and the registration number of the car was circulated. A patrolling beat Constable spotted the car outside a public house called 'The British Lion' in Hackney Road (another illustration of the value of good, observant policing). The public house was raided by Metropolitan Police officers together with Elphinstone Dalglish and Detective Chief Inspector Stewart Fraser from the Glasgow police, and Boyle was arrested. A great deal of publicity has been given to Boyle's subsequent conviction and conduct in prison, including production of a play and television programmes. I am told that he has put his violent past behind him; I certainly hope so, and if so I wish him well.

Then there was James Latta. A well-known Glasgow solicitor, Latta often defended criminals. A major social scourge in Glasgow in the 1960s was unlicensed moneylending. The rates of interest were so high that repayment of the debt was virtually impossible. In addition, the terms of a loan usually included a penalty clause in the event of default. Behind many such moneylenders were the strong-arm tallymen employed to 'persuade' debtors to keep up their payments. The 'tallymen' were the spiders of a vast web in which many poor people were caught up – rarely able to free themselves once they had taken that first step of borrowing money to provide for themselves and their families. The evils of this system became

45

widespread and increasingly directed by well-known criminals. During the investigation into the death of 'Babs' Rooney, evidence of this network began to come to light and as a result Tom Goodall, my Detective Chief Superintendent, gave me the task of doing something positive about it. Goodall was head of the Glasgow CID at the time and he was one of the greatest detectives I have known. He had all the qualities needed to make a first class investigator, including a complete dedication to his work. To him, the greater the crime the greater the challenge. His instinct and flair to reconstruct a crime were uncanny. To ignore his advice as to what he surmised had occurred was to place yourself at risk of ending up with an unsolved crime. He would have gone further in the service if it had not been for his premature death in 1969.

The assignment he had given me was as open-ended as any assignment could be. I gathered a good squad of detectives to help me, and visits were made to a number of well-known public houses in the Gorbals to 'read the riot act'; telling those present, many of whom were caught up in these rackets in one way or another that it had to stop. In one place I stood on top of a table and told my audience that we were well aware of the tallymen system, and what was happening; that I believed some people involved were present and that if it did not stop they would suffer the consequences. There was no need to draw pictures for them. They knew that we meant business. I ended with a plea for those who had information to pass on to get in touch with me. They listened in stony silence.

To my surprise, however, a man did make contact within hours and this led to the arrest of Latta and a number of associates of James Boyle for attempting to pervert the course of justice by suborning witnesses in order to get accused persons acquitted. Latta and others were convicted and given salutary sentences, which did a great deal to check the activities of the tallymen. It was this success that brought me the nickname of 'The Hammer', an epithet used about me in connection with the case by the Scottish *Daily Express*.

After eighteen months in the Flying Squad, Tom Goodall told me that I was to be transferred to Special Branch, and my reaction was, 'I don't want to go. Why would I want to go to Special

Branch?' He made it very plain that the move was not optional: 'You're going there to find out what the buggers do.' Apart from being an invaluable experience, it motivated my application for the Senior Command Course – after all you can have too much of a good thing.

The Police College has had its problems since being established in Hampshire soon after the last war, but it has played and continues to play a fundamental role in moulding the police service. It is where promising young constables can be sent and prepared for accelerated promotion, and where selected senior officers can be prepared for the highest ranks in the service. But the College is more than this, for high standards are set there for the whole service and progressively disseminated throughout all forces. There were one or two interesting characters on my Senior Command Course, but none more than a young Chief Inspector from Greater Manchester by the name of James Anderton. One of the youngest members on the course, he was even then a positive, highly principled classmate – an outspoken man, with no fear of controversy. I found him excellent company, and the two of us struck up a friendship. Our families visited each other and we spent holidays together. Later on, after my appointment as Deputy Chief Constable of Dunbarton-shire, we met less often.

Jim Anderton's enjoyment of the cut and thrust of public debate has led him into controversy which has tended to cloud the fact that he runs a very good police force. Some would say he has become too 'political' and at times that has been my view. Police chiefs cannot escape the political context; they have to work within it. But the need for impartiality and evenhandedness is paramount. An admirer of Bob Mark, Jim has occasionally chosen to involve himself in publicly debating issues which I believe go beyond the remit of chief officers. This may well prove to be an obstacle to his ambition of becoming Commissioner of Police. I hope not.

On my return to Glasgow after my six months' Hampshire sabbatical, during which I had been promoted to the rank of Detective Chief Inspector, Tom Goodall put me in charge of a special squad to tackle serious crime in the city. I was deep in the middle of one such case when he came to see me and asked if I knew that there was a vacancy for a Deputy Chief Constable in the nearby county force of Dunbartonshire. He told me to apply. My reply was that I was not interested. I saw myself as a career detective, perhaps at some time in the seat that Tom Goodall occupied as the Detective Chief Superintendent in operational charge of Glasgow's CID.

In characteristic words Tom told me not to be stupid and to apply. He had set me thinking, but it was not until the last day for applications to be submitted that I hurriedly threw my application together, getting Tom Goodall's secretary to do the typing for me. I took it home with me, showed it to Isabel and then set out by car to the central post office to ensure that the form would be submitted in time. It was pouring with rain and the car ran out of petrol. I was soaked to the skin but finally reached the post office and posted the application. When I arrived home I said to Isabel that if the problems I had faced getting the application in were anything to go by, I could forget all about it. Much to my surprise I was shortlisted for interview.

There were three other candidates shortlisted for the post, and we were separately interviewed by the full police committee of Dunbartonshire. My surprise at being shortlisted grew yet further when I got the job.

Tom Goodall had clearly seen something in me that I had not seen in myself and his persistence was largely responsible for my application. During the time I had my application under consideration a Chief Inspector colleague in Glasgow came and asked if I had applied. He told me that the Dunbartonshire Police Authority were looking for a man of about fifty years of age with thirty years' service: his own qualifications. He was not even shortlisted. I have never been sure why I got the job. The other men who were interviewed were well qualified, but I believe that my brief Special Branch experience (which, as I have explained, I did not welcome at the time) was an important factor, for William Kerr, the Chief Constable of Dunbartonshire, had been a Special Branch officer in Glasgow before taking up his appointment.

'A small step for man, a giant step for mankind.' It was with these words that Neil Armstrong stepped out onto the surface of the moon. The reverse was true when I went from Glasgow to Dunbarton. It was a giant step for me but a small and relatively insignificant step for mankind. For twenty-two years I had been strictly an operational policeman, mainly engaged on detective work. Certainly I had been involved in the administration of many major crime investigations, but for the first time I found myself concerned with policy-making, administration and control of a police force – entirely different responsibilities.

I have often been asked the question, why had it taken twenty-two years for me to move forward to senior rank? And what was it that had led Tom Goodall to push me upwards? The answer to the first question is the easy one: at the time in question you could pass, as I had, the police promotion examinations and be efficient at your work, but seniority was almost an absolute prerequisite for promotion. The answer to the second question is more difficult and perhaps not for me to judge. It was perhaps that as a detective I always saw a job through to the best possible completion, that I sought to keep an open mind, that I welcomed different points of view and that I had never been a 'yes-man'. Perhaps above all it was because my bosses had seen in me a capacity for decision-making and leadership.

William Kerr, the Chief Constable of Dunbartonshire, was a character. On reflection he was – and this is an understatement – something of an autocrat. He ruled his force, including his senior officers, in imperial style. Most stood in awe or fear of him. He would congratulate you one minute on a job well done and tear into you the next for something quite trivial. He was not a well man and I am sure that contributed to his unpredictability.

I already had definite views on man management before I went to Dunbartonshire, and my experiences there strengthened them. Management, leadership, call it what you will, is certainly not about unpredictability. Certainty of purpose and judgment, consistency of action and direction, clarity of communication: these are its essence. An effective and efficient police force obviously needs good management. Perhaps more than most organizations police forces need senior officers who not only understand the needs of operational officers, but do not lose sight of their importance within the overall scheme of things. Police authority and power is invested in each officer individually, and each man and woman's point of view is important. If Tom Goodall was the man who taught me much about detective work, it was Willie Kerr who taught me much about being a chief police officer, although not always directly. My time with him was particularly instructive about relationships with police committees. I am frequently amazed today when I hear certain police chiefs trumpeting about the politics of their committees. In Dunbartonshire we had a large joint committee, consisting solely of local politicians – no tame magistrates to help out. Conservatives, Liberals, Socialists, Scottish Nationalists and Communists made up that committee. Arnold Henderson and Finlay Hart, both Communists, were great believers in law and order and supportive of the police: not uncritical but supportive. On one occasion when I was asked to chair a Salvation Army musical festival in Clydebank Town Hall I looked up to the gallery where the two of them stood amongst other civic dignitaries and caught them both singing lustily the hymn 'Stand up, stand up for Jesus'. At the next meeting of the police committee they took me to one side and jokingly swore me to secrecy. It is on that kind of personal level that good relationships stand or fall.

Politicians are elected to take on responsibility for the determination and control of public policy. They not only have a right to a say in policing procedures, they have a duty to say it. As the professional element in the equation, the role of a Chief Constable in committee is to ensure that the committee does not operate on a basis of ignorance and is fully aware of any legal, structural or organizational factors which may constrain the decisions of the police committee. Success is largely a combination of personality and commonsense. I have always had a good rapport with any police committee on which I have served. Such rapport is a vital element in providing an effective policing service.

On arrival in Dunbartonshire I found that they were just

commencing a reorganization and from the outset I was deeply involved in it. Major reorganization has been the story of my life; in Glasgow, Strathclyde and again in London.

Dunbartonshire Constabulary was only a small force. It employed around 400 police officers and 130 civilians. But, and you might expect me to say this, it was the best of the smaller Scottish forces. Willie Kerr enjoyed being in the van of policing and encouraged the trial and implementation of any new method which might make the force more efficient and able to provide a better service to the county's residents. Service to the public was something Willie Kerr consistently stressed and in that respect I have tried to emulate him throughout my own chief officership.

The Dunbartonshire reorganization had been sparked off by a Scottish Office circular to all forces with the objective of increasing the size of divisions. Chief Superintendents were given geographically larger areas to command; the number of divisions was reduced and a Chief Superintendent post was absorbed. As a result of the reorganization my substantive rank, Deputy Chief Constable (which is a position as opposed to a rank) was upgraded from Chief Superintendent to Assistant Chief Constable.

Not long after my arrival in Dunbartonshire Willie Kerr suffered a terrible accident. He was extremely interested in introducing a helicopter to British police work and arranged a helicopter trip to assess what value one might have for the county. Police headquarters were part of the County Hall complex and the helicopter landed on a lawn behind County Hall to pick us up. We flew down the Clyde, out across the Firth and landed in Arran for lunch. The flight back took us via Loch Lomond and we landed on the island of Inchmurrin in the middle of the loch before heading back to headquarters. We landed again behind County Hall and as we got out of the helicopter, Willie Kerr walked round the back of the aircraft into the rear rotor blades. He suffered very severe head injuries, lost an eye and lost partial use of an arm. He was lucky to survive. But survive he did and eventually came back to work.

The accident was investigated by Superintendent Pat Hamill, the man who was to succeed me later as Chief Constable of

Strathclyde. In the aftermath of the accident, it was understandable that the purpose of the day was lost and helicopters were never again considered as an adjunct to policing in Dunbartonshire. But despite Willie Kerr's accident the potential that helicopters offered did not escape me, and motivated me to establish London's first Police Air Support Unit when I became Commissioner.

During Willie Kerr's time in hospital and convalescing I was effectively Chief Constable, an experience I would have gladly foregone if it could have meant the accident not taking place. Nevertheless, the experience was invaluable and it may have had something to do with the invitation I received from William Smith, Aberdeen's Chief Constable of the day, to go and visit him. He made it plain that I should not leave it too long, so I went within a few days. With William Smith was the Chairman of his police commit-tee, Dr Norman Hogg. I learned that Smith was shortly to leave Aberdeen to become HM Inspector of Constabulary for Scotland. Both he and his Chairman asked me to apply for the vacant post in Aberdeen. Of course they emphasized that there was no guarantee of my getting the job, but they thought the possibility was high. I was flattered and said so, but I asked for time to consider the offer as I wished to talk with Isabel and my daughter before committing myself.

A few days later, whilst still reflecting on the approach from Aberdeen, I received a communication from Councillor Anderson, Chairman of the Glasgow police committee, telling me that Sir James Robertson, Glasgow's Chief Constable, was to retire, and asking if I was interested in returning to my parent force. He had heard that I had been approached about the Aberdeen job. It was no contest. Every prodigal wants to return home, and I applied for the post of Chief Constable of Glasgow. The intervening weeks be-tween application, interview and acceptance were the longest of my career. Would I fall between two stools? Willie Smith understood my dilemma and later, as HM Inspector of Constabulary, he proved to be a great friend and mentor.

Five men were interviewed by a sub-committee of the Police Authority to see who would succeed Sir James Robertson: the late

James McLellan, Chief Constable of Lanarkshire; Donald McInnes, Chief Constable of Perth and Kinross; Adrian Clissett, Assistant Chief Constable of Leeds, later Chief Constable of Hertfordshire; Stanley Bailey, Assistant Chief Constable of Staffordshire, later Chief Constable of Northumbria; and myself. The interviews took place on 6 January 1971 and my appointment was confirmed by a meeting of the full Corporation two weeks later. On 7 April 1971, just under nine years after my first promotion to Detective Sergeant (a rank which had taken me over sixteen years to reach) I returned to Glasgow as the new Chief Constable. (Perhaps it's not how you start but how you finish that counts.)

The move from Glasgow to Dunbartonshire had been a big step in my career. The move back to the city where I had grown up and learned the art of policing was a daunting one. No moment was more daunting than sitting in my headquarters' office on that first morning facing my senior colleagues. James Kelso, my Deputy and three Assistant Chief Constables, William Ratcliffe, William Rae and Elphinstone Dalglish: all four had been my senior officers in both the uniform branch and CID. I do not know how I appeared outwardly; inwardly I was extremely nervous. Any fears I had were groundless. They supported me to the hilt despite some of the changes I later made not being entirely to their liking.

Also looking down on me that morning were photographs of past Chief Constables, from the first, James Smart, to my immediate predecessor, Sir James Robertson. Among them was the famous Sir Percy Sillitoe. Those three in particular had made magnificent contributions to law and order in Glasgow. I wondered whether they would view my own term of office with approval or not. What I did not know then, was that I was to be the *last* Chief Constable of Glasgow.

Even at that early stage I was determined, with no disrespect to those who had gone before me, to take a long hard look at the force and see what changes needed to be made. The time was right and many in the force were not only ready for change but welcomed it. My examination, to which many contributed but none more so than the Head of Research and Planning, Peter Ross, resulted in the reorganization of divisions, a fresh look at recruitment and training, the expansion of research and planning, the introduction of a press and public relations office, and the establishment of a community involvement department. This was the start of a number of new initiatives, which included the introduction of a computerized command and control system.

Because of the size of the force and the resources at its disposal the Glasgow force has always been to the forefront in policing, both in Scotland and beyond. Many officers from other forces came to see what we were doing in the use of computers for operational policing and to look at our community involvement work. Prominent among them were officers from John Alderson's force – Devon and Cornwall. They clearly liked what they saw, took many of our ideas back to their own force and even enlisted the aid of Evelyn Schaffer, the Principal Clinical Psychologist at the Douglas Inch Centre, who had been instrumental in helping to establish the Glasgow Community Involvement Department.

Three people were of great help to me throughout my time as Chief Constable. They were Mrs Agnes Ballantyne, the Chairman of my police committee, James Kelso, my Deputy, and Elphie Dalglish who became my Deputy when Kelso retired.

Jimmy Anderson, who had encouraged me to apply for the Glasgow post, was a Tory. In the May elections following my arrival, the Conservative Party lost control of the Corporation, and he was replaced as Chairman of the police committee by Mrs Agnes Ballantyne. Small, fiery, warm, outgoing, practical, wise: that was Mrs Ballantyne, an experienced local Labour Councillor who represented the Provan ward of the city and who had the ability to get things done. Once she was convinced that a policy or innovation was in the best interests of the citizens of Glasgow you would always have her support.

Kelso and Dalglish, both wonderful raconteurs, were just the right men for me. I was a young, forward-looking, forceful, sometimes brash, chief officer who wanted everything done yesterday, and they never hesitated to pull on the reins and advise me in the art of the possible. Tall, debonair Kelso had a sardonic sense of humour and was never short of a ready quip. His advice on any aspect of policing was always worth listening to. He had been my Chief Inspector when I was a Constable.

I had known Elphie Dalglish from joining the service. He and I came up through the CID together. We had worked alongside on cases and knew each other's strengths and weaknesses as well as any two people could. He was both academic and practical. A decisive, assertive man, he could spell out the principles of policing and back them up with practical experience. A loyal friend (and still is), Elphie was never frightened to criticize me when he thought it necessary.

In 1974 Mrs Ballantyne handed over the office of Chairman of the police committee to Mr Bashir Maan, the first Asian anywhere in Britain to hold such post. Bashir was the owner of a string of liquor stores. He taught me much about Britain's new Commonwealth minorities and continued to be a help to me when I later moved south to London. At his instigation and often in his company I ate many curries (not my favourite dish) in the furtherance of good race relations.

The passing of the Local Government (Scotland) Act in 1973 signalled the demise of the Glasgow City Force, with its proud history dating back to 1800, and there was great sadness in the force. And great speculation as well about who was likely to lead the new Strathclyde Regional Police Force. Seven forces were caught up in the reorganization – most of Argyll, all of Ayrshire, Dunbartonshire, Glasgow City, Lanarkshire, Renfrew and Bute and a part of Stirlingshire. Strathclyde, with about 7000 police and many civil staff, serving a population of over two and a half million (more than half of Scotland's total population) was to be the biggest force in Scotland and second only to the Metropolitan Police in the United Kingdom. The upheaval caused by regionalization was massive; the planning required was extensive. The reorganization necessary to establish the Strathclyde region created a local government unit which was too unwieldy and divorced from the people living in the region. But the promptness with which the policing of the new region was effectively established surprised and impressed political leaders of all parties and attracted a good deal of favourable comment.

The new force came into being on 16 May 1975 with the announcement of my appointment as its chief officer being made nine months earlier. Dalglish was appointed as my Deputy and the months that followed made great demands on both of us. Working parties were formed to deal with every aspect of the administration of a new large modern police force. Each group prepared reports which had to be carefully considered before final approval.

Elphie Dalglish and I visited every corner of the new force before its inception to meet police officers of all ranks, and the officials and councillors of the many authorities affected by the reorganization. The very size of the area made this quite a task.

The planning of the new force revealed a great many differences in practice and policy between the seven forces. Amazingly, one force had no force orders (i.e. handbook of guidance for its officers), on the assumption that they could work better without them. If anyone was in doubt about the action to take they had to phone Headquarters. In creating rules of guidance for any organization great thought and care are needed. Somehow flexibility has to be built in. In a large and geographically diverse police force such as Strathclyde an order which might be right for an urban area would not be right for a rural one. Flexibility was vital. We did not always achieve it.

Strathclyde has something like ninety-two offshore islands within its boundaries. Visiting one of the larger of those islands I met a perplexed Sergeant. Studying force orders he had read an instruction which required him to visit or see his Constables at least twice during each shift. He was in charge of five Constables who were spread out across the island, linked by a ten-mile network of narrow winding roads. In trying to live within the order the man was going round in the proverbial circles. Before he disappeared, I put him right and on my return to Glasgow arranged for that particular order to be rewritten.

In the main the new Strathclyde Force settled down well – give or take the odd birth pain. My time as its chief officer was short-lived, for in March 1977 I travelled south to become Commissioner of the Metropolitan Police. My successor was Patrick Hamill. My Deputy, Elphie Dalglish, had never served outside Glasgow and under rules recently introduced by the Scottish Office (in parallel to those of the Home Office) he could not succeed me. He had all the necessary qualities and it remains my ever-long regret that government policy prevented him from taking over my chair.

3

Mark's Successor

BY JUNE 1976 I had been Chief Constable of Strathclyde for fifteen months and I had reached a stage where I was beginning to think not only that God was in his heaven – which I have always believed – but that all was becoming reasonably right with my particular world. It had been a hard slog but it now appeared that the new regional force was taking shape, despite its political, geographical and operational diversity. Although I am not one for resting on my oars, I saw the way ahead being as smooth as a policeman can ever reasonably expect.

How wrong can you be! Man may propose but as always God disposes. That very month I took a telephone call from Robert Armstrong, then head of the Police Department of the Home Office; his message was that the Home Secretary, Roy Jenkins, wanted me to go and see him to explain and discuss the new computerized command and control system. It had been installed and operating successfully at Glasgow Police Headquarters since March 1976. I was not born yesterday; and although I was more than a little proud of this control system, which was said at the time to be the best in Britain and probably in the world, the invitation seemed unlikely. I had not been a detective for over sixteen years for nothing and 'the nose' for things which are short of the whole truth, something all good detectives develop, began to twitch. I knew for instance that if Roy Jenkins, with all his other cares of state, really wished to be briefed about computerized command and control systems, there were experts close at hand in his own Police Department who were more competent and qualified than I. What business then had the Home Secretary in hand that made it necessary to invite a Scottish Chief Constable to his office in London?

It so happened that within days of receiving the invitation Richard (Jimmy) James, the Undersecretary in charge of police support services in the Police Department, made one of his fairly frequent visits to Glasgow Police Headquarters. We had tea together, and like a good policeman I began carefully to sound him out to see if he knew anything. He was prudent in his replies, but then what civil servant is not; however by the end of our conversation I was thoroughly convinced that something more was stirring than the computerized tape of a command and control system! As an aside, this strange chain of events had another outcome which was unexpected at the time. This was that Jimmy James, who was to be appointed later as the Receiver for the Metropolitan Police District and thus become one of my two deputies during my first years as Commissioner, became and has remained a close friend.

My suspicions were alerted further when I saw Roy Jenkins. With him, that day in July, were Sir Arthur Peterson, the Permanent Secretary, Robert Armstrong and Sir James Haughton, HM Chief Inspector of Constabulary. They had certainly not come along for some ordinary piece of police business.

It was a strange interview. Roy Jenkins did not make any direct reference to his real purpose which, as I learnt later, was to form a view as to my suitability for appointment as Commissioner. Instead he talked about Glasgow, which he seemed to know well (and now knows even better) and of its problems, questioning me all the time about how I dealt with public order, race relations, terrorism, inner city tensions, drug trafficking. And he sought my view on such matters as the treatment of prisoners and capital punishment.

It was a long and friendly discussion. I cannot recall my exact replies to his questions, but after the interview the Home Office officials told me that what I had said was well received. They also explained that, after further consideration by the Home Secretary of all possible candidates, it could be that I would be invited to accept appointment as Commissioner of Police. In reply I was just as

59

circumspect, indicating that without committing myself in any way at that stage, I would of course be highly honoured if such an offer were to be made. 'Well,' said James Haughton, 'it's up to you to make up your mind.' Yes indeed; as I left for home that was my one thought.

Of course my heart and mind leapt at the possibility of being Commissioner of Police, with New Scotland Yard as my headquarters. The most important and renowned chief officer post anywhere, head of the greatest police force in the world, and working at a headquarters which was an international byword. All this for one who had spent his boyhood in the tenements of central Glasgow, and was holding a rank of Chief Inspector just eight years before. My head was turned towards London, but acceptance was not a simple matter. The appointment frightened me not at all. For I thought I knew myself and my capabilities well enough, without harbouring any false modesty, to do the job if it was offered me. I paused a while nevertheless at the fact that, if appointed, I would be the first Commissioner from a working class background. Commissioners up to the end of World War II had largely been men of distinguished rank in the armed services, and included names like Viscount Trenchard and Viscount Byng. Even more recent Commissioners like Sir John Nott-Bower, Sir Joseph Simpson and Sir John Waldron had all come from public schools, and from backgrounds vastly different from my own.

I was a Scotsman, born and bred. All my roots were in Glasgow. I could truly say, 'I belong to Glasgow'. What, therefore, was I about in contemplating going to head the premier police force in England? Isabel, my wife, also came from Glasgow. All her relatives and friends as well as mine were there. Her Christian church-going and mine had been in Glasgow all our lives. How would we find a stay in a city 'of alien corn' where at first we would have virtually no close friends? As a family we were very content – happy and at one. We had just had a new house built to our requirements in Pollokshields, Glasgow. A lovely house, we were justly proud of it. Heather, our daughter, was living at home and had recently begun to work as an occupational therapist in a Glasgow hospital. Going south would mean leaving Heather behind and giving up our new home.

It was not an easy decision. As in the past, Isabel took the line that as a policeman's wife she would go with me, wherever the job took me. It was typical of the support she has always given me. About two years later a journalist on the *Daily Mail* inferred, in the slick way journalists have, that I might be considering resigning because Isabel was unhappy and wished to return to Scotland. It was an example not only of the total untruths that journalists can write but also of how hurtful they can be.

Heather took the same line as her mother. For myself, I decided that if I was to be offered the most important and the most responsible police post in the world, I should accept. To decline the offer for domestic reasons or for reasons of my own comfort would have been wrong. I would have had difficulty in living with myself in the future, facing the thought that I had turned down a great opportunity solely for personal comfort. Despite some uncomfortable moments during my time as Commissioner I never once regretted accepting the challenge of the job. I was also mindful of the story in St Luke's Gospel about the need to make the maximum possible use in this life of such talents as God has given to each of us. So, as a family, we decided that if the offer became a firm one, I should accept it.

A most frustrating period followed. First, Roy Jenkins left office in August on being designated President of the European Economic Commission. His successor was Merlyn Rees, and shortly after he moved in we had a re-run of the earlier interview. At that meeting I made it known that if offered the post of Commissioner I would accept.

So far so good, but then came a further exasperating delay. First, Home Office officials recommended that on grounds of equity and to show that all was fair play, other possible candidates should be interviewed. There were few others in the field. John Alderson, Chief Constable of Devon and Cornwall, previously an Assistant Commissioner in the Metropolitan Police, was thought by the press to be one candidate. He was not called for interview either by Roy

Jenkins or by Merlyn Rees. Another name floated by the press was Philip Knights, Chief Constable of the West Midlands, who was seen during the selection process. Other names were mentioned and possibly considered but there were two in a special category. The first was the incumbent Commissioner, Robert Mark. He would not be sixty until March 1977, and it was open for him to remain as Commissioner if this was the Home Secretary's wish. Despite the furore which had been raised over the establishment of the Police Complaints Board and despite his views about the financial losses that would accrue if he were to remain in the post, it is my belief that he was half expecting to be asked to stay. No such invitation was forthcoming; nor is it ever likely to be, once a Commissioner has told the Home Office that he intends to go.

The second apparently strong candidate was Colin Woods, Deputy Commissioner, formerly Commandant of the Police College and an officer with many years' service in the Metropolitan Police. It was common gossip in the Met that he was ambitious to become Commissioner. In my view his candidature was badly and unkindly handled. Robert Mark made it known to the Home Office that Woods had his strong personal support. Shortly afterwards information was leaked to the press that Colin Woods was to be the next Commissioner. *The Sunday Times* reported it and, given the high reputation of the newspaper, it was assumed by many that the report was accurate. It certainly led to letters of good wishes being sent to Colin Woods and flowers to his wife. It was unfair and hurtful not least because, as I understand it, there was no real prospect of Woods being appointed Commissioner. When he was made Deputy Commissioner, he had been told by the Permanent Secretary at the Home Office that he would not be eligible for the higher post.

Tension and rumour continued. Uncertainty trod its insidious path all the way to Glasgow. Obviously, I wanted the matter settled as quickly as possible. This was not to be, but I was sustained during this period by Robert Armstrong and Jimmy James, who counselled me to bide my time and – in the words of Mr Asquith – to 'wait and see'. I took their advice, difficult as it was and contrary as it is to my nature, which is to get a decision and action taken as quickly as possible. Finally the matter was resolved. On 28 October I received a letter from Merlyn Rees formally asking whether I would be willing to take the post as Commissioner when Robert Mark retired. I replied in the affirmative.

What had expedited the letter was not far removed from farce. Because of the erroneous article in *The Sunday Times*, Colin Woods was invited to the Home Office where he was told plainly that he was not getting the job. He asked who was and was told, David McNee. Naturally he then telephoned his wife to let her know what had been said. A little later Percy Hoskins, that distinguished journalist of the *Daily Express*, called the Woods' household by telephone and was told in turn by Gladys Woods that Colin was not going to be the next Commissioner but that I was. Later in the same evening Leonard Murray, a lawyer friend of mine in Glasgow, telephoned me to ask if a report by Percy Hoskins due to appear in that night's edition of the *Daily Express* was correct. I played for time and got in touch with Robert Armstrong. The next day saw the official Home Office announcement. It was as simple and as slightly absurd as that. When it came to my own departure, the circumstances surrounding its announcement gave me a strong feeling of *déjà vu*.

A few weeks later I came to London to have preliminary discussions at the Home Office. Afterwards I walked the streets of London, aware that this was probably the last time that I would do so without attracting attention. I savoured the freedom of being able to sit in a café drinking coffee, unrecognized.

Robert Mark invited me to London to talk a few weeks before I took up office and kindly arranged for me to have a series of very informal meetings with the heads of the police and civil departments of the Yard. I appreciated these arrangements, which contrasted sharply with the cold and unhelpful reception he had met when he first went to New Scotland Yard. Everyone went out of their way to be helpful, kind and hospitable although one wiseacre did warn me that if I was accompanied to the lift on the eighth floor, where the

Commissioner has his office, it would be prudent to make sure that the lift was there when the doors opened.

I learnt later that reports had reached London that Isabel and I were opposed to drinking alcohol and that we held the view that any social occasion should be wholly teetotal. The prospect of a 'dry' Commissioner for years to come, I am told, spread a good deal of alarm and despondency throughout the force, nowhere more than in the ranks of the CID. I think that during our participation in various introductory parties, Isabel and I did much to dispel that alarm, showing that we did enjoy hospitality and good company in a normal relaxed way. I also now know that at these parties I was under close and continuous surveillance – 'to drink or not to drink' clearly featured largely in the minds of those present, particularly some looking for promotion.

It was also at this time that the national press began to refer to me widely as 'The Hammer'. This was a bit of nonsense. During my time as Chief Constable of Glasgow and Chief Constable of Strathclyde, I was never known as 'The Hammer'. It was years previously, when I was a senior detective in Glasgow, that a caption in the Scottish *Daily Express* had appeared as follows: 'McNee Hammers the Underworld'. Between the announcement that I was to succeed Bob Mark and his departure I declined to give any interviews to the press, not least because Sir Robert was still in office. Faced with this, the press turned back to such previous reports as they had about me. They dug out the earlier newspaper caption and dubbed me with the title of 'The Hammer'. It is not a title I sought but if, in dealing with serious wrongdoing, crime and violence the cap fitted, I wore it cheerfully enough.

It was not the only nonsense written about me at the time. An article appeared in another paper on 30 October 1976.

And yesterday I heard the story of the inspector who was carrying a large electric typewriter – part of a haul of stolen goods – from a van into police headquarters.

'I tripped on the steps and the thing came down heavily on my left foot, which was in bandages because of gout,' the

64

inspector recalled. 'Naturally I let out a choice expression. Unfortunately, McNee was holding the door open for me.

'I can tell you, I've never had a dressing down like that. He even called me a sinner!'

In fact, his appointment as head of Britain's second largest police force in 1971 was followed by a rush of resignations.

Officers took exception to his iron rule. He banned, for example, the tradition of men celebrating promotions with a 'wee dram' at the police station.

'We are police officers,' McNee told a superintendent who protested. 'Our probity must be 100 per cent. This isn't just a job – it's a cause.'

He even takes exception to officers of different ranks being on first-name terms, on duty or off.

One senior officer made the mistake of sending him a postcard from Jamaica, where he was on holiday.

'He called me in when I got back,' the man said yesterday. 'He came right to the point. He wanted to know where I had got the money for such an expensive trip.

'I told him I'd had a win on the pools. I even showed him the correspondence between myself and the pools company. He just sort of nodded. And left me with the feeling that as a policeman I had no right to gamble.'

None of these stories had any real basis and it would not have been worth the effort to try to discover where they originated. All that is certain is that there was very little that a person in my position could do about them.

I took up my post as Commissioner on 13 March 1977. It may be of interest, particularly as it continues to be a matter of much political debate, to say a little about the office of Commissioner and the relationship between the Commissioner and the Home Secretary, who is the police authority for the Metropolitan Police. It is important to have very much in mind that in a provincial police force in England and Wales, the chief officer works with a police committee consisting of elected representatives of the local authority and nominated local magistrates. This is not so in the Metropolitan Police where, partly because of the national importance of the force, the relationship has remained, as it originated in 1829, between the Commissioner and the Home Secretary, in other words with a senior cabinet minister of the political party forming the Government. My experience of policing in London and outside leaves me convinced that the special arrangements for political responsibility for the Metropolitan Police are wholly right and proper and work well to the benefit of London's citizens.

I do not need to provide a history of the Metropolitan Police and its Commissioners: that has been done by others. Suffice to say that the office of Commissioner dates back to 1829 when Robert Peel at last successfully achieved the enactment of his Bill to establish a disciplined police force for London. Two Commissioners were appointed at that time – Colonel Sir Charles Rowan and Sir Richard Mayne, both outstanding men to whom this country and Londoners in particular owe a great deal. That too is another story. From the time their partnership came to an end, one Commissioner only has held office. I was the twentieth in succession.

The preamble to the 1829 Act states that '. . . it is expedient to substitute a new and more efficient system of Police which, acting under the immediate Authority of One of His Majesty's Principal Secretaries of State, shall direct and control the whole of such new system of Police . . .'

There is no statutory definition of the extent to which the Home Secretary's authority extends over the Metropolitan Police. Lord Denning, when Master of the Rolls, set out the position in his judgment in the case of *Regina v Metropolitan Police Commissioner ex parte Blackburn (1968)*. He said:

> I have no hesitation in holding that like every constable in the land he (the Commissioner) should be and is independent of the executive. He is not subject to the orders of the Secretary of State, save under the Police Act 1964 the Secretary of State can call on him to give a report, or to retire in the interests of efficiency. I hold it to be the duty of the Commissioner of Police, as it is of every Chief Constable, to enforce the law of the land. He must take steps so to post his men that crimes may be detected and that honest citizens may go about their affairs in peace. He must decide whether or no suspected persons are to

be prosecuted, and, if need be, bring the prosecution or see that it is brought, but in all these things he is not the servant of anyone save the law itself. No Minister of the Crown can tell him that he must, or must not keep observation on this place or that, or that he must or must not prosecute this man or that one. The responsibility for law enforcement lies on him. He is answerable to the law and to the law alone.

'Amen' to that say I, because independence of action in respect of law enforcement by police and the political impartiality of chief officers of police linked with accountability to the courts is at the very heart of democratic government and freedom under the law.

Of course that is not the end of the matter, for not only has the Home Secretary considerable statutory and regulatory responsibilities for the Metropolitan Police but in addition, if he is worth his salt, he takes a close personal interest in the force. He will expect, for instance, to be kept informed by the Commissioner about the strategic plans for the force and about proposals for dealing with matters such as public disorder demonstrations and racial problems. This is commonsense. For, apart from other considerations, it is the Home Secretary who has to deal with questions and debates in the House of Commons on what the Metropolitan Police has done, or failed to do, in its general policing of London or the handling of a particular incident.

There is clearly room for dispute over the extent to which the Home Secretary and his Department should be kept informed. There is also scope for disagreement over plans and policies. History shows that in the past some Commissioners and some Home Secretaries have not always had a satisfactory working relationship.

Much might be said about this important constitutional issue, but to my mind it fundamentally depends on the personalities and good sense of the men in power; the Home Secretary and the Commissioner of the day. If they are jointly determined, as they should be, to secure the best possible policing of the metropolis and to get on together to this end, all will be well. If they seek other interests, or put personal or party political considerations first, disagreements are bound to arise. Then the force and the citizens of London are the losers.

I cannot answer for my predecessors but I will say that the relationship between Merlyn Rees and myself could not have been bettered. He fully understood my position as Commissioner. He understood the needs of the force. He gave me his wholehearted support. He had my respect and total confidence. I did my best to keep him fully informed, confident in the knowledge that my operational independence and discretion would remain unfettered.

When a Conservative Government came to power in 1979, William Whitelaw became Home Secretary and the same excellent relationship continued, including working closely together during the major police and political operation involved in the siege of the Iranian Embassy. We had our disagreements, not least over the need for a public inquiry after the Brixton riots and his handling in the House of Commons of the Buckingham Palace incident – but personal relations remained good.

This is perhaps the more remarkable since the two Home Secretaries, Merlyn Rees and William Whitelaw, were two very different types of men from very different backgrounds. Merlyn Rees was born into a Welsh mining background, educated in state schools and at the London School of Economics, and became a teacher and lecturer before being elected a Labour Member of Parliament for Leeds in the 1960s. William Whitelaw was educated at Winchester College and Trinity College Cambridge, followed by service as a regular officer in the Scots Guards. After distinguished war service, he went straight into Parliament as a Conservative MP.

As Commissioner I was soon aware that policing London is different from policing elsewhere. Police officers in London are much the same as police officers in other parts of the United Kingdom, for all forces have their share of the good, the indifferent and the bad. The problems which Metropolitan Police officers face are also for the most part not exclusive to London. However, it is the scale and the gravity of the problems which confront London's police and the Commissioner, linked with a number of special responsibilities, which set the Metropolitan Police apart.

Let me end this chapter with a quote from a police historian, Sir John Moylan (a former Receiver for the Metropolitan Police), who wrote: 'The appointment of Commissioner of Police of the Metropolis is among the most difficult upon which Ministers have to advise the Crown, and the holder of it is perhaps more exposed to criticism and the vicissitudes of fortune than any other member of the public service.' After five and a half years as Commissioner I cannot disagree with that.

4

McNee of The Yard

ARRIVING AT THE FRONT DOOR of New Scotland Yard is a forbidding experience for anyone. It is particularly so on the day of arrival of a new Commissioner.

Even on a normal day the front entrance of the Yard is not a peaceful place. You say 'Good morning' to the officer on duty outside the building and then push your way through revolving doors to a reception area where there are always scores of police and civil staff, some arriving for work, others on their way out on various commitments, and visitors from all over the world. You walk past memorials for those from the Metropolitan Police who died in the World Wars, including an ever-burning flame of remembrance, and possibly meet an officer called 'the Back Hall Inspector': a misnomer if there ever was one! It stems from the nineteenth century when the headquarters of the Metropolitan Police was in Great Scotland Yard with an entrance in Whitehall Place. A police inspector with the primary responsibility of examining persons arrested during the night was on duty in a hall at the back of that building, and the title of 'Back Hall Inspector' has continued, although the post now has very different duties.

The day of my arrival was certainly not a normal day. A barrage of cameras faced me on either side as I came to the front door. Journalists shouted questions, and behind them was a crowd of people attracted to the scene by the hubbub. On the other side of the door, staff had gathered to get a first look at their new boss. I was glad to reach the lift and get to my office. But there was to be no respite there. I changed quickly into uniform and went straight to the force briefing room for a press conference. The room was packed with reporters from scores of newspapers, from home and abroad, together with microphones and television cameras. Questions flew thick and fast, as many about my personal life as about my new job. I cannot recall all my replies, but the main theme of that inaugural address was my aim to make the streets of London safer by putting more policemen back on the beat.

After the conference a crop of major problems awaited me; this first meeting with the world press underlined one of them. Robert Mark was the first Commissioner, indeed the first chief officer of police, to 'go public'. In the past chief officers and policemen had generally been members of a 'silent service', but Bob Mark made extensive and successful use of the media to present police views on a wide number of issues. He did so in several ways. One was to invite the press and other sections of the media into the midst of the force. A second was to allow officers of all ranks to speak to the press or television about incidents in which they had been involved. Of greatest impact was his decision to speak forcefully in public to bring the problems faced by police officers, particularly in connection with the prosecution of offenders, to the attention of ordinary men and women. This he did effectively, not least in a Dimbleby Lecture early in his time as Commissioner, and in consequence the media and the public had become progressively to have different expectations about public pronouncements by chief officers of police. Other chief officers followed Robert Mark's example without, in my view, having his ability for public expression or being so surefooted in dealing with impromptu questions put by skilled reporters.

For myself, I decided to speak out publicly about important issues which affected the police as and when the need arose, but otherwise to stick to my professional last and not to try to match the gift for appearance on television which Robert had in such generous measure.

More serious problems related to the condition and morale of the force. It was not good, and in some respects the force was in turmoil. On arrival as Commissioner I found great uncertainty everywhere in consequence of proposals put forward by the Deputy Commissioner – Colin Woods – and supported by Robert Mark as Commissioner, that the existing twenty-four divisions of the Metropolitan Police District, whose boundaries were aligned for the most part with the boundaries of London boroughs, should be grouped into eight 'super' and largely autonomous districts. I understood the thinking behind this well enough: it was to decentralize operational control from New Scotland Yard. But the reasons which had led to the proposals being made, the way in which they had been mishandled, and the misunderstandings which had been allowed to arise inside and outside the force brought opposition from all sides and an outcry about my ears.

They were in fact proposals which had been formulated nearly ten years previously. In 1967 PA management consultants had reviewed the management and organization of the force. Their recommendations were presented and considered, some were accepted, others including the Super-8 idea were shelved. After lying dormant for so many years, including most of the time Robert Mark was Commissioner, they were resurrected during the latter half of 1976. Bob Mark had indicated he was to retire and the selection of a new Commissioner was in process.

I soon became acutely aware of the upheaval the pursuit of the project caused. The introduction of far-reaching changes in a large organization is always a delicate operation, calling for great skill. The mishandling of Super-8 was a classic example of how not to do it. Commanders thought their authority was being undermined. Constables and Sergeants thought they were going to be shunted all over the place. Headquarters staff thought they were going to be sent off to distant parts of the metropolis. Local authorities thought they were going to lose important and close links with local Commanders.

Worst of all, rumours suggested that the proposals involved the closure of over sixty police stations; this really caused an uproar. I received a deluge of protests from all parts of London, including those from a delegation from Belgravia who came to see me at

Scotland Yard in a pony trap, and from the film star Miss Lee Remick who came to the defence of St John's Wood Police Station. I have to admit that I rather enjoyed this visit and, for the record, St John's Wood Police Station is still open. Stickers appeared in windows in many streets of London with the words 'Save our police station'. It was of no consequence that the station in question had few, if any, callers.

The whole exercise – nicknamed Rufus* – created a storm, not a jot of which was of my making, which blew around me for some months after my arrival. The eventual outcome was that I fully maintained, and even enhanced, the role of the twenty-four District Commanders, and built on the responsibilities of the existing four Area Deputy Assistant Commissioners, each of whom took responsibility for a quarter of the metropolis. Very few stations were closed. The role and numbers of staff at some of the less important stations were reduced and that of others enhanced. These new arrangements were substantial but they were also understood and largely accepted by local authorities, local communities, the public and the force, who with inevitable police humour called this scheme 'Son of Rufus'.

The force was also disconcerted and unsettled for other reasons, one of which was the aftermath of extensive investigations into corruption, particularly within the CID. These had started with serious allegations of corruption published on the front page of *The Times*, which led to great publicity and later dissatisfaction with the outcome. Other serious allegations, including that of the involvement of police officers in drug trafficking, had followed. Again the result was unsatisfactory. Close to my arrival had been the disclosure of major corruption by senior CID officers, including those holding Commander rank, arising from trade in pornography. Known colloquially as the Humphreys Inquiry it produced an outstanding investigation by a team of officers under the leadership of Gilbert Kelland – then a Deputy Assistant Commissioner. A large

* The name RUFUS came from the official title of the exercise – Reorganization of the Force Structure (RFS)

number of officers were charged, appeared at court, and were convicted and disciplined.

The publicity surrounding these cases disturbed public confidence, and police morale, particularly within the CID, was badly shaken. I took a number of measures progressively to put this right, of which the most significant within months after my arrival was to make Gilbert Kelland the Assistant Commissioner in charge of the CID, with three new Deputy Assistant Commissioners under him.

This was but one part of my construction of a new team of senior officers. Within twelve months of my arrival, nearly all the most senior posts had seen a new appointment. Pat Kavanagh had become Deputy Commissioner, Wilford Gibson had taken over the uniform branch (A Department), John Wilson B Department, Gilbert Kelland was head of C Department and John Gerrard became responsible for recruitment and training (D Department). Jimmy James's appointment as Receiver for the Metropolitan Police, head of the civil staff, had only shortly preceded my arrival at the Yard. It was a strong team, with many of the best characteristics of a closely knit family. Each of them played a notable part in the events which followed. Later on I was able as retirements occurred to maintain a good team with the appointment of Geoffrey Dear and John Dellow as Assistant Commissioners and Alec Gordon Brown as Receiver.

At the same time I began to reorganize my headquarters. For decades the departments of the force had been self-contained units, operating under autonomous heads and largely independent of each other. This was to change and co-operation greatly to increase. The structure of the New Scotland Yard building did nothing to help in this. It is divided into nineteen separate floors with poor inter-communicating lifts which encouraged separation detween departments and branches. The building had not even been constructed in the first place as a police headquarters. It was being erected in the late 1960s as an office building for commerce when it was taken over as the new headquarters of the Metropolitan Police, superseding the historic building on the Embankment – the then Receiver, incidentally, getting into hot water with the Public Accounts Committee of the House of Commons for arranging this.

At the time of my appointment there were architects, engineers, solicitors and other civilian staff sharing the building with operational police officers, and this too was not sensible. I drew up plans with the Receiver for turning the New Scotland Yard building into an operational headquarters, including the provision of a major computerized command and control system. We were also successful in obtaining a nearby building to house civil staff who had to work closely with the police.

At operational level, too, police morale was generally low. The reason quite simply was that while demands on the police had grown markedly heavier, police pay and conditions of employment had worsened. The level of police pay in relation to levels of pay in other forms of employment had been satisfactorily established in the early 1960s following the recommendations of the Royal Commission on the Police. But this relationship had been progressively eroded to such an extent that by the time I took up office there was a real threat of a police strike. No one wanted this, least of all the police. But police officers had watched one group of workers after another force up their pay by use and threat of strikes, and faced with central and local government opposition to comparable increases in their own rates of pay, they drew the inevitable conclusions. A police strike would have been contrary to the law. That in itself would not have prevented it; particularly when police officers saw miners and other trade unionists breaking with impunity the industrial legislation of the day. The last police strike had been in 1919. Responsible leaders of the Police Federation told me that 1977 could well see another if something positive was not done to prevent it. I was in no doubt about the gravity of the situation, particularly in London where policing had become more and more onerous and the strength of the force was thousands below the number required for policing the metropolis adequately.

The strength of feeling in London was demonstrated at the rowdy Annual General Meeting of the London branch of the Police Federation in October 1977. Held as usual at Central Hall, Westminster, it was attended by the Home Secretary – Merlyn Rees – and myself. The hall was packed from end to end and it was soon apparent that the huge numbers of police officers had clearly not come just to welcome a new Commissioner. Steve Barrett, Chairman of the London branch of the Federation spoke first, in a hard-hitting and rousing speech. Merlyn Rees had to follow this and he was loudly and frequently heckled as he spoke. I spoke last and, though given a much fairer hearing than the Home Secretary, the occasional need to indulge in repartee served as a reminder that I was speaking to a turbulent audience.

By coming to speak at the meeting Merlyn Rees had acted more courageously and properly than his hostile audience knew. Shortly after I had become Commissioner, James Callaghan, then Prime Minister, had seen me at 10 Downing Street to bid me welcome and to make known his support. The previous day he had seen the national leaders of the Police Federation (with whom he had previously been closely associated for some years as their parliamentary adviser). He considered they were being unreasonable in continuing to talk of strike action if police pay did not increase substantially, after he had given his word that matters would be put right as soon as possible. Merlyn Rees had personally worked hard to achieve this and knew, when he attended the Central Hall that evening, that in a few days the Cabinet were likely to approve a committee being set up under a High Court judge to inquire into police pay and conditions. The Cabinet, however, had not met formally to agree this and Merlyn Rees did not consider it proper to divulge at the meeting what was being proposed even though, had he done so, he would have been cheered and applauded instead of receiving shouts of criticism and abuse.

Characteristically he came and took it on the chin. It was the performance of a brave and upright man, and when I spoke I said so very plainly. Much to the credit of the majority of those present, this brought a round of applause for Merlyn Rees. Police officers are generally fair-minded people, with a well developed sense of fair play, and I was encouraged by the numbers of officers who came up to me later and roundly condemned the actions of those who had heckled and shouted. A few days after the meeting, the Home

Secretary was able to announce the appointment of a committee under Lord Edmund-Davies to undertake as a matter of urgency a review of police pay and conditions of service, with the Government committed to accept its recommendations. This had had my support from the outset.

It did not take me long after becoming Commissioner to be convinced that the nature of policing in London justified Metropolitan Police officers being given a substantial pay lead over their colleagues in other forces. I put this as forcibly as I could in my written evidence to the committee, concluding with these words: 'The sum of my approach is that I earnestly hope that the committee will first recommend for the police service at large a major increase in pay, and in my view nothing short of a very substantial award would be justified, and will also give recognition by a substantial increase in London pay differential to the heavy burdens and special commitments which fall to the Metropolitan Police.' I emphasized this further in oral evidence to the committee and linked it with the acute manpower shortage of the force which had persisted for more than fifty years.

In an excellent report Lord Edmund-Davies and his committee recommended a substantial increase in police pay generally, and at the same time recognized the special difficulties of London by recommending not only the retention of the existing pensionable London weighting but also the payment of a new non-pensionable allowance of £650 a year.

These recommendations were accepted by the Government and progressively implemented. The importance of our representations and the subsequent resolution of the problems of police pay and conditions cannot be exaggerated. It was a turning point. All possibility of a strike vanished. Police morale was restored, and the status of the police service in relation to other forms of employment and in the community at large was raised to where it should be.

For me personally, the recommendations of the committee were a turning point in my home life. They led to my being moved from our home in Tadworth to an official residence in central London. Although my wife and I were sorry to lose our own home, the central location enabled me if need be to move quickly to the operational headquarters of the force or to any scene of police action.

London police officers now felt reasonably satisfied that they were being adequately remunerated for an increasingly difficult job. As a consequence, recruitment began to surge forward. Young men and women of good quality came in increasing numbers to fill the empty ranks of the force. When I became Commissioner the strength of the Metropolitan Police was about 22,000. In my last year as Commissioner manpower rose to over 26,500. Never previously in its history had it been over 23,000. In organization, in morale, in satisfaction with the job and later in numbers, the force was gradually rebuilt to cope with the demands which were to be placed upon it by the disorders of Grunwick (with which the force was already dealing on my arrival), of Lewisham, of Notting Hill and of Southall, by the siege of the Iranian Embassy, by the IRA bombings and by the Brixton riots. It was just as well.

5

Order and Disorder

IT WAS ALMOST MIDNIGHT on Monday 23 April 1979. I was still at my desk. Police resources had been hard pressed that day in Southall where the National Front had held a parliamentary election meeting at the Town Hall, deep in the heart of London's largest Asian community. There had been violence towards the police, who as always had had the job of holding the ring, but towards the end of the day the crowds began to disperse and the attacks on police to diminish. As the Duke of Wellington might have said, it had been 'hard pounding' but a peaceful end seemed in sight and I was thankful that we had been able to deal with a complex problem with less difficulty than I had foreseen.

The phone rang. It was John Dellow, then Deputy Assistant Commissioner for that part of London. A man injured during the demonstration had died in hospital. His name was Blair Peach. My premature mood of self-congratulation was swept away, all my experience told me an event of grave concern was on hand.

It had been clear from the outset that the National Front election meeting was a potential powder-keg. Southall's substantial Asian population, mainly Sikh, was apprehensive about the future. Many were genuinely uneasy over suggestions being made at the time about the repatriation of immigrants and restrictions on the admittance of relatives, and there was a quite unjustified feeling that the authorities tacitly approved of National Front policies. A small hard core of extremists – from both ends of the political spectrum – use every opportunity to challenge authority and prey on the fears,

79

anxieties and passions of people. Southall was heaven sent for them. In a frightened, uncertain and divided community there was ample opportunity to work on people's fears and misunderstandings, to foster discontent and plant the seeds of violence.

The presence of the National Front, who advocated repatriation and seemed intent upon stirring up racial hatred, was an outright affront to Southall's Asians. I could not see the Asian youth, who had in recent years begun to form their own, separate organizations and were generally more militant than their elders, accepting it quietly. The fact that the local council had given permission for the meeting and that the meeting was both lawful and the constitutional right of a candidate seeking election to Parliament was no bar to protest and disorder. No matter that the odious policies of the National Front and their use of Southall Town Hall was likely to provoke violent reaction; as Commissioner of Police I had no power to prevent the meeting taking place.

It is not the role of police in Britain to exercise that kind of political judgement. That was made quite plain by Lord Scarman in his inquiry (into the Red Lion Square disorders) when he empha-sized:

> The police are not required in any circumstances to exercise political judgement. Their role is the maintenance of public order – no more, no less.

And in an answer to those who criticize the police for not having prevented a particular event on the grounds of its objectionable political character, Lord Scarman wrote:

> This criticism, though in many cases it springs from deeply and sincerely held convictions, is misconceived. The police are not concerned with the politics of a demonstration; if they were, we should be a police state. Their duty is to maintain public order and to act, if need be, to prevent or suppress a breach of the peace.

This and other guidance laid down in his Report became the conventional wisdom which shaped the Metropolitan Police approach to public demonstrations and protests. It was so in the spring of 1979 when the National Front organized its election meeting at Southall.

Opposition to the meeting was organized by a co-ordinating committee of Southall organizations, operating from the premises of the Indian Workers' Association (IWA). I was told that it was the President of the IWA who invited the Anti-Nazi League (of which Blair Peach was a member) to Southall to help mobilize local opposition to the National Front. Whether this is so, or whether the League offered its services, has not been established, but there is no disputing the significant part they played in the events that were to follow.

It was an ominous sign when local police liaison officers were excluded from an otherwise public meeting called to formulate the strategy and tactics of the demonstration to be held in opposition to the National Front. At this meeting the local Council were condemned for allowing the Town Hall to be used by the National Front and two proposals were made. First, a protest march should be held on Sunday 22 April – the day before the National Front meeting – and, second, the people of Southall should be called upon to 'close down' the borough on the day of the meeting from 1 p.m. so that when the National Front arrived they would find a 'ghost town'. Had this latter proposal been carried out it could have been highly effective; it would have deprived the National Front of any opportunity to stir up trouble and would have shown the real insignificance of their support. Such a passive tactic did not suit the mood of the meeting. Others pressed for a sit-down demonstration to prevent the National Front using the Town Hall and their voices carried the day. From that moment confrontation was a certainty.

Local police called a meeting with the community leaders and appealed for reason and calm. They explained in particular the constitutional and legal rights of a parliamentary candidate. Pointing out that as it was a meeting which was planned and not a march, there was no law under which it could be banned. They underlined the lasting harm that could be done to community relations within the borough if confrontation continued to be the aim. At the same meeting police officers were told that some persons would be

81

coming to Southall on Monday 23 April with the specific intention to cause breaches of the peace. When the person giving this information – a man holding down a responsible position within the community – was asked to name these people, he said that was for the police to find out. The same man subsequently declined my invitation to see me during my own inquiry into the events at Southall.

The Socialist Workers' Party and Social Unity – an international Marxist group – gave the protest campaign publicity in their respective journals. So did the *Morning Star*. Violence was incited. One article (in the journal of the Socialist Workers' Party) hinted at it: 'We will not be intimidated by police. We will use any means necessary to stop the meeting.' And in the same edition the National Secretary of the Anti-Nazi League wrote: 'The Nazis must not be allowed to get anywhere near Southall Town Hall. For the Nazis to appear in Southall is an act of blatant and criminal incitement. Our reaction needs to be overwhelming and decisive.' There was much else said to the same effect. One man later told me that he was personally warned to stay away because 'there was going to be a rough house'.

So we came closer to the day of the meeting. The day before saw 2–3,000 people on a march organized by the IWA. It began at Southall moving to Ealing Town Hall to hand in a petition accompanied by a good deal of disarray and discussion between the groups making up the march. Two black youths were arrested for obstructing the police; this led to the marchers stopping outside Southall Police Station where they sat down blocking the road until the two youths were released – after being charged and bailed. As the march got under way again it split into two quite separate sections, with the more militant younger element displacing their elders at the front of the march. By now it was evident that Monday would be a difficult day.

And it was. Nearly 3,000 police were deployed in Southall to keep the peace on that black Monday. Blair Peach died. Twenty-five members of the public and ninety-seven police officers received hospital treatment for injuries. Race relations suffered a severe setback with repercussions spreading far beyond the boundaries of Southall.

The first police contingents came on duty at 11.30 a.m. For the protestors the day began at about 1 p.m. with the stewards of the demonstrators being called by their leaders to a hastily arranged meeting to which other members of the Asian community were invited. A member of the Anti-Nazi League was elected Chief Steward. I was later informed that when the violence erupted in Southall High Street one of the demonstrators was calling out in English for people to be orderly and in the next breath calling out in Punjabi for people to attack the police. If true, that man was clearly guilty of incitement. I was never able to verify the truth of it, but it is an illustration of how communication and language barriers can and do hamper police work and the process of investigation and law enforcement.

The plan was to place cordons of police officers around the outer area of the Town Hall and then to allow a limited number of demonstrators to come through to pre-arranged positions within sight of the Hall. Contingency plans had been prepared for sealing off the area if serious disorder broke out. By 1.30 p.m. groups of people had begun to gather near the Town Hall. From then on the numbers began to build up. The first flare-up and attack on the police began at 3 p.m. and police strength was increased. Damage and violence continued and at 4 p.m. the decision was taken to implement the contingency plans. Cordons of police moved across the roads and the area round the Town Hall was sealed off. By this time there were around 2,000 demonstrators on the scene. From 6 p.m. onwards, concerted and extremely violent attacks were made on police ranks. Bricks, smoke canisters, lumps of wood and concrete, paint, even folding chairs were thrown. Shop windows were broken. A police officer was stabbed.

Members of the National Front began to arrive for their meeting at about 7.30 p.m. No more than sixty people were allowed into the Town Hall, including twenty members of the public. The meeting was peaceful and lasted about ninety minutes. Following the departure of the National Front the demonstrators dispersed, police cordons were removed and by 10 p.m. traffic was flowing again. It was while the meeting was going on that Blair Peach was found with a head injury that was to prove fatal.

At about 7 p.m. a group of young Asians had gathered in front of a police cordon across the Broadway and started throwing missiles. A constable was hit in the face by a brick and his jaw was broken in three places. Assistance was called. A unit of the Special Patrol Group arrived and chased the group of Asians down a side street. It was then that Blair Peach was found injured. A New Zealander, a school teacher, Blair Peach was a political militant of the left wing. He was no stranger to protest and counter-protest and was particularly fervent in his opposition to racism and fascism. An ambulance was called and he was taken to Ealing Hospital where he later died.

As soon as I heard about his death I appointed David Powis, the Deputy Assistant Commissioner who headed CID operations, to investigate it. He brought in John Cass, one of the force's most experienced detectives, and assembled a team of detectives to help him. A rigorous and comprehensive investigation followed. It involved the questioning of nearly every police officer on duty at the time in the area where Blair Peach was found. Full use was made of the skill of pathologists and of forensic science. When all the evidence was assembled it showed that Blair Peach had died from a blow to his skull, which was thinner than most. The evidence pointed to the fact that the blow had been struck by a police officer. It is unlikely, however, that a police truncheon would have been heavy enough to inflict the injury. It is more probable that some other implement was used and although no direct evidence came to light to support it, one theory was that the injury was caused by a police personal radio.

It was one thing to identify that the blow had been struck by a police officer. It was quite a different matter to establish which one out of all those involved in the turmoil of clearing violent demonstrators from the Broadway. The investigation certainly narrowed down the number of suspects and the investigators had their suspicions. But suspicion is one thing, evidence to satisfy a court of law is another. The burden of proof does not shift because the suspect is a police officer. Every piece of evidence that could be found was put to the Director of Public Prosecutions; I was not surprised when he concluded that it was insufficient to justify judicial proceedings. Inevitably the allegations of 'whitewash' and 'cover-up' began. The position would have been very much easier if a police officer or officers had been charged. It would then have been a matter for the courts. Some officers would have been freed from suspicion. The Metropolitan Police would have been freed from unjustified accusations. This must have occurred to those who criticized us but it did not suit their book to acknowledge it.

Having set up a top level investigation into the circumstances of Blair Peach's death, I also decided to conduct personally an inquiry into the events surrounding the Southall demonstrations. It was, as far as I am aware, a unique course of action for a Commissioner to take. Some of my fellow chief officers thought I might be creating a dangerous precedent. I did not agree. The disorders had been very serious and I felt that a personal inquiry by the Commissioner would indicate the grave view that we took. I spent eight days interviewing people from Southall and police officers involved in the events. Of all the members of the community that were invited to take part, six declined. Mine was not the only inquiry. With the Home Secretary deciding not to set up a judicial inquiry, an unofficial inquiry was set up under the chairmanship of Michael Dummett, Professor of Logic at Oxford. The Metropolitan Police was invited to give evidence and criticized by Dummett for refusing to do so. That was hardly a logical reaction to the political realities of the situation. How, when the Home Secretary, the police authority for the Metropolitan Police, had declined to set up an official inquiry and was lending public support to my own personal inquiry, could I be expected to accept? Acceptance would have been tantamount to a public disagreement with Merlyn Rees. And I certainly did not disagree with him on the question of an official inquiry.

From beginning to end, the police had sought to maintain the law, preserve the peace and defend the constitutional rights of both the parliamentary candidate and his party members and of those citizens who wished to demonstrate peacefully. For their pains they had endured long hours of duty. They had been abused, buffeted and stoned; afterwards they were the target of hectoring accusations. The one consolation was that the Home Secretary took the view, as I did, that there should be no public inquiry. He too may have been influenced by the comments of Lord Scarman (in his Report on the Red Lion Square disorders):

> Public inquiries cannot, and should not, be held after every disorderly demonstration; police officers concerned with public order need to develop a continuing capacity for analysing, assessing and learning from their own operations.

This is exactly what is done. After all major demonstrations a comprehensive de-briefing takes place to see what lessons there are to be learned for the future.

One of the criticisms made at the time was that there were too many police officers on duty in Southall on Monday 23 April. I have to reject that criticism. There was clear evidence, justified in the event, that the meeting would attract several thousand determined demonstrators to prevent it. Since we did not have firearms, gas or water cannons as a means of controlling the protest, the presence of police in large numbers was essential.

With the benefit of hindsight, however, and I emphasize that, it is possible to see that misjudgements were made in the planning of the police operation. It now seems likely that the police cordons which sealed off the area around the Town Hall made matters worse by increasing the frustrations of the demonstrators and making communication with responsible leaders more difficult. The irony is that this concept of maintaining a sterile area free of demonstrators, as was done in the immediate vicinity of Southall Town Hall, stemmed from Lord Scarman's observations about the disorders at Red Lion Square in 1974:

> In the light of the events of the 15th June the police would be wise not to allow a future counter-demonstration to come so close to the object of its opposition.

Sensible advice, which had been applied successfully on a number of occasions. This time it merely made matters worse.

Much has also been said about the importance of making use of local officers and I agree with that. But in major operations involving thousands of demonstrators and 3,000 police officers, such an objective is not always easy to attain. The size of the demonstrations at Southall clearly precluded any possibility of the local District Commander being able to cope with the day's events without outside help. The directions therefore were that the Town Hall would be his sector of responsibility and, had events turned out as planned, it could have been local officers who would have dealt with the most sensitive incidents of the day. It did not happen that way. In the event the local police officers were mainly inside the cordoned area, out of contact with the bulk of demonstrators.

This is wrong, as local officers must be to the fore on the day of any demonstration. Just to illustrate how complex events can be, the unplanned isolation of local police officers from the worst disorders and conflicts of the day was in fact beneficial in helping to rebuild good community relations. The direct albeit unintended result was that hostility was not directed at local police but at those officers brought in from outside – and particularly at the Special Patrol Group.

It was inevitable that there would be criticism of the use of the SPG at Southall, and some of it extravagant, for example that made by Len Murray, General Secretary of the Trades Union Congress when giving a lecture at the Metropolitan Police Cadet School on 22 May 1979. Among other criticisms, he said:

> When the police act in their home neighbourhood they have to live with the consequence of what they do if they antagonize sections of the community. The Special Patrol Group are under no such restraints and their methods are giving rise to fears that we are developing, in all but name, a distinctive French-style riot police. I recognize that people are seconded to the Special Patrol Group for limited periods and are not permanently appointed as they are, say, to the French CRS. But there are

clear dangers in using a mobile reserve group of this kind and I hope these are recognized by the police.

To suggest that any police unit in Britain remotely resembles the CRS is irresponsible. It may suffice for me to quote back Len Murray's own words spoken in defence of the TUC and attacking the view that trade unions are above the law. He said:

> This picture is totally false. It is based on a few incidents – sometimes including violence – which we ourselves have condemned and which are utterly untypical of trade union activities. It is a concoction of what are not even half truths, presented as a description of trade union methods. It is much resented by active trade unionists. The truth is entirely different.

My comment is – for 'trade unions' substitute 'Special Patrol Group'.

The Group was first formed in 1965, when it consisted of 100 officers, split into four units, based in different areas of London. Its function was to act as a mobile reserve, intended to provide assistance for divisional officers in respect of any duty, but primarily to concentrate on the twin problems of housebreaking and hooliganism. As time went by, because of their ready availability, the SPG were increasingly used in connection with demonstrations and disorders. In some ways the use of the word 'Special' in the title of the Group is a misnomer. For the officers are no different from the majority of their colleagues, except in so far as they are selected – from among volunteers – for their crime-fighting aptitude.

Following the death of Blair Peach at Southall, I asked Pat Kavanagh, the Deputy Commissioner, to carry out a thorough review of the Group and the way it was being used. He made a number of recommendations, including the establishment of three extra Chief Inspector posts to improve supervision, the limitation of the period of service on the Group to a maximum of four years, wider and improved training, incorporating community relations training, and the attachment of local liaison officers to the Group

88

when working on divisions. I decided the name should be retained, mainly on the grounds that a change would be detrimental to the morale of the Group, since it would almost certainly be interpreted as a victory for their more vociferous and unreasonable critics. The strength of the Group was increased and their primary task was emphasized as responding to changing crime patterns and major emergencies. From that point on the SPG could only be committed to public order duties with the express authority of a Deputy Assistant Commissioner or someone even more senior.

Between 1977 and 1982 the political criticism of the SPG, which began to be voiced during Robert Mark's time, became more strident. In addition to Len Murray's speech at the Cadet School, the TUC passed a motion at its Annual Conference that same year calling for the SPG to be disbanded. And in June 1980 thirty-two Labour MPs put down a Notice of Question calling for the Government to arrange a debate on:

> the role of the Special Patrol Group, which although originally intended as an anti-crime squad, has been used extensively against political demonstrators and industrial pickets, and which, heavily equipped and armed for anti-terrorist work, has been used repeatedly against civilian targets, so that there is no publicly agreed authorization for its current role which has never been sanctioned by public opinion or parliamentary debate.

A good deal of nonsense has been talked about the SPG, much of it in ignorance, some of it half-truth and some deliberately dishonest. The transgressions of a few officers have been seized upon and used to belabour all SPG officers who are, in the main, men and women deserving of society's gratitude, not their brick-bats.

Following Southall I was not long to be left in peace. Other serious disorders followed. All Commissioners of Police have their share, but if I mention Notting Hill, Southall, Ilford, Lewisham, Grunwick and Brixton, it shows that I had a very full share.

It is important to get these events into historical perspective. Violent demonstrations, disorderly meetings and riots have long been a feature of British life. In 1833 Sir Robert Peel's new police had to contend with a mass political meeting at Clerkenwell which led to one officer being stabbed to death and many others being injured. It was in dealing with the violence then that the force first won the seal of public approval for their steady conduct, and this set a tradition, which it is essential to maintain, of minimum force in dealing with demonstrations.

The Victorian age is often thought to be an age of order and respectful behaviour; in fact terrible riots took place, such as those in Trafalgar Square in 1880 when the cavalry were mobilized, and in Hyde Park in 1885. The halcyon Edwardian days before World War I also saw violence linked with industrial disputes. As did the period around the General Strike of 1926. In the 1930s there were the riots incited by Sir Oswald Mosley and his Blackshirts against London's East End Jewish community. It is also important to recognize that most demonstrations take place peaceably and properly and in co-operation with the police. It is only a few that hit the headlines.

The right to protest and demonstrate may not be set down in parliamentary statute, but it is enshrined as one of Britain's fundamental political freedoms, and is certainly well established by historic custom and practice. The rise of television with its visual impact and emphasis on conflict and controversy makes protest an even more effective means of drawing attention to issues. Today it is at least open to question whether demonstration – as a means of expressing views in public – is as necessary as it was in the past when there were no newspapers with mass circulation, when there was no television or radio, when there were no democratically elected representatives of central and local government. But question it or not it is here to stay; and in a pluralistic society such as our own we can expect a high incidence of protest.

It is important to remember, however, that whilst freedom to demonstrate is part of our liberty, its exercise can and in London often does impose severe restrictions upon the freedoms of other people. A long line of demonstrators moving through the streets restricts the freedom of the men, women and children who have their homes in these streets, making it impossible for them to get out. Pedestrians are inconvenienced, shopkeepers have their trade restricted. Those who travel by bus or car do not travel as freely as they expect to. Those who want to go to work, faced by an industrial dispute or demonstration at their work place often cannot. At another level police officers have their freedom restricted by having to turn out at weekends instead of being at home with their families.

If the right to demonstrate is part of the nation's freedom, it is important to remember that it is a right which all should be free to exercise if they so wish. You might think that a statement of the obvious, but as Commissioner of Police I often found that some, especially on the extremes of politics, wished to be wholly free to demonstrate for their own causes but were not willing to allow this freedom to those with strongly opposed views – the cry going up that the police should not allow a particular march to be held.

Demonstrations, especially where there is a real prospect of major violence, put the police under pressure, and in London the Commissioner is at its centre. How the pressures build up is well illustrated by what happened when the National Front announced their intention of holding a march on Saturday, 13 August 1977, through the streets of Lewisham, an area densely populated by black people.

The situation locally had been exacerbated earlier by the arrest of twenty-four black youths for street crimes. This had led to a 'defence committee' being set up with the active assistance of the Socialist Workers' Party, followed by demonstrations against the police. A march was then held on 2 July by the Socialist Workers' Party during which their members clashed with supporters of the National Front: some fifty arrests were made, mostly from the ranks of the National Front. Against this background, news of the pro-posed National Front march in August was not welcomed by the Lewisham Borough Council. They made their concern known to the local police Commander and he in turn reported to me. I was faced with a serious and complex issue, involving strong political and racial elements. It was an issue I could have well done without in the first six months of my Commissionership, but it had to be faced.

Next on the doorstep were the representatives of the National Front and of a body calling itself the All Lewisham Campaign against Racism and Fascism. We met them separately on 26 July.

A third meeting took place when three local Members of Parliament, Roland Moyle, Christopher Price and John Silkin, together with the Mayor of Lewisham, the Bishop of Southwark and the Reverend Naylor all came to New Scotland Yard to register objection to the proposed National Front march and to ask me to recommend to the Home Secretary that the march be banned. They saw the Assistant Commissioner Wilford Gibson and David Helm, who was Deputy Assistant Commissioner (Operations) at the time.

We had decided that our policy should be to follow the guidance given by Lord Scarman in his Report on the Red Lion Square disorders. He had dealt in particular with the criticism that 'in view of its political character and provocative nature the National Front should have been prevented by police, not protected by them', and he had rejected this criticism forcefully. He wrote in his Report:

> It is necessary to understand the true nature of this criticism in order that it may be rejected as itself a menace to our liberties. It assumes that the police should be directed to prevent a demonstration taking place not because of any threats to public order but because the views being propagated by the demonstration are regarded as odious by others. The police cannot be allowed to do any such thing, unless Parliament expressly requires it to be done. Parliament has not forbidden the streets to the National Front and, were the police to do so, they would be usurping the political function of Parliament.

The relevance of these words to the proposed march through Lewisham were fully discussed with the Members of Parliament and other members of the deputation, and they were each given a copy of that extract from Lord Scarman's Report. I gave careful consideration to their representations, but I do not think it can have come as a surprise when, a few days later, each member of the delegation received a letter from me informing them that I would not seek a ban. I explained that I understood their fears but confirmed that I would not be seeking to recommend that the march should be banned because I believed that attempts by coercion or force to suppress a lawful demonstration to be not only wrong but illegal. To give way to such threats would not be just to defer to mob rule but to encourage it.

So the pressure and emotional content of the issue built up. Opponents of the march vented their fears in newspapers and on television about the violence and disorders which might arise, giving publicity to the plans of the National Front and making sure that the violence they predicted would in fact materialize.

Naturally I discussed the matter with Merlyn Rees. He understood the complexities of the issue and appreciated the reasons for my decision. The same could not be said of local Church leaders, some of whom kept strange company and others who made sure that they were not personally going to be involved in any exercise of authority to preserve good order.

I am saying this only to illustrate how decent, well-meaning people like local clergymen can allow emotion to overrule reason. One particular priest came to see me in my office in New Scotland Yard, a red handkerchief ostentatiously hanging out of his breast pocket. He spoke vehemently against the policies of the National Front (which was not what was at issue) and went on to tell me that lots of missiles were stored ready for use on the day. When asked where these missiles were hidden, he blustered and did not reply except to say, as he prepared to leave, 'By the way, Commissioner, I shall be on holiday in Spain on the day of the march.' I asked in reply whether he was washing his hands of all responsibility in the manner of a Pontius Pilate. Within twenty-four hours missiles had been used in earnest.

Before then a final attempt to secure a ban on the march was made by the Lewisham Council with an application to the High Court for an Order of Mandamus. At a hearing two days before the march, Mr Justice Flynn was in no doubt that he had the power to grant an Order of Mandamus if:

93

(a) I had failed to take account of all relevant matters or

(b) I was of the opinion that my powers under the Public Order Act were not sufficient and nevertheless had failed to seek the consent of the Home Secretary to make an order banning the march or

(c) I took a view of the situation which was hopelessly untenable in the circumstances.

His judgment was that I had properly applied my mind to all the relevant considerations, taking into account the times of the marches, the availability of police to control any likely situation, and the history of previous occasions. Conscious of the fact that I was keeping the situation under continuous review, he made no Order of Mandamus, and awarded costs against the Council. It was reassuring to have my decision not to seek a ban on the march ratified in the High Court, but there was no satisfaction in knowing that this was yet a further expense for the people of Lewisham who also had to bear the heavy costs of the disorders.

So the march, or rather marches – one by the National Front and one by the All Lewisham Campaign against Racism and Fascism (ALCARAF) – went ahead. In addition to 1,000 in reserve, over 3,000 officers were deployed between 9 a.m. and 7 p.m. and they showed great courage and determination in the impartiality with which they carried out their duties. The violent attacks on them were well-organized and at one stage there was a hail of missiles, including bottles and bricks, coming from roofs and high windows. The viciousness of some of the weapons and the use of ammonia from plastic bottles and water pistols bore the hallmark of violent political protest on the Continent and carried forebodings for the future. Mounted police were in action and the new plastic protective shields for foot constables were put into use for the first time.

Two hundred and seventy police officers and sixty members of the public were injured. 210 arrests were made. Great damage was done to private and police property.

While I was visiting one of the injured police officers in King's College Hospital, he pointed out a young man lying in a nearby bed, head bandaged, reading the *Socialist Worker*. He was one of the demonstrators. On my way out I stopped to speak to him. He told me he was a student from York. Indicating his injured head I asked what had happened and he told me that he must have been hit by a police officer. Not unnaturally I pressed him further, only to discover that he had not seen anyone hit him. He had blacked out and did not know what had happened. We chatted amicably for a little while before I left him with the observation that he might spend his time more profitably by returning to his studies in York.

In the light of the outcome at Lewisham, should I have banned the march? There is no clear answer to that, but first let the question be seen in its historical context. Lawful demonstration is part of the liberty of the nation and a ban is a denial of that liberty; this is illustrated by the fact that during World War II there was a permanent order of prohibition on marches. After the war, bans on marches in the Metropolitan Police District had been imposed on twenty-one occasions between 1945 and 1952, but for the fifteen years following 1952 there had been four orders only, the last ban being implemented in 1963 for two days.

When the orders had been made they were generally complied with, and were largely effective in preventing disorder. The major exception was the demonstration organized by the Committee of 100 in the early 1960s favouring nuclear disarmament, when thousands of people sat down in Trafalgar Square. On that occasion 4,000 police were employed and more than 1,300 persons arrested. Two orders also in 1962 and 1963 were ineffective inasmuch as although no march took place, meetings were held leading to disorder.

Gradually, then, a tradition of non-use of bans had been developed in favour of restoration of greater freedom of demonstration. This was also an indication of how the police service had responded to a society which had grown increasingly sensitive to its democratic rights and increasingly concerned about the powers of the state.

It had also been recognized by the police that bans can encourage minority groups to threaten violence with the object of silencing political opposition. This had been well explained by the late Aneurin Bevan, a man hardly well-known for support of right wing views. When in 1936 Parliament was considering the Public Order Bill (now Act), Bevan spoke in the House of Commons and said:

> So far from this Bill preventing the growth of the kind of organization to which we take exception, it is a Bill to confer the maximum amount of publicity upon the most undesirable element. It puts into their hands the liberties of all the rest of the political community. All that has to happen is for a certain party to misbehave in such a manner as to cause a breach of the peace and reasonable apprehension, and the liberty of meeting and procession is forthwith removed from all other political parties in that borough.

Certainly a ban would not have prevented disorder on Saturday, 13 August 1977. Against people determined to ignore it, a ban creates only additional problems of enforcement. A public meeting, without a march, would have been sufficient excuse for violent opposition, as illustrated by what happened at Southall.

Moreover, the National Front had informed my officers that if a ban was imposed, they would march outside the area of the ban or hold a meeting. A ban might therefore have relieved the Borough of Lewisham but it would have left the Metropolitan Police – or perhaps some other force – less well prepared to deal with the inevitable public disorder. We took the view that it was better to know what the National Front intended and to have their co-operation if serious public disorder was to be contained. Despite the disturbance, the damage and the casualties I was in no doubt at the time, and my mind has not changed, that the decision not to recommend a ban of the Lewisham march was the right one.

As Commissioner I had a clear duty not only to protect people's right of lawful demonstration but also to uphold the rule of law on the streets of London. At no time during my Commissionership had I any intention of abdicating my responsibilities in the face of groups who sought to achieve their ends by violent means, come what may.

Having said that, life does not stand still and each future occasion had to be judged by past events. What happened at Lewisham was now part of the record to which I had to have regard in deciding whether or not to apply to the Home Secretary for a ban. Clearly the level of violence displayed at Lewisham had added a new dimension to what, regrettably, must now be expected. The ugly face of politically motivated anarchy displayed on the streets of Lewisham made it possible now to envisage circumstances where a ban might have to be sought to protect the public and police alike.

It was this consideration among others which I had in mind when looking at the public order situation likely to arise in connection with a parliamentary by-election being held at Ilford shortly after the Lewisham disorders. A National Front candidate was among those seeking election and his supporters wished once again to march through Ilford. There were also prospects of violent opposition to the march.

The proposed march was to be through an area where a large Jewish community and a substantial Asian community lived and worked. Immediately, publicity about the event grew widespread and 1,500 members of the National Front were expected to come from all over Britain to join as demonstrators. The extreme left wing responded as at Lewisham with opposition being marshalled by the Redbridge Campaign against Racism and Fascism (RCARAF) and the Anti-Nazi League, which had close links with the Socialist Workers' Party. The Communist Party also put up a candidate.

Clearly a re-run and more of the events of Lewisham was intended and this time an Order was sought, and approved by the Home Secretary, to prohibit for two months from 24 February 'all public processions other than those of a religious, educational, festive or ceremonial character customarily held within the Metropolitan Police District'. It had to be broad-based and of some duration in order not to be discriminatory, and quite a few organizations seeking to promote their causes by marches in different parts of London were surprised to find that they were caught by the ban.

The ban did not prevent the need for large numbers of police officers to be on duty on the day because the National Front immediately announced their intention of going ahead with a meeting at Ilford County High School but substituting 'mass canvassing' for a march. This was, of course, all constitutionally and legally proper, but to avoid disorder some 6,000 police officers were on duty in the area, largely in cordons round the school.

There was some counter-demonstrating but, either because of the show of police strength or because of the ban, the numbers involved did not exceed a few hundred, and the day ended quietly.

Was the ban necessary? We shall never know the answer to that because no one can say what would have happened if the National Front march and the counter-marches had taken place. All that can be said is that all of us who lived in London were the losers. The freedom to march had been taken away, shops and houses were barricaded in Ilford against the possibility of violence, and 6,000 police officers were taken away from areas all over the metropolis where they should have been getting on with their ordinary work of policing and protecting the public. The London ratepayers had to pay a lot of money to meet the extra cost of the large police deployment. It all had very little to do with the citizens of Ilford and Barkingside, who suffered a great deal of intrusion into their lives.

Two last words on the Lewisham marches. Nothing of what I said at the time or have said since means that I find the racism of the National Front any less repugnant than the malign seeking of violence by the Socialist Workers' Party and groups of similar ilk. For their part the National Front showed no kind regard for me: they put me on their 'hit list' and called me the 'Tartan Muppet'! What I do say is that ample powers exist under the Public Order Act and other legislation to restrict and deal with any display of racist messages. Indeed, at Lewisham when the National Front produced some sixty posters which had an anti-mugging theme with a racial bias they were told by police officers that action would be taken against them if the posters were displayed. None were. Perhaps the last word about my impartiality can lie with my daughter. She telephoned me from Glasgow to say, 'Dad, you must have got the balance about right – both sides are abusing you!'

Secondly, less than three years before the events of Lewisham, Robert Mark was able to observe that history showed a general avoidance of extreme disorder in London. The underlying reason, he said,

> ... is perhaps our long-standing tradition of changing governments without bloodshed or turmoil, and freedom of expression unsurpassed elsewhere. This has allowed a unique relationship between the people and the police, who traditionally depend on goodwill rather than force in carrying out these duties . . . The police have never had any special weapons or equipment for crowd control . . . demonstrators in this country rarely have recourse to lethal weapons.

How quickly change can come about. It was no easy decision in 1976, after the excessive violence and police injuries of the Notting Hill Carnival, for the Metropolitan Police to break with long-standing tradition and seek authority for protective shields. The cascade of bricks, the many offensive weapons and the use of ammonia showed all too sadly how the wheel had turned. It has turned further since.

Whilst the ban imposed as a result of the National Front's intended march at Ilford was the first such ban for fifteen years, it was not to be the last. In fact it was the first of twelve bans I asked for and had granted by the Home Secretary. After Ilford, however, it was three years before another ban was imposed. Again it was prompted by National Front activity. This time they proposed to hold a march through Deptford only weeks after a tragic fire had killed thirteen local black youngsters. The Brixton riots, which came only days after the ban ended, would have paled into insignificance against the disorders that such a march would have attracted had it been allowed to go ahead.

The first five bans were all of an extended period of four weeks or more. They covered all processions, other than those of a religious, educational, festive and ceremonial nature and applied to the whole of the Metropolitan Police District. The bans were of a general nature to avoid any suggestion that we were (in Lord

Scarman's words) 'usurping the political function of Parliament'. This policy did not meet with everyone's approval; particularly opposed to it were supporters of organizations who were inadvertently caught up in the ban and prevented from holding their own marches. Prominent among these were Monsignor Bruce Kent and the CND. In May 1981 their application for leave to apply for judicial review of my Order banning marches was refused. The Court of Appeal upheld that decision and unanimously held that the Order I had made prohibiting processions for twenty-eight days from 25 April was valid. Nevertheless, reading between the lines of the judgements of Lord Denning and Sir Denys Buckley, it was clear that greater selectivity in drawing up the Order would be acceptable.

With this in mind, in October that year when the National Front proposed a march through Thornton Heath, where early that year Terry May, a young white man had been killed during an affray between black and white youths, I applied for a selective ban limited to the Borough of Croydon for a period of four days. It must be admitted that I had by this time become even less patient with the activities of the National Front and the equally odious British Movement and decided that the threat of civil disorder posed by their marches could no longer be allowed to interfere to the same extent with the political freedoms of other citizens. That remained my policy in applying for bans during the remainder of my time as Commissioner. If I was to stand accused of political bias that, I decided, was a cross I would have to bear.

At Southall, at Lewisham, at Ilford, at Brixton and at other such events there was one common element, virtually one common cause for the great disorders: race and racism. There was one event only involving great confrontation with the police where race was not the key issue – Grunwick. Although there the employees were Asians, the issue at the heart of the dispute was an industrial one.

There was much that was unbelievable about the facts of the Grunwick dispute. Would any TV producer accept a scenario of fiction which ran as follows? The greatest and most famous police force in the world, always alleged by its critics to be racist, struggles might and main each day for months under scrutiny of all the media, to convey a small group of frightened Asian workers in a double-decker bus into a small factory managed by a rich Anglo-Indian against the massed opposition of white trade unionists. The scene of this great action? The backstreets of the rather sad suburb of Neasden in north west London, famous only for being the regular butt of the satire of *Private Eye*. Pull the other leg indeed, but this is precisely what happened.

It was a problem which I inherited on becoming Commissioner, and it was a major and testing one. Seven Asian workers walked out of a small photo-processing laboratory in Neasden on 20 August 1976, complaining about bad pay and poor working conditions; within three days the number of strikers had risen to about 140, including about forty-five students, and their cause had been taken over by a white collar union: the Association of Professional Executive and Computer Staff (APEX). Roy Grantham was the secretary of APEX. Another leading figure was Jack Dromey, Secretary of the Brent Trades Council, who acted as close adviser to the strike committee. The employer at the factory was George Ward, an Anglo-Indian, who came to Britain in 1948, started as an office boy, qualified eleven years later as a chartered accountant, started the Grunwick venture in a mews in 1961, and by 1976 was a millionaire.

At the heart of the dispute was George Ward's wish to continue employing Asian workers and non-union workers at rates of pay determined by himself, whereas the trade unions wished to see the factory manned by union workers paid at nationally agreed rates of pay.

The dispute in my view would have proceeded along routine lines without major violence if there had not been deliberate outside intervention, much of it for political reasons. The situation was not helped by the presence of public figures such as Len Murray, who not only took part in the marches outside the factory but also joined the picket line. Roy Grantham addressed the TUC in September 1976 and obtained unanimous promise of support. Later Shirley Williams, Fred Mulley and Denis Howell who, as well as being

Government ministers were also members of APEX, all decided to join the picket line. Their presence was given a great deal of publicity. I have no doubt at all that the three Members of Parliament did what they did for the best motives. I also know that Shirley Williams and the others in no way supported the violence. But whatever the intentions the impression was that Parliament, the Labour Party and the TUC supported the dispute. It was police officers who had to meet the cost of that. Political extremists, like the Socialist Workers' Party, saw a chance to build a small local situation into a national one, to challenge the Government and authority and to secure confrontation between pickets and police.

George Ward, too, did not remain idle. He obtained the support of John Gorst, Conservative Member of Parliament for the area in which the Grunwick factory was located, who was also a public relations consultant. Groups like the National Association for Freedom also came to his aid.

Attempts to cut off supplies to the factory failed, with Ward flying in chemicals and other materials from his factories in Holland and West Germany. Jack Dromey recommended more aggressive tactics, aimed at marshalling such massive pickets at the factory gate that Ward would have to capitulate to the demands of the trade unionists, as had happened in 1971 at the Saltley Coke Depot in the West Midlands where Arthur Scargill and large numbers of miners had their way at the factory gate.

At Grunwick on 13 June a mass picket of 700 demonstrators faced the police outside the factory gate. The entire footway and road became blocked and when the workers started to arrive they were pushed, jostled, abused and spat on. Eggs and flour bombs were hurled at the police. Eighty-four arrests were made, and the workers got safely through the gates. The number of pickets grew to 1,500 and the now famous double-decker bus began to be used daily to take the workers into the factory. Each day this bus under heavy police escort made its laboured journey to the gate of the factory and the shoving, the shouting, the obscenities, the spitting and the hurling of missiles began. It was a daily ritual watched on television by audiences at home and abroad.

In my experience there is often an element of farce in the midst of the gravest of situations. It occurred at Grunwick when Roy Grantham, the APEX Secretary, was invited to enter the Grunwick factory to address the workers in the presence of representatives of the press, to see the conditions within the factory (which he had never visited) and to ascertain in person if the workers there wished to be members of a trade union. Grantham accepted the offer. He went inside, climbed onto a table and began to speak to the workers as arranged. But something must have gone wrong for the workers, mostly women, began to shout that they were going to take his trousers off and throw him out into the street. George Ward rescued him and he fled the factory in a rage telling the press that mass picketing would continue indefinitely.

On 21 June seven Members of Parliament took post on the picket line: Ian Mikardo, Joan Maynard, Dennis Skinner, Martin Flannery, Joan Lestor, Denis Canavan and Audrey Wise. Mrs Wise was arrested for obstructing the police and subsequently convicted. The most difficult day came on 23 June. Arthur Scargill, in those days President of the Yorkshire branch of the National Union of Mineworkers, appeared outside the factory, accompanied by large numbers of supporters. They had come by coach from all over the country. As Scargill and these men first paraded on the Neasden street it seemed that their intention might be to secure another 'Saltley': to overrun the police lines, halt the bus carrying the workers and close the factory. Many people were arrested that day; among them Arthur Scargill. At the magistrates' court he was defended by Queen's Counsel and found not guilty. An application for costs was refused. Following Scargill's case a number of other miners who had been arrested at the same time appeared in the same court. No defending lawyer was provided; all without exception pleaded guilty.

That was also the day when a most serious injury was suffered by a young police officer going to the assistance of another officer who had made an arrest. He was struck on the head by a bottle thrown from the crowd, and lay unconscious and spreadeagled on the ground with a serious head injury. The photograph of this gravely injured officer was widely published by the media and illustrated something of the violence police officers were having to face. When I visited the young officer in hospital on the same day he told me it was obviously not a decent trade unionist who had thrown the bottle at him but a lout.

23 June was also the day on which Maurice Jones, a friend of Scargill and Editor of the *Yorkshire Miner* was arrested for using threatening words and behaviour likely to lead to a breach of the peace. He was charged, fingerprinted and released on bail. When the time came for Jones to surrender to his bail it was found that he had fled to East Germany with his family, leaving behind a letter in which he alleged that while detained at Wembley Police Station he had been interrogated by Special Branch officers who had made threats against him and his family. This is completely untrue. At no time did any Special Branch officer even speak to him. He was in the presence throughout of the uniformed officer who arrested him, and nothing was known at the station of his political background.

A newsreel film of the day shows Arthur Scargill being released from Wembley Police Station and on the steps of the station Maurice Jones can be seen applauding Scargill as he comes out and walks down to the newsmen. Jones is smiling happily even though, according to his story, he, his wife and his child had all been threatened by the police inside the station a few minutes earlier. More significantly, Jones made no move to tell the assembled press there and then of what he later said had happened inside the police station.

Events became singularly strange thereafter. First, Scargill flew off to join Jones in East Germany where he had sought asylum. Second, on 24 July reports reached the police that Jones was coming back to London; it was also learnt that arrangements had been made for the media to be represented in strength when he arrived. A Chief Inspector and other officers waited at the terminal of Heathrow Airport. Shortly after 1 p.m. Jones came out with his wife and daughter, with Arthur Scargill and Richard Briscoe, an official of the NUM. As Jones reached the terminal barrier he was arrested by the Chief Inspector on a warrant issued by the court. Jones said he was not moving until he had seen his solicitor and he was told that this could be arranged at Heathrow Police Station. Jones continued to refuse to move and eventually officers had to carry him away kicking and struggling to a nearby room. Once inside, Jones immediately became quiet and was joined by his wife and daughter. A little later he walked quietly to Heathrow Police Station where he was joined by two solicitors acting for him. Two policewomen stayed with Mrs Jones and her daughter to help her with her luggage, which had been wrongly routed, until she was collected by a friend in a car.

About 2 p.m. on the same afternoon, Scargill and Briscoe came with Richard Kelly MP to complain about the manner of Jones's arrest. They had five journalists with them. All except the journalists were seen by a Chief Superintendent and written statements were taken. At 4 p.m. Jones was taken to Wembley Police Station and detained pending appearance the following day at Willesden magistrates' court. That evening his solicitor applied to a judge for Jones to be released again on bail. The application was refused.

When Jones appeared in court his solicitor asked for a remand on bail and this was granted once Jones's passport had been taken from him and a surety of £1,000 had been obtained. Finally, on 29 September, Maurice Jones appeared at Barnet magistrates' court with Counsel acting for him. He was found guilty of using threatening words and behaviour likely to lead to a breach of the peace and he was fined £50. He appealed to the crown court against conviction and sentence. A Queen's Counsel was engaged on his behalf and the appeal was heard on 4 January 1978. It was dismissed.

Those are the basic facts of Maurice Jones's arrest and the events that followed. They bear little resemblance to the report put out by Tass at the time of his flight to East Germany. Broadcast in Russian on Moscow Radio, Tass gave their own distinctive slant to the arrest:

Several Members of Parliament have announced their intention to raise in the House of Commons the question of the illegal persecution of Maurice Jones, Editor of the official paper of Britain's Yorkshire coalminers. This was reported on Sunday, 17 July, by Arthur Scargill, the Yorkshire miners' leader, who read out a letter from Jones at a press conference in Barnsley.

On 23 June Maurice Jones was on a picket line outside the Grunwick photo-processing laboratory the workers of which have been waging a struggle for eleven months now for the recognition of their right to form a trade union. Their courageous struggle is supported by all categories of the working people in Britain, but the authorities took the side of the employers, and the police have made repeated arrests of the pickets. Maurice Jones too was taken to a police station and charged with 'insulting behaviour'.

Maurice Jones was intimidated and blackmailed by plain-clothes policemen, who hinted that his two-year-old daughter may become a victim of a road accident and that the residence permit for his Finnish-born wife may be terminated. The policemen made no secret of why they were blackmailing the newspaper editor. One of them said that no authority could afford the luxury of allowing a 'dangerously attractive' newspaper like that edited by Maurice Jones to politicize such a vital group as the miners.

Because of the threats to his family, Maurice Jones has had to 'emigrate' from Britain, together with his wife and daughter. In a letter sent to Scargill from the GDR, he writes that he could not put his family at risk. The story of Maurice Jones clearly shows what the much-vaunted 'democratic liberties' in Britain are worth and how the workers' hard-won right to strike is being violated.

Meanwhile, at Grunwick the double-decker bus continued to carry its workers daily to the factory through massive physical opposition. On some days the numbers of demonstrators was simply enormous. On 11 July for example, 20,000 were estimated to be present. It was all to no avail, and finally a demonstration was planned for 7 November by the strike committee which they called 'The Day of Judgment' – a code name which speaks for itself. Massive numbers were assembled outside the factory and the violence against the police was very bitter. Many arrests were made, and the busload of workers once again passed safely through the factory gates. The demonstrators became so frustrated that several thousands of them marched to Willesden Green Police Station and picketed the building. A delegation was allowed inside the station and they said they had come to protest against the actions of the police. I suspect that the real cause of their anger was that they had been out-manoeuvred by the police. From that day on the opposition outside the factory gate began to diminish and the numbers to dwindle, until finally the dispute expired with a whimper and peace returned to the streets of Neasden.

During the most violent week of the dispute I had gone to the scene of operations and walked down the police lines, talking to officers waiting for the violence which would break out when the hired bus arrived. Shouts of abuse greeted me on every side from the trade union pickets and members of the Socialist Workers' Party. They at least showed a proper recognition of my rank for as soon as I was seen, up went the cry 'Chief Pig!'

The Home Secretary, Merlyn Rees, was not so fortunate. When he visited Grunwick he was roundly condemned by local residents. The encouragement given to the industrial dispute by Labour supporters had led to havoc being played for months with the peace and quiet of their normally tranquil back streets. I recall in particular one man coming in his shirt sleeves to the front door of his house and calling to the Home Secretary to come over. When Merlyn Rees did so, the old man told him that he had been a Labour supporter for fifty years and never had he expected to see a Labour Government encourage a dispute and then fail to deal with the disgraceful scenes which were happening in the neighbourhood.

The issues raised by the Grunwick dispute were taken to the High Court and important questions were raised relating to industrial disputes and picketing, but this is not the place to rehearse them. It is, however, worth mentioning the role of police. The police are there to keep the peace; to allow those who wish to work to do so without intimidation and to allow strikers to picket peacefully and lawfully. The suggestion is not infrequently made that the law is deficient and I am not against a revision of the law if it helps to clarify enforcement and other issues. The truth is that the current law works well enough provided the parties to a dispute observe it – which is what happens in the great majority of industrial disputes. It is only when emotions are aroused, perhaps by persons not directly involved in the industry concerned, and the rules are broken that trouble starts.

Grunwick, Lewisham and then Southall each in its time seemed to be the peak of London's disorder. But the real crescendo was still to come.

6

Race and Riots

On 11 April 1981 the racial tensions which had smouldered just below the surface of life in London's deprived inner city areas finally erupted into flame. Predictably it happened on the streets of Brixton, which had for years been the focus of black politics both within London and the country as a whole. If the location was predictable so was the immediate cause of the violence – antagonism toward the police.

The scene was set on the evening of Friday, 10 April; disorder broke out following an incident in Atlantic Road, when two police officers (one of them a woman) went to the aid of a young black man who had been stabbed. Confrontation with the black community was no rare event for Brixton's police officers. For a decade or more arrests of black people had increasingly carried with it the possibility of concerted opposition from other black people, who often had no connection with the person arrested other than the commonality of their skin colour. The fact that on this occasion disorder occurred following an attempt by police to help an injured black youth only underlined the sad state of the relationship between Brixton's black community and Brixton's police officers.

The trouble on Friday lasted no more than ninety minutes; its effect was to heighten tension and suspicion. It led directly to an increased police presence in Brixton on the following day; an increase over and above the 112 officers who were already being employed locally on 'Operation Swamp' – designed to 'swamp' the locality with plain clothes police officers to combat the high level of street crime that Brixton was suffering. This operation was a direct response to the demands of local residents. Reports from victims indicated that street crime in the area was being committed pre-dominantly by young blacks. Afterwards the name took on unfortunate and unintended connotations, and in truth it was neither a sensitive nor sensible name for the operation. I later made it clear that the practice of giving operations a title was to stop.

Two officers employed on 'Operation Swamp' were unwittingly to become the trigger to Brixton's riots when, late on Saturday afternoon, they stopped a black man on suspicion of possessing cannabis. Working in plain clothes they saw the man, sitting in the driving seat of his car, put something into the top of his sock. The location was once again Atlantic Road; cannabis was not unknown in the area. As it happened, when the two officers questioned their suspect it turned out that he was a mini-cab driver; innocent of the officers' suspicions he was wisely hiding his money in his sock. By the time the officers found this out a group of thirty to forty black men had gathered and begun to shout abuse at them. One of the group was arrested. By now other officers patrolling nearby had been attracted by the noise and disturbance. A police van arrived and the arrested man placed inside. The crowd had grown and now numbered around 150. Hostility towards the police gathered force. First stones, then bricks were thrown. Police vehicles were over-turned and fired. At 5.45 p.m., just one hour after the stop on the mini-cab driver, the first petrol bomb was thrown. Brixton was literally aflame.

Smacking of the sectarian disorders of Northern Ireland but more closely paralleling the race riots of the United States, the destruction was greater than anything London had seen since the days of the blitz. From a police viewpoint it was much like a war, but it was a war which had to be fought by a police service accustomed to traditions of defensiveness in combating disorder. Despite the lessons we ought to have learnt from the Bristol riots a year earlier, we were still ill-equipped to deal effectively with the violence of urban riots. What we lacked in weaponry, tactics and strategy, however, was more than compensated for by the courage and fortitude of the 7,000 plus police officers – men and women – who were called in to quell the disorder.

The violence came to its peak on the Saturday evening, but the disorder continued until late on Monday 13 April. At 11.34 p.m. the final call was received for police to deal with a smashed shop window. The information was false; the riots were over. Between 6.10 p.m. on Friday 10 April and 11.34 p.m. on Monday 13 April 1981 in a small area of Brixton 415 police officers and 172 members of the public were injured. 118 police vehicles and 61 private vehicles were damaged. 4 police vehicles and 30 private vehicles were totally destroyed. 28 premises were seriously damaged by fire and a further 158 premises were attacked. 779 crimes were reported and 285 people were arrested. British policing was put squarely under the spotlight of public scrutiny. An example was set – as the 'Bristol now, Brixton next?' graffiti of the year before had suggested it would be – that did little to discourage the widespread outbreaks of disorder which occurred across Britain during July.

There is a danger that the impression left by the news coverage of that weekend will become more vivid and dramatic than the reality of events. Let me try, therefore, now that time has intervened, to put the main elements into perspective. The disorder was limited to a very small part of one inner London borough. There were no deaths. Compared to the race riots in the United States during the 1960s and compared to disorders elsewhere in Europe, Brixton was small beer. The international interest the riots attracted was an indication of the relative tranquillity we enjoy in this country – to the envy of much of the rest of the Western World.

On that fateful Saturday, I was the guest of Hertsmere Borough Council at their annual dinner in the Borehamwood Civic Hall. The Mayor was coming to the close of his welcoming address to which I was to reply, when Don Hanson, the local police Commander, passed a note telling me about the start of the riots and the fact that I was required back at New Scotland Yard. My reply to the Mayor's welcome was, to say the least, brief. I explained that I had to leave, that it was not because of anything the Mayor had said, but that rioting had broken out in Brixton. I left the room to a standing ovation, which had nothing to do with the quality of my speech, but was a spontaneous expression of people's concern, sympathy and support for officers facing up to the dangers and trials of policing.

I walked across the road to Borehamwood Police Station and telephoned Wilf Gibson, the Assistant Commissioner in charge of uniform operations. He quickly spelled out the gravity of the situation and I lost no time in returning to New Scotland Yard. There I was brought up to date with developments and later I left with Pat Kavanagh and Wilf Gibson for Brixton Police Station.

The worst of the violence had abated and I walked round speaking to as many operational officers as possible, assuring them of support and trying to maintain morale. Even at that early stage it was evident that we had lessons to learn about how best to control our manpower resources. In their anxiety to help colleagues, police officers from all over London, many of whom were off duty, had responded to calls for assistance and headed for Brixton Police Station. The station became inundated and unable to cope with the number of officers arriving. The resources of men and equipment available took too long to assemble and organize. One of the hard lessons of the riots was the need for a location, separate from the local police station, to which manpower and resources can be directed as they arrive. Reinforcements can then be collated, policing needs assessed, duties formulated and directions given away from the operational hubbub that will inevitably take over the local divisional police station.

That weekend London's police officers were the target of stone throwing and petrol bomb attacks. Many showed, individually and collectively, a calmness and bravery that is beyond praise. Lord Scarman wrote in his official Report on the riots that the events had led him 'to marvel at and be thankful for the courage and dedication which was displayed by members of the police and emergency services in Brixton over that terrible weekend. They stood between our society and a total collapse of law and order in the streets of an important part of the capital. For that they deserve, and must receive, the praise and thanks of all sections of our community.' Well said, but in the torrent of words which poured forth in

Parliament, in newspapers and on television and radio, police officers heard a great deal of elaboration and comment on criticisms expressed in Lord Scarman's Report, but mighty little of 'the praise and thanks of all sections of our community'.

Just how much London and the nation owed to police officers in Brixton is well illustrated by the conduct and character of one particular Chief Superintendent who, with a handful of officers prevented disaster.

Chief Superintendent Robinson and his men were in the thick of the disorder at the junction of Effra Parade and Railton Road. He had twice been struck in the face by missiles and sustained injuries which in normal circumstances would have been sufficient to send him to hospital. He and his men were under pressure and in danger of being overrun. Lord Scarman's official account was that:

> At about 9 p.m. Mr Robinson's north cordon was temporarily overwhelmed by the crowd attacking it. Many officers were injured, some of them seriously and some police shields were captured by the crowd. The officers (now some 25 to 30 in number with about 10 to 12 shields between them) fell back to the north side of the junction with Effra Parade where they managed to re-form a line. This meant, however, that the cordon and the crowd were virtually on top of the fire appliances and firemen. A fire officer said to the Chief Superintendent that he and his officers would have to withdraw. Chief Superintendent Robinson told the fire officer that reinforcements were on the way and asked him to remain a little longer, to which he agreed. But considering the situation, it seemed to Mr Robinson that extraordinary measures were necessary if he was to save the position and prevent his officers or the firemen being further injured or even killed. He took a hose from a fireman, ordered other officers to do likewise and turned the jets on the crowd. The action achieved the effect Mr Robinson desired. The crowd fell back and the firemen were able to continue to fight the fires.*

* para 3.70 Scarman Report. HMSO Cmnd 8427

While I was at Brixton Police Station, Chief Superintendent Robinson came into the room where I was with the local Commanders. He had just returned from hospital where his facial injuries had required plastic surgery and the insertion of many stitches. His face was still bloody and he was dishevelled, but not downhearted. He was in uniform and prepared to return to duty.

I asked him if there was anything I could do or get to help him, and in reply he said that he would appreciate a tot of whisky. I went over to the Commander's drink cupboard and poured out a glass for him. Mr Robinson asked if he could have it without water, but he forgot the effect that neat whisky would have on the painful injuries inside his mouth. His first mouthful probably put his fortitude to the test more than anything he had suffered so far that evening. At least it was the only time I saw tears in his eyes.

I will add a postscript to this account of the conduct of a brave and outstanding police officer. At the National Staff College for the police, a course, called the Senior Command Course, is held for police officers of Superintendent and Chief Superintendent rank who are considered likely to be worthy of appointment to the most senior ranks in the service. This is an important course and extensive arrangements are made for the selection of suitable candidates. Some time after the Brixton riots, Chief Superintendent Robinson, who is a university graduate, applied and was selected by the Met to attend an extended interview for final selection to that course. The National Selection Board turned him down because they considered that he lacked all-round experience. An operational officer until the force sent him to university, then Chief Inspector entrusted with the task of setting up social studies in the training school, a Superintendent in the Community Relations Branch, a Chief Superintendent in command of Kensington Division, all this over and above his performance at Brixton – and yet John Robinson was felt not to have sufficient all-round experience.

The local Commander of the district was Brian Fairbairn and his predecessor had been Len Adams. As is the fate of front line Commanders, they received an undue share of criticism and comment either from those wise after the event or from armchair critics who have never come within a mile of a missile-throwing, menacing mob on the rampage in the hours of darkness. I stand foursquare in saying that Fairbairn did a magnificent job in marshalling resources and in containing the violence. And what did Adams do? As soon as he heard report of the outbreak of disorders, he made haste to get to Brixton to see if he could help and sustain his successor. Such is the spirit, nourished over 150 years, of the Metropolitan Police.

Lord Scarman and others have criticized Adams and Fairbairn for not getting alongside and consulting local community leaders sufficiently. I do not want to drag out all the pros and cons of this issue again for yet more debate, nor, I am sure, do Adams and Fairbairn, so let me limit what I want to say to the comment that good community relations, like marriage, depends upon a two-way commitment. Married men may perhaps confirm my view that it is not easy to get alongside your wife, if your marital partner has no intention of making this possible. And when community relations break down, the fault, as in a broken marriage, rarely lies with one party only. No one denies that police officers made mistakes and did things that contributed to the state of affairs in Brixton. But the fault was not theirs alone. Too often Ted Knight, as Leader of Lambeth Council, and others were given to criticize publicly the local police, which did nothing to make the task of police in the community less difficult.

I stayed late at Brixton Police Station and on the following morning – Sunday – I was in touch with the Home Secretary. He had been kept informed of the progress of events, and a meeting was arranged for the early afternoon. As I arrived at the Home Office, I ran into a bevy of television cameras and reporters. They caught me on the wrong foot and in answer to a question I said that in my opinion the riots were not spontaneous; that the use of Molotov cocktails indicated outside organization and the possibility of conspiracy. Act in haste, repent at leisure. In fact there is no evidence to show that the disorders *started* other than spontaneously, but once under way there were of course, as Lord Scarman found, people ready to take advantage of them.

William Whitelaw's reaction when we met was that the riots

were going to be a difficult political horse to ride. He made it clear that he was considering an inquiry, although at that stage he did not indicate what form it was going to take.

Together he and I visited Brixton. We toured the damaged area, but avoided locations where police officers were still dealing with troubles and especially with potential looters; neither of us intended to be the spark that ignited another round of violence. The Home Secretary spoke with Brian Fairbairn and his senior officers who gave him their assessment of the situation and tried to estimate how long the trouble might continue. In the event their prognosis was more pessimistic than the reality, but it was a measure of how we all felt that weekend. Our dark feelings only deepened as we visited hospitals to see officers who had been injured. The many vicious head injuries I saw that day made me determined that police officers should have equipment to give them greater protection from injury and enable them to deal more effectively with serious public disorder.

For me Brixton was a watershed. I had always believed that maintaining the traditional image of the unarmed, conventionally dressed British bobby was of major importance in maintaining the peace and preventing violent disorders, for it attracted public sympathy. I still hold to the importance of maintaining that traditional image, but not where it means police officers suffering serious injury. What I saw at Brixton and in the nearby hospitals convinced me that the time had, alas, come when police officers must be equipped with protective clothing and provided with special equipment to deal with riots. It may also have left its impression on the Home Secretary, for after the disorders in July of that year he was quick to accept publicly the need for police officers to have additional equipment – offensive as well as protective – in order to deal with the disorders effectively. Lord Scarman made the same recommendation in his Report on the events at Brixton. It was a sad day for Britain that forced us to this conclusion.

In addition to this, operational lessons were learned that led to the force drawing up new contingency plans for dealing with disorder, which included the rapid reinforcement of local units as necessary. Substantial changes were also made in training. The new arrangements proved their worth several times before I retired.

On Monday the Home Secretary called me to a meeting at the Home Office. On arrival I found Sir Brian Cubbon, the permanent head of the Home Office and Robert Andrew, head of the Police Department, already present. With little ado the Home Secretary told me that later that same day he would be announcing to Parliament his decision to appoint an inquiry under Section 32 of the Police Act 1964. This effectively meant that the inquiry into the events at Brixton would concentrate upon policing and not extend in depth to the wider social, political and economic context. The limitations of this were subsequently acknowledged by Lord Scarman who, a year after completing his inquiry, wrote in *The Times* on 25 November 1982:

> The Brixton inquiry was an inquiry into policing. It was ordered by the Home Secretary under a power given to him by the Police Act 1964. But it was clear from the beginning that the specific policing problem could not be understood, let alone solved, unless it were studied in its social setting. All this is now common knowledge and is accepted equally by police and community leaders.
>
> No doubt it was recognized by the thoughtful long before the report was published one year ago.

I was, to say the least, unhappy at what the Home Secretary had to say, and told him plainly why. Some faults certainly lay at our door but there were faults elsewhere also. I put it to him that there were many other factors, social, political, economic and racial which needed to be examined and taken into account. I added that after the battering which the force had received over the last two days, morale was hardly likely to be improved by an announcement that there was to be an inquiry into the conduct of police.

Some fairly cool discussion followed, which disclosed pretty clearly the supporting advice Brian Cubbon had already given to the Home Secretary. Finally the Home Secretary asked me bluntly whether I was saying that there should be no inquiry at all. I replied that I was saying no such thing, only that if there was to be an inquiry it should not be confined just to the policing of Brixton but extended to a much wider field.

The Home Secretary then told me that he had already asked Lord Scarman to conduct the inquiry under the Police Act: he added that he was sure that Lord Scarman would have regard to wider issues. This, however, was moonshine, for however the proposal was dressed up (and I was sure that it would be well dressed up) it was, to use Lord Scarman's own words, to be 'an inquiry into policing'. It was also clear to me that I had been called to the Home Office meeting not to discuss what might be arranged, as a Commissioner of Police might reasonably expect, but to be informed of what the Home Secretary had already agreed with his civil servants. It was an acrimonious meeting and as I left the Home Office that morning it was the only time in my many visits there that I was not escorted to the lift or the front door by a civil servant. After what I had just witnessed at the meeting I was glad to keep my own company.

The thought kept pressing in on me that the police were to be the political scapegoats. Later in the day the Home Secretary announced his intentions to the House of Commons. Admittedly, the options open to the Home Secretary were few. But having decided to hold an inquiry, the procedure laid down by the Tribunals of Inquiry (Evidence) Act 1921 was surely the most appropriate in this case. With Parliament resolved on the necessity of an inquiry, the subsequent tribunal would have had all the powers and privileges of the High Court. Alternatively, the Home Secretary could have set up an informal inquiry with wide terms of reference; of course such an inquiry would have had no power to sub-poena witnesses. A Section 32 Police Act inquiry has sub-poena powers and that may have been a factor affecting the decision. But the choice of this narrower type of inquiry left me with the lurking suspicion – and it haunts me still – that the Home Secretary was playing a close political hand, having been dealt cards to play which provided a measure of protection for the Home Office, amongst others.

A wider inquiry would have looked at the immigration policies and practice of the Home Office, at the initiatives and achievements of the Community Relations Department of the Home Office, and at progress made in criminal law reform and other social measures. All this, set in the much wider context of successive governments' dealings with unemployment, housing, welfare and social services in inner city areas and of the major cuts imposed on local authority and welfare services. An inquiry covering these matters could lead to an embarrassing outcome at a time when the Government's fortunes were low. Was it for these reasons that the police were put into the dock? Perhaps I am being unreasonable and seeing shadows where none exist because of my disappointment over the Home Secretary's decision.

About three months later Margaret Thatcher set an example, as she has set an example in much else, of how the police can be encouraged, supported and sustained in what they are trying their best to do, whatever the difficulties. Twelve weeks after the riots of April, violence again erupted on the streets of Brixton. It was Saturday, 11 July and the Prime Minister came to New Scotland Yard with her husband in the early evening expressing a wish to meet the police officers and civilian staff at work coping centrally and locally with what was happening. She had a word of support for everyone she met, and always a smile of encouragement which masked the anxiety she shared with us as to whether we were going into a re-run of those events of April.

Again, as had happened before at moments of high drama, comedy intervened. I had been officially briefed that Mrs Thatcher would not be staying long at New Scotland Yard as she had another engagement. This advice was incorrect but I did not know that at the time. So, thinking we were working to a tight schedule, I propelled the Prime Minister at a rate of knots around the control staff at New Scotland Yard so that she would meet as many people as possible within the limited time. This involved a series of high speed introductions. No sooner had she begun a conversation with one person than I presented another to her. Not unnaturally the Prime Minister began to look somewhat bewildered. Finally she said gently to me, 'Sir David, do we really have to rush around like

119

this? It's not as though I'm going anywhere else tonight. I intend to be here until the early hours.'

Seven hours in all she stayed with the Metropolitan Police, contributing every minute of the time. We sat together watching the Brixton situation on the police television monitors, pictures from cameras at the scene of the action and in the police helicopter overhead. We watched groups of youths massing, and police officers moving quickly to prevent a large mob forming. The Prime Minister remained glued to the screens. Then as darkness intervened and the cameras closed down, she asked to visit Brixton. We went together to Brixton Police Station where she spoke to police officers who had been in the thick of it, and also to the civil staff providing non-stop refreshments to these officers. Many of the civil staff were West Indians and they were as appalled as any of us at the rioting and violence on Brixton's streets. The visit included a tour of Brixton by car to survey some of the damage done by rioters and looters. 'What a waste,' the Prime Minister said, 'what a tragic waste,' voicing her concern particularly for shop keepers whose livelihood was threatened. 'The rioters must not be allowed to get away with it. People who behave like this are criminals, no more and no less.'

Information about such criminals and a stock of petrol bombs they were allegedly storing up at addresses in and around Railton Road was behind the police raids in Brixton on 15 July. I had agreed to the application for the warrants in the full knowledge that tension in the area was running high after the year's second round of anti-police violence. I knew that the execution of the warrants was a potential flashpoint for further disorder. That possibility did much to dictate the timing of the operation in the early hours of the morning. But information from what I was assured was a reliable source about petrol bomb factories in Brixton indicated that someone was set on violence anyway. I considered then – and still do – that not only were the raids justified but also that to have ignored the information and done nothing would have been tantamount to burying my head in the sand, in the vain hope that the problem might go away. It would have been a dereliction of duty. What I could not justify, nor did, nor would I seek to, was the way in which the raids were carried out. Considerable damage was caused, much of it apparently gratuitous. No petrol bombs were found. Of the seven people arrested, one was charged with obstruction and the other six with drug offences.

I appointed Geoffrey Dear, then a Deputy Assistant Commissioner, to investigate the raids and any complaints arising out of them. Following a preliminary visit to the area, he reported to me and we took the unprecedented step of paying compensation for damage, virtually on the spot. But no amount of money could compensate for the unprofessional and undisciplined way in which the raids were carried out. It smacked of revenge and led to a further outbreak of violence in the area. Condemnation and criticism came at us from all quarters, and rightly so. Police officers who take the law into their own hands in the pursuit of justice forfeit all right to the protection their office affords them. Quite plainly on this occasion officers were not well briefed, they were not adequately supervised and the operation as a whole was not properly controlled. Communication, somewhere along the chain of command between New Scotland Yard and Brixton, had broken down.

To return to the inquiry by Lord Scarman, discussion of his Report has been extensive and I want now to make two or three comments of my own.

The first is that, as foretold, the decision to restrict the inquiry to an investigation into policing had the anticipated effect on police morale. This was not because of the way in which the inquiry was conducted but because police officers of all ranks, and especially those who had been on duty in Brixton during the riots, felt that they were being 'got at' and that they had been let down by those in authority. What other country would follow injury to over 400 police officers sustained in dealing with riots, with an inquiry into the way those officers, their colleagues and the force as a whole conducted themselves and into virtually nothing else? It is one of the prices we pay for democracy, and within a democracy it is unfortunately the price to be paid for being a policeman and not a politician.

Second, so far as policing is concerned, the central problem is, of course, how police officers conduct themselves and carry out their duties on the streets. This is at the very heart of policing and has been so from the outset of the history of the Metropolitan Police. In 1829 the instructions of the first Commissioners of the force were that:

> He (the officer) will be civil and attentive to all persons, of every rank and class; insolence and incivility will not be passed over . . . He must be particularly cautious not to interfere idly and unnecessarily; when required to act he will do so with decision and boldness.
>
> He must remember that there is no qualification more indispensable to a police officer than a perfect command of temper, never suffering himself to be moved in the slightest degree by any language or threats that may be used; if he does his duty in a quiet and determined manner, such conduct will probably encourage well-disposed bystanders to assist him should he require it.

A year later those instructions were reinforced:

> No Constable is justified in depriving anyone of his liberty for words only, and language, however violent, towards the Police Constable himself is not to be noticed; the Constables are particularly cautioned not to answer angrily, or enter into altercation with any person while on duty.

These instructions have remained valid throughout the history of the force. The antipathy towards the police that undoubtedly exists among a minority of black persons will be overcome only by the pursuit and attainment of standards of behaviour such as those demanded by the Commissioners over 150 years ago. The words of Rene Webb, the Director of Brixton's Melting Pot Foundation, summed up the problem succinctly in giving evidence to the Scarman inquiry: 'We do not object to what they do so much as the way they do it.'

To meet that requirement the service has to recruit men and women of the right calibre; it has then to train them properly –

throughout their careers, they have also to be well supervised and given positive leadership. Where officers fall short of the high standards expected of them they must be in no doubt of the consequences, which in the ultimate may mean dismissal.

As regards training, it took me a few months only after becoming Commissioner in 1977 to realize that despite the accolades that the Metropolitan Police Training School had received from home and abroad, all was not right. My first visit to Hendon was when I went there to be interviewed by members of the ethnic press. They had been invited to take a look at developments in police training and it had been arranged that the culmination of their day would be an interview with the new Commissioner. The outcome of the meeting was very favourably received by the ethnic press and others. Unfortunately the honeymoon period was all too short.

Whilst at Hendon I took the opportunity to talk to some members of the staff. There was nothing I could specifically point at or put my finger on but the feel of the place was not right. I decided then to put my intuition to the test as soon as possible. A straight line is defined as the shortest distance between two points; that may be so but the direct approach is not necessarily the most effective. So I asked Evelyn Schaffer, the clinical psychologist who had helped me set up Glasgow's Community Involvement Department, to take a look at community relations training in the Metropolitan Police. Police training is so interlinked that an examination of one aspect inevitably requires the researcher to take a look at training in the round. Evelyn's directness brought out the very worst kind of defensive parochialism in some Metropolitan officers. But she had the support of those in the Community Relations branch of the force and in the event her comparatively brief critique became the catalyst for a comprehensive review of recruitment and training by a high level body with outside representatives, which included a member of ICI with experience of personnel selection and training. This review, set up in 1978, reported in 1980 and led to many important changes in the process of recruitment and in all forms of training.

It is clear from the section on training in his Report that Lord

Scarman was considerably influenced and impressed by the innovations introduced following the review. He went to the heart of the matter when he wrote: 'Above all, the central theme in all training must be the need for the police to secure the consent and support of the public if they are successfully to perform their duties.' This had been the very purpose of the review, whose recommendations I had put into effect promptly. Lord Scarman, writing a year after publication of his Report, gracefully acknowledged this: '. . . it would be unjust to ascribe these developments in training to the publication of the Report. That helped, of course, but Sir David McNee had taken hold of training and started a revolution in ideas and practice before the riots of 1981. It was, I believe, his greatest achievement as Commissioner.'*

Linked with training of all officers is the special work of Community Liaison Officers of the Metropolitan Police who are appointed for each of the twenty-four districts of the force. Each of these officers is specially selected and trained and all police Commanders are told to give full support and priority to their work. Their task is, of course, to keep in close touch with local communities, to explain to them the role of the police, to sort out misunderstandings, and in particular to establish a two-way consultation with leaders of minority groups. These men and women are generally well-regarded within the community. But without executive command responsibility they are often seen, particularly through the eyes of the black community, as 'front men' who carry little weight operationally. An ability to produce the goods in operational terms is a decisive factor in cementing relationships. The implication is that divisional Chief Superintendents are the people who should be assuming responsibility for police/community relations rather than some specialist officer who is part of staff as opposed to line management.

More successful is the extensive programme by police liaison officers for visiting schools and for close association in particular with schools with large numbers of black youngsters. It is along this

* *The Times*, 25 November 1982

124

avenue that the best hope for the future lies, linked with the work which many police officers undertake in their spare time at youth clubs and other such places. Contacts of this kind and other initiatives that have been developed in an attempt to bring police constables and young people closer together are important adjuncts to operational policing. They are the oil that makes the wheels of policing turn more freely.

In 1979 I launched, with the help of the Midland Bank, the Football Association and some distinguished footballers like Trevor Brooking and Ian St John, a five-a-side football competition for schools all over Greater London. Over 50,000 youngsters participated under arrangements made locally by Metropolitan Police officers, with the knock-out matches leading to a finals night at Wembley Arena. It has now become an annual event.

This brings me to my last point on the Scarman inquiry and Report. The inquiry was spread over about three or four months and led to a number of conclusions and recommendations. Clearly in such a limited time, Lord Scarman could not go in depth into all the many strands which had led to the riots. The Report was therefore to be an invaluable basis for discussion and progressive development.

One of my first moves after publication of the Scarman Report was to arrange a two day seminar at the Hendon Training School for all senior officers from the rank of Commander upwards in the Metropolitan Police (about 100 officers in all), for initial discussion of the recommendations in the Report. Lord Scarman accepted my invitation to attend this seminar, and we both spoke and took part in the detailed discussions which followed. As he left, the officers stood up and applauded him from the room. It was an illustration of how police, despite all their bitterness about the way the Home Office had limited the scope of the inquiry, had responded to Lord Scarman's approach and to the demands of the future.

I wondered, as Lord Scarman left Hendon that day, how many other organizations would be holding seminars and taking positive action as a result of his inquiry. For the one overwhelming lesson of the riots is that we all have a responsibility in the preservation of public tranquillity. Lord Scarman has subsequently recognized the major initiatives made by the police but he added, 'Sustained effort by everyone will be needed, if the success, which now seems possible, is to be achieved.'

It was surprising that in his Report on the Brixton riots, Lord Scarman made no mention of what has become known as the Deptford Fire. Yet the death of thirteen young black partygoers just down the road from Brixton in the early hours of Sunday, 18 January 1981, when a fire swept through the terraced house at 439 New Cross Road, brought about a change of mood and a sense of unity within the black community not previously seen.

How far this new psychological climate was a precondition to the disorders three months later none can say but there can be no doubt that it worsened police relations with black people; yet another brick had been placed in the growing wall of racial discontent.

Our problems started as a result of the initial reports about the fire, which almost without exception attributed the cause to a fire-bomb; witness the *Daily Telegraph*: 'A fire-bomb hurled through a window of a terraced house during an all-night West Indian birthday party killed nine people and injured at least 30 others . . .'

The subsequent forensic evidence did not support the theory of a fire-bomb, but by that time the damage was done. The belief was widely held amongst the black community that the fire was caused by a petrol bomb thrown through the window of the house and that this attack was racially inspired. Evidence came to light which indicated that a fight had taken place, that the furniture in the front downstairs room was damaged, that the room was ransacked, that the seat of the fire was in the centre of the front room and that the spread of the fire was accelerated by the use of paint thinner. All this came out at the inquest but it did nothing to dispel the belief of a racial attack. Indeed the inquest itself was a rowdy and disruptive affair. *The Sunday Times* summed up the situation: 'Even if the cause of the Deptford fire in which 13 young blacks died last January is finally established, the proof will almost certainly come too late. Mutual suspicion between blacks and police is now so great that many people in the area will simply not believe the outcome of the investigation.'

So strong were the feelings of the black community that they assembled in their thousands to march in protest through London from Deptford to Hyde Park. Commentators likened the protest march to the black civil rights marches in the United States during the 1960s.

Later that month in an address at the Church of St Lawrence Jewry I tried to reassure people that there was no cover-up and that our aim was to find out the truth as to how the fire was started. Invited to give one of a series of speeches billed under the title 'The State of the Nation' I was asked to talk on the broad theme of law and order. In dealing with the Deptford tragedy I said:

> Co-operation and the confidence of the public are the essence of effective policing. Without them we cannot do our job. Witness the difficulties that are currently inhibiting the investigation into the recent tragic deaths of thirteen young black people in a fire at Deptford. This is not the time or place to go into detail of that incident.
>
> Sadly the militants have turned the tragedy into a *cause célèbre*. They have used it to play upon the fears of the minority communities. Police have been accused of a cover-up. To that charge I say this: the Metropolitan Police has but one aim; that is to find the truth as to how those thirteen young men and women died. And nobody should be in any doubt about that. There is no cover-up. There will be no cover-up. But we cannot get at the truth without the help and support of the black community.

My words either fell on stony ground or perhaps failed to reach the right audience, for sixteen days later the Brixton riots began.

In his examination of policing in Brixton, Lord Scarman described the 'policing dilemma' thus: 'The essence of the policing problems . . . is as simple to state as it was, and remains, difficult to resolve; how to cope with a rising level of crime – and particularly street robbery (in the colloquial phrase "mugging") while retaining the confidence of all sections of the community, especially the ethnic minority groups.' The Scarman Report offered no immediate solution to this dilemma because there is none. But the level of crime requires immediate action by the police. Those who are committing crimes in Brixton or anywhere else in London cannot be allowed to do so without prompt police counter-action. Equally the residents of Brixton must have confidence in the police to deter and detect potential attackers, robbers and burglars. This is particularly so for the most vulnerable in society such as the old, or those living alone, or those who have to walk through darkened streets, or work or shop late. Do these people regard police presence and police activity on their streets as hostile?

Where I part company with Lord Scarman is that he seems to be implying in his Report that there is a level of crime in an area like Brixton which is acceptable as the price to be paid for racial harmony. I have posed the question above more than once and never had a straight answer in reply. I know what my answer is and I know what answer would come from those who are robbed, threatened, attacked and put in fear in Brixton. It is too simplistic to see the preservation of the peace and law enforcement as separate issues. They are part of the same process, inextricably linked by the threads of police discretion. When levels of street crime in an area are high, the peace is not under threat; it is already disrupted and short term expediency through a policy of non-enforcement is likely to lead to even higher levels of crime and even further disruption of the peace. No crime is acceptable. A major omission of Lord Scarman's Report is a substantial consideration of the victim's viewpoint.

I had the same criticism of the mounting campaign, which was eventually successful, to repeal Section 4 of the Vagrancy Act – the 'Anti-Sus Campaign' as it became known. Section 4 prohibits suspected persons lingering about in a street or like place with intent to commit an offence. The offence was *not*, and it is important to emphasize this, merely the forming of a criminal intent; it required positive evidence of this intention in the form of a series of overt suspicious acts. The standard of proof required to convict a suspected person was the same as that for the conviction of any other

EARLY LIFE   Aged 3.   In the Boy's Brigade.
In the Navy.   On the beat in Glasgow.

PROMOTION AND RESPONSIBILITY

Chief Constable of Glasgow.

Appointment as Commissioner of the Metropolitan Police.

Sir David with Merlyn Rees and the High Commissioner for Bangladesh in 1978.

With William Whitelaw, Home Secretary.

With Margaret Thatcher at Scotland Yard.

RIOTS AND DEMONSTRATIONS
The Notting Hill Carnival, 1978.

Police with ersatz riot shields at Brixton, 1981.

The bus carrying workers through the picket lines at Grunwick, 1977.

A policeman wounded by a bottle lies outside the Grunwick factory gates.

TERRORISM AND VIOLENCE
Sir David with PC Philip Olds, permanently paralysed while intercepting an armed robbery.

The end of the six-day siege of the Iranian Embassy, 1980.

Sir David with PC Trevor Lock, hero of the Iranian Embassy siege, and his wife.

Policemen give emergency treatment to a victim of the IRA bomb in Regent's Park, 1982.

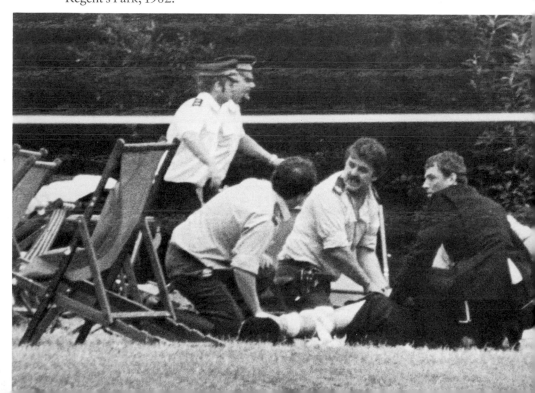

The Royal Wedding: bridging the barrier.

offender, the burden of proof lying with the prosecution to prove their case beyond reasonable doubt, with the intention of the accused often being the central issue as in many other alleged criminal offences.

Much energy was expended by individuals and organizations in promoting the 'Anti-Sus Campaign'. Myth, rumour and prejudice were fermented in the process. The campaigners alleged in particular that arrests under Section 4 did great harm to the relationship between police and black people, and particularly young black people, in London. Support was forthcoming from those who in my view were unable to accept that the problems of race relations are complex and deep-rooted, and sought instead some instant solution.

Nowhere, in all the publications and propaganda produced during the campaign, was there any substantial evidence to justify repeal of the statutory provision, and much of what was put forward was based on alleged accounts of unidentifiable incidents between police officers and black youngsters. The campaign certainly did not help the course of police relations with the black community. On the contrary, encouragement of rumour and myth increased the difficulties faced by police officers in dealing with black youths.

The pressure for repeal of the 'sus' law certainly did not come from the law-abiding in Brixton, nor indeed from people anywhere who were rightly concerned about the safety of themselves and their children and the protection of their homes and property. I would ask, moreover, whether the repeal of this law has led subsequently to greater harmony in Brixton and other areas.

Let us examine what evidence there is. The campaign drew its main inspiration from the contention that the arrest figures of the Metropolitan Police showed that the force discriminated against black persons. There is, however, no getting away from the fact that black youngsters are involved in street crimes, and the reality of this was of major concern to me during my time as Commissioner. Part of the problem facing me was that the crime level was used by right wing extremists to besmirch the reputation of the black community as a whole, without any justification whatsoever. Despite the high level of involvement of young blacks in London's street robberies and thefts, that criminal element is a very small minority of the black community as a whole. Moreover, when one takes into account that 70% of the black community live in the more deprived areas of the capital and that the black community is very young, the level of involvement is no more than might be expected. The dilemma is always whether to expose the facts to public debate and risk an increase in racial tension or say nothing and be accused of covering up important social phenomena.

As a general rule I took the line that we would only release crime statistics in response to parliamentary questions and requests from Members of Parliament. In March 1982 I agreed that we should include mention of the figures in the overall crime statistics when they were publicly released by Gilbert Kelland, the Assistant Commissioner in charge of the CID, at his annual press conference on crime. Crimes of street robbery and violent theft from the person had increased alarmingly during 1981 and the reported high level of involvement of black offenders in these crimes was giving cause for concern. Admittedly, these street offences amount to only a small percentage of the overall crime figures but their effect upon the emotional climate and life of the city is out of all proportion to their actual numbers.

There were signs of a growing dissatisfaction both inside and outside the service with our apparent inability to deal with the problem. The media, both press and television, were suggesting that we were deliberately standing back from the street crime issue in order to preserve the fragile peace that had existed within the inner areas of London since the riots of the previous year. The fact was that we were exploring a whole range of options that would help us to deal with street criminals without provoking violent disorders. The signs were that we were gradually overcoming the crisis of confidence that existed within the black community towards police. I felt that the time was right to make the facts public. If the level of black involvement in crime was to be curtailed it would need the wholehearted condemnation of London's black community, and without public debate of the issue I could not foresee that forthcoming. So it was decided to release the figures.

The purpose of the exercise was lost, at least in part, in the ensuing public furore. The figures were presented with very little comment after Gilbert Kelland's observation in his press release that –

> Coloured persons are disproportionately involved in this type of crime, but it must be emphasized that these criminals and crimes are respectively only a minority of the total coloured population and of the total number of offences. It does not mean of course we have that number of offenders, because frequently on arrest we find that the robber had committed a number, even into double figures, of this type of crime.

His general statement had concluded with a call for the help of the community as a whole in dealing with the problem of street crime. Other than that, his only additional comment came in response to questions by Peter Burden, crime correspondent of the *Daily Mail*, about the reason for the release of the statistics and whether police were soft-pedalling on law enforcement:

> Let me try and answer your questions, Mr Burden. These figures, it is true, have been released for the first time. Statistics are difficult. They have been compiled for a number of years in this category of description of the assailant by the victim and they have been released in Parliament in bits and pieces relating to this borough or that borough. There is a demand, the police feel, for this information from the public and by you, ladies and gentlemen of the media, on behalf of the public, and as they are available it was considered important, if the position is to be understood and if you like to prevent gossip and rumour and miscalculations, to publish them.
>
> The second part of your question I must say I don't quite follow, about going 'soft'. I do not think the figures released bear any relation to going soft. The attempts to combat crime within the Metropolitan Police area have been consistent. We have not been obviously as successful as we would have

wished. But again, as I stressed, now it is everybody's problem and it is too simple to say, yes the police can solve it.*

With hindsight – always more accurate than foresight – I think I might have insisted that we gave the total picture, drawing out in particular the social and political circumstances of the figures, instances of racial harassment, figures showing the extent to which the black community was under attack, the racial tensions that existed, the precarious nature of community life in many parts of London and the difficulties of policing those communities with the ever-present possibility of violent disorder.

I received many letters – some congratulatory, some condemnatory – about the issue. David Lane, Chairman of the Commission for Racial Equality, wrote to express his concern about the balance of the presentation and felt that it had contributed to what he described as 'very crude reporting in some newspapers'. He feared that the support of the black community, far from being enhanced, was likely to be diminished, and regretted that our intention to publish crime figures in this way had not been mentioned when he had met the Deputy Commissioner toward the end of February. My reply to him outlined the purpose of presenting the statistics and voiced my subsequent reservations as to its effect.†

The one thing all that illustrates is how difficult it is to discuss this highly complex and sensitive issue in public in a rational and reasonable way. Until we can begin to talk calmly about these matters I fear that we have not seen the end of riots, and the problems of race are no doubt with us for a long time to come. I have set out some of the issues as I saw them as Commissioner and see them today and you may be asking why, if I felt so strongly and sincerely about them, I did not make them known more forcibly in the years before the Brixton and other riots occurred.

The short answer is that I did make them known, over and over again, right from my first press conference on arrival at New

* Extract from Questions and Answers at the annual Metropolitan Police Statistics Conference, held on 10 March 1982
† see Appendix I

Scotland Yard. The following is a short extract from one major speech I made two years before the riots:

Since the early fifties many people from the new Commonwealth have come to London, settled and raised their families. Today it is estimated that they and their children (and in some cases their children's children) number about ten per cent of London's population; and seventy per cent of them live in the deprived inner city. Poverty and deprivation bear heavily upon ethnic minorities and fuel the fires of racial tension and conflict. Parallels have been drawn between the situation in London now and that which existed in the major cities of the United States at the time of the race riots in the 1960s.

The black community is also a young community; and youth and deprivation are bound up with the commission of crime. Chuck Colson has already discussed the determinist view that delinquency is a response to deprivation. To suggest that deprivation is a justification for crime is to deny man's freedom of choice and to insult millions of people who are poor, deprived and honest. I agree with him that there is autonomy and choice in human affairs, and that delinquency is not a blind or helpless response to deprivation, despite the fact that it has become intellectually fashionable in some quarters to regard it so. Nevertheless, the connections between crime, youth and deprivation bring police officers into open conflict with black youngsters committing crime. Mutual animosity, suspicion and distrust grow. Myths develop about police harassment on the one side and black criminality on the other, and become accepted as fact . . . with a tradition of policing that relies heavily for its effectiveness on public support and goodwill, the task of policing West Indian and Asian communities (the young Asian is barely less critical than the young black) is both difficult and volatile.

It is of course fertile ground for extremists who seek to make political capital out of racial issues. Whether from the left or the right of the political spectrum, the extremists feed off each other and keep London's multi-racial melting pot at boiling point. Solutions to the racial tension, which is fast becoming an integral part of inner city life, are vital to the future well-being of everybody – black, brown, white, West Indian, Asian, English or Scot.

I was of course giving the same advice as forcibly and still more specifically in private to the Home Office. There is no comfort for the people of Brixton that these words were not heeded, but one can but ask whether, if social conditions there and elsewhere had been put right, the riots would still have taken place.

7

Terrorism and
the Siege of the Iranian Embassy

IF THE 1970s can be described as the decade of the terrorist then the 1980s have so far shown no sign of being different. All too often London's streets became a battleground on which there were serious casualties.

Since 1973 when the IRA extended its campaign to the mainland, with car bombs exploding outside the Old Bailey and Great Scotland Yard, London has been the scene of more bombings, shootings and persons injured as a result of terrorist activity than the whole of the rest of Britain. Between 1973 and 1982 in London there were 252 bomb incidents, nineteen terrorist shootings, fifty-six deaths and 805 persons injured by acts of terrorism. 138 arrests were made in connection with these incidents.

The Metropolitan Police experience of terrorism goes back to 1829, but particularly to March 1883 when the Special Irish Branch was formed to counter the Irish Fenian dynamiters who were then putting down bombs in London. It is an experience which includes:

The murder of Field Marshal Sir Henry Wilson by the IRA on the steps of his Belgravia home in June 1922.

The declaration of war by the IRA in January 1938 followed by a series of bombings. Those hostilities culminated in August of that year with a bicycle bomb in Coventry killing five people and injuring two.

The detection and arrests in 1971 of young anarchists of the

Angry Brigade, whose activities prompted the formation of the Bomb Squad, now styled the Anti-Terrorist Squad.

The terror in the Tower of London in 1974 where an IRA bomb exploded killing one and causing injuries, some of them severe, to thirty-seven, including a number of children.

The major explosion in the Houses of Parliament in 1974.

The murders in 1975 of Ross McWhirter and Professor Gordon Hamilton Fairley.

The Balcombe Street siege in 1975.

In addition to the evil work of the IRA, the Metropolitan Police experience includes series of atrocities by terrorists from the Middle East and the Continent, stretching back to 'Peter the Painter', the Sidney Street siege and beyond.

The grisly tale was to continue right through the six years I was Commissioner. I had been in post only a few days when three Yemeni diplomats were assassinated outside the Royal Lancaster Hotel. The murderer was subsequently killed by German security forces whilst rescuing passengers from an aircraft at Mogadishu which he had helped to hijack. When I went on an official visit to Saudi Arabia with Merlyn Rees, we had an audience with the King, and the first question he put to me was why had I allowed his Yemeni friends to be killed outside a London hotel. I had to spend a little time in explaining some of the problems of maintaining the peace in every part of a city the size of London.

In 1978 a lull of two years ended with the IRA detonating bombs in British cities, including two car bombs in central London. We believed the intention was to plant a further bomb in a crowded London store a day or so before Christmas. The effects would have been appalling and I ordered that the West End should be saturated with police officers. The attack did not materialize and Christmas passed without incident.

Further IRA activity however was not long in coming. 1979 saw not only the murder of Lord Mountbatten in Eire, but the assassination of Airey Neave MP, at the Palace of Westminster.

Airey Neave and I had met earlier in the year, in the company of

Lord McAlpine, and I had tried to persuade him to have a personal protection officer because of the known threat to his life. He made it clear that if as an Englishman he could not walk the streets of London freely, then life for him was not truly worth living. I pressed him to reconsider his decision, but he would not. Although I wished he would take my advice I understood and respected his view. A few weeks later we were guest speakers at a major lunch given at the Dorchester Hotel by Lord McAlpine. He gave me a copy of his recently published autobiography, and when I opened it I saw that the flyleaf was inscribed in his own hand to me with the words:

> To David McNee
> In the hope that the rule of
> law will be maintained and
> racist tyranny be defeated.
> Airey Neave

1979 ended with a major operation by the Metropolitan Police against the IRA followed by a number of important arrests and the discovery of arms and bomb-making materials in Greenwich. One of those arrested was Gerard Tuite, who escaped from Brixton Prison while awaiting trial. This and the start in October of the hunger strike by Republican prisoners in the Maze Prison in Belfast made further attacks inevitable. They were not long in coming. Explosions, casualties and damage were inflicted at a Territorial Army centre in Hammersmith and at a gasworks in Bromley-by-Bow.

So the evil went on with a coach of Irish guardsmen being blown up as their vehicle approached Chelsea Barracks. General Pringle was severely injured in his car as he left his home in Dulwich; Kenneth Howorth, a Metropolitan Police explosives officer, was killed by a bomb which went off as he examined it. A large bomb exploded at the home of Sir Michael Havers, the Attorney General, and another at offices of the Royal Artillery in Woolwich. Finally, during the last months of my time as Commissioner, bombs exploded in Hyde Park killing soldiers of the Household Cavalry.

Underneath a bandstand in Regent's Park a second device detonated causing deaths and injury to the bandsmen and their audience.

Those were the main events. During the same years there were other explosions, other incidents; incendiary letter bombs and similar devices.

Let me not give any impression that the IRA were able to press home their attacks on Britain with impunity. They had the greatest difficulty in mounting their operations because of the efficiency of the police, and the pressures which were maintained on them despite a number of obstacles placed in the way of police operations. The IRA would have liked to have been much more active in London because of the great publicity value of explosions there. But intelligence, searches, detention of suspects, arrests and other measures made this impossible. There were long periods when no IRA activity took place because of preventive police action, most of which for obvious reasons was not made public. In the years 1973 to 1982 the Metropolitan Police made 138 arrests for IRA and other acts of terrorism in London, recovered over 60 weapons, 800 pounds of explosives and 4,500 rounds of ammunition.

Acts of terrorism were not confined to the IRA. During my time as Commissioner, London was frequently used for bloody acts of violence by Middle Eastern terrorists – acts for reasons which had little to do with Britain but which were committed in London because of the worldwide publicity which they would ensure.

Following the shooting of the Yemeni diplomats in 1977, two Syrians were killed in December of that year when a bomb exploded in their car. In January 1978 the London representative of the Palestine Liberation Organization was assassinated. In July a grenade attack was made on the Iraqi Ambassador outside his Embassy, and in the same month a former Prime Minister of Iraq was shot dead at the Intercontinental Hotel. In August, following the Camp David talks, a gun and grenade attack was made on the El Al airline staff as they left their coach outside the Europa Hotel.

1980 was the year of the Iranian Embassy siege, but in addition two bombs exploded in a room at the Mount Royal Hotel killing the Arab occupant; it was in police terms a 'self-inflicted' injury. And so it went on all the way to the savage shooting of Shlomo Argov, the Israeli Ambassador, as he left the Dorchester Hotel. Mr Argov had been attending a dinner organized by the De La Rue Company for ambassadors and others at which I was present.

As I left, a secretary of the De La Rue Company told me that a man had been shot outside the hotel. At such times you remember at once that whatever your rank, you are a policeman with a policeman's responsibilities. I hurried outside to find Mr Argov lying in the gutter with a bullet wound in his head.

He was being tended by Lord Richardson, who had been at the dinner. Lord Richardson is a most distinguished doctor and a former medical consultant to the Metropolitan Police. I did what I could to assist him and help in other ways. For such a distinguished man and a Commissioner of Police to carry out together basic medical and police duties wearing full evening dress and regalia must have been, as an occasion, unique.

I was impressed and pleased at the efficient way in which the force acted to bring the situation under control and surround the area. One of the assassins had already been shot by a Special Branch officer, and the others were caught while making their way through Brixton.

What is one to make of these events, which were being repeated over the same years in Paris, Rome, Amsterdam and other capitals of the world? Let me record some thoughts which close and direct experience with terrorism has given rise to.

The aim of the terrorist is to have his way whatever the opposition and no matter how right or reasonable the opposition may be. No matter that the terrorist is representative only of a minority group. He does this by creating a state of uncertainty and by putting fear and terror into the hearts and minds of people. In so doing he strikes at the core of civilized society.

It is therefore for society, for us all, to face and rebut the threat and reality of terrorism. In London the co-operation of the public was magnificent. They reported anything of suspicion, responded to police requests for information, and withstood the impact of death, destruction, injuries and shock with great fortitude. Individuals often acted with bravery in helping to deal with terrorists.

In the terrorist field the media have an important role to play as channels of information and persuasion. The press, radio and television keep the public alert, encourage them to keep the police informed, and advise on what should be done if they receive letter bombs or come to hear of explosive devices. In this way the media helps both to apprehend the terrorist, restrict his freedom of action and reduce the risk of death and injury.

But it is not a smooth road to travel and from time to time programmes or articles, however well-intended, provide terrorists with unwarranted publicity. One possible effect is that as well as inflating the terrorist's sense of self-importance – and making him the more dangerous thereby – a report may contribute to the growth of a terrorist organization by giving it enhanced credibility.

It is one of the dilemmas facing a country enjoying the benefits of a free press. Terrorism is, of course, a proper matter for public debate. The problem is knowing precisely where the boundaries of the debate are to be drawn, in order to ensure that the debate does not itself contribute to the evils under discussion. This is a dilemma which impinges on many areas of police operations and it is one that is not always resolved satisfactorily, particularly insofar as the police are concerned.

A similar dilemma arises with regard to the courts. As each terrorist is caught and brought to trial, the evidence put before the court virtually tells all. As the case unfolds, the failing of the terrorist in making his attack or covering his tracks, and the ingenuity of his pursuers, is laid bare to public view. There is no need to be in court for the details will sooner or later be graphically reproduced in newspapers or books. Terrorists learn from what they hear or read, and they use what they learn to avoid repeating their errors. Freedom of expression in the press and elsewhere is a freedom of the highest importance, but it has a consequence that the terrorist, or his successors, can be better equipped to attack again.

Are the consequences of freedom of reporting in this field, including the parading of police techniques which so readily enhances terrorists' knowledge, too high a price to pay? Should it be so easy to learn police tactics and practices? Should there be closed courts and limits on reporting to minimize the risks of disclosure? Those who are horrified at the very thought of such measures should also recall the horror of the explosions at Chelsea Barracks, Hyde Park and Regent's Park. The growing expertise of the Irish terrorists was demonstrated there by the diverse type of device used against different targets, with different methods employed to trigger them.

To secure our safety we must also exploit to the maximum the benefits of being based on an island with the ability to keep some control at the points of entry. Irish terrorists have been thwarted several times by the logistical difficulties of getting supplies to their units in this country. It is obviously most convenient for them to gather their supplies in Eire and then transport them to Britain. If this movement of supplies could be checked, the units would be starved of the means of attack. But this can only be achieved by more stops, more searches and greater infringement of personal freedom. Once again a dilemma for our society.

Let us remember that the most effective measure for prevention of terrorism is good intelligence. To be forewarned is indeed to be forearmed. Intelligence is the very life-blood of good policing and during my time as Commissioner, the Central Intelligence and Surveillance Branch was expanded. In this field some inaccurate information will inevitably be gathered. We all give credence at times to information about people, places and events which is later proved wrong, and not every informant, however reliable in the past, can provide accurate facts every time. The onus is on the police to check the information so far as possible before it is used by, for example, obtaining a search warrant, establishing an association, or putting a suspected person under surveillance. The crux of the issue rests in the action taken, not in the gathering of the information.

In the wake of the cry for liberty for the individual much damage has been done to the obtaining of good intelligence. This is demonstrated by the effects of the Freedom of Information Act in the United States of America. The testimony of many eminent persons concerned with law enforcement is that the provisions of this Act have been debilitating and working in favour of criminals, including terrorists, to the detriment of the law-abiding. For example, use is often made of the Act not to advance justice and truth, but rather to protect and conceal criminal activity. Enactment of similar provisions in Britain should be resisted, not of course because the principle of keeping accurate information is wrong, but because of the unintended consequences for the protection of ordinary citizens.

Central to the control of points of entry to our island is the Prevention of Terrorism Act. Described as a Draconian measure by some, I have no doubt that most people see the measure as necessary, and indeed desirable. The Act has stood the test of regular scrutiny by Parliament and by eminent members of the judiciary. It is certainly a vital part of the police fight against terrorism, both in the field of prevention and of detection. Although the number of people excluded from entry to the country under the Act are low compared to the number of people stopped and questioned, this should not be regarded as weakening the purpose or effectiveness of the Act.

Activity under the provisions of the Act leads to a good deal of information being obtained. For obvious reasons this information cannot be made public, nor can those who give it be identified, and in such circumstances the public need to trust their police, and have trust in particular that the police will not abuse the powers given to them under the Act. I certainly agree that checks are necessary and the review undertaken by Lord Shackleton and Lord Jellicoe was testament both to the effectiveness of scrutiny, to the lack of abuse of its powers and to the need for retaining the Act.

I always had to keep in mind that terrorism was international, and that London's streets were an especially suitable arena for its practice. I learnt that any incident with a political background taking place on the other side of the world – be it the Middle East, South America or wherever – could lead, often in a very short time, to violent action in London even though the citizens of London were in no way involved, and were probably not even aware of the dispute.

Terrorists are not normally resident in Britain – they come to

London for a specific purpose only. Their weapons and explosives also are imported. I am satisfied that these were reaching Britain with the help of diplomatic missions sympathetic to the aims of the terrorists concerned. Use of the 'diplomatic bag' is abused. This is well-known and there has been positive proof. The Foreign Office under successive governments has known this. Little has been done to put a stop to it. I understand the arguments advanced for inaction, many of which are political, but I think we should look again at some of the diplomatic missions and demand a higher standard of probity, or the removal of the diplomatic concessions which are being abused.

As regards terrorists coming in from abroad, we should examine entry more closely. This was brought home to me by the shooting of the Israeli Ambassador, Shlomo Argov. His assassins did not arrive from abroad a few days before; they had been students in Britain for some months prior to the shooting. A search of one of their rooms revealed a pistol and ammunition, and evidence of dedicated terrorist activity.

This man was registered for study at a School of English. To what extent is student entry to Britain being used for purposes other than for education, such as for political activity, for social and family reasons, for crime and disruptive aims? Tightening the criteria on which entry is granted and checking regularly on the continuing validity of the reasons for entry may be controversial, but it would provide a practical control which would help to reduce terrorism.

Terrorists are also able to escape too easily from the scene of their violence to another country from which they cannot be brought to justice. There are extradition treaties and international agreements on terrorism between nations, but not all countries are signatories to these treaties and agreements. Those which do not sign are often nations which give refuge to terrorists. Politics too can thwart extradition proceedings, as has happened in Holland and Eire. Or the judicial process can grind on painfully slowly, as happened in the United States when application was made for the extradition of the Irishman Quinn. This does nothing to encourage effective law enforcement. The failure of nations to bring terrorists to justice, wherever they are, is intolerable and needs attention. The remedy does not of course lie in the hands of the British Government acting alone. But it is an area requiring unremitting pressure by our Government for redress of the present deplorable situation whereby murderers of innocent persons can find refuge because of omissions and inadequacies in agreements between nations.

On the credit side is the excellent police liaison which exists between West European countries. At New Scotland Yard there is a European Liaison Section which secures the rapid dissemination to Europe of details of incidents, persons, materials and trends. This co-operation is vital, given the international links between terrorist groups which can orchestrate simultaneous attacks in a number of countries.

In general these international links between police forces are excellent, operating without formality, with detectives getting in touch directly with each other as appropriate. Home Office officials are also in touch with their counterparts in other EEC countries, special arrangements being made for dealing with terrorism and information about terrorists. To further facilitate co-operation and exchange of knowledge, and with the agreement of police forces on the Continent, I launched in 1979 a series of annual conferences of chief officers of police of the capital cities of Europe. I was host in London to the first of these conferences. The subjects of common interest which were discussed each year always included aspects of terrorism, and there were benefits for us all to be had from sharing knowledge and experience and creating close contacts for the future.

Another welcome step forward has been the introduction of legislation in Eire allowing proceedings in United Kingdom cases to be heard in the Irish courts. Proceedings against Gerard Tuite were the first of such cases. Extradition however would be preferable, because trial on 'home' ground enables the victim or victims of the crime and witnesses to feel more secure. Furthermore the evidence is tested against known and accepted standards of proof.

What of the future? I am afraid that I must say that it is bleak.

International tension, conflict and confrontation is at a premium. There are many groups who see the use of tactics of terror as a means of advancing a cause. There are countries which overtly or covertly support terrorist activities. These are countries where training facilities, weapons and explosives are provided for those who undertake these activities.

Bombs and similar devices will continue to be favoured by terrorists, for they capture the publicity and involve minimal risk for the terrorist. Detonation by remote control or command wire means that the risk of identification and arrest is low. Provision of materials and planning for this form of attack is difficult, but the wanton destruction and panic caused achieves one of the main aims of terrorism: massive publicity.

As regards other methods, firm action by governments and increasing expertise by police has diminished the earlier interest of terrorists in hijacking aircraft carrying passengers. For similar reasons the taking of hostages and a consequent siege may be less likely.

Assassination has also not been a frequent offence on the British mainland, but it could be more widely used in the future; the Irish National Liberation Army, for example, have made it known that they regard assassination of people of public standing to be a means of pressing their political aims. The attempted assassination of the Israeli ambassador, Mr Argov, was also committed for political reasons.

With careful planning, assassination can involve few risks, for assassins require very limited resources and the offence can be difficult to investigate afterwards. Fortunately the record of the Metropolitan Police in the apprehension of assassins is high and this has been the best deterrent. It has mostly been achieved by a good early response at the scene of the attack by patrolling officers. Indeed an early response was our main strength in the metropolis. This is the purpose in particular of the Diplomatic Protection Group of the force, and the policy, organization and activity of the Group is directed very much to this end. Although no person with inner knowledge of the situation would willingly predict a decline in future of terrorist activity, on the past record of the Metropolitan Police, people can be confident about the ability of police to provide a high level of vigilance to prevent it, to handle it efficiently if it happens and to arrest those responsible. The continued success of the Anti-Terrorist Squad, an outstanding success in my time under Commanders Duffy, Richards and Hucklesby, is the best guarantee against an increase in terror.

In the end you come back to the publicity factor. Publicity of almost any kind is regarded by terrorists as worthwhile. They see it as an essential life-line not only for their cause but for recruitment. If the terrorist could be denied publicity, the life-line would be severed and the effects might be remarkable. But I am afraid that this is pie in the sky because it would once again involve restricting the reporting of news.

The most favourable publicity is given when terrorism succeeds. The greatest damage is done to the fight against terrorism by those nations who submit to terrorist demands or allow terrorists safe passage through their countries. The defeat of terrorism requires a firm, unequivocal stand by each and every government against terrorist demands, whatever they may be, from start to finish, linked with effective control of the incident.

Nowhere was the effectiveness of this response to terrorism more effectively illustrated than by the handling of the Iranian Embassy siege in 1980.

The blast of an explosion shatters the quiet of residential Kensington. Smoke pours from the window of a stately Victorian building. All round are scores of police officers. A hubbub of journalists are watching and waiting, perched on top of a mechanical jungle.

Elsewhere people are watching television, engrossed in the exploits of John Wayne or enjoying championship snooker. Suddenly the pictures on the screen change to show hooded figures storming that same building. Inside the building a police constable begins a death struggle with armed terrorists.

This was the end of the siege of the Iranian Embassy which lasted from 30 April to 5 May 1980. A unique situation, never previously encountered in the history of British policing and not least remarkable because from beginning to end a police officer in uniform – and armed – was in the heart of the building in the hands of determined terrorists. It was certainly not the kind of scenario which, even in my wildest dreams, I had contemplated when I travelled from Glasgow to London three years earlier.

There have been other notable police operations, including those when hostages have been taken and held by violent men. The siege at Spaghetti House, Knightsbridge, in September 1975 and the siege at Balcombe Street in December of the same year are two which come readily to mind. But the events at the Iranian Embassy were unique in the experience of the British police service.

First, the occupation of the Iranian Embassy and the taking of hostages was undertaken for political purposes. The planning and action were carried out with careful deliberation by well-trained terrorists, whereas the sieges at Spaghetti House and at Balcombe Street came about by chance. The former because criminals were interrupted while engaged on a robbery, and the latter because three Irishmen, members of the IRA, took random refuge in a block of flats whilst being pursued by police officers. Second, the siege of the Iranian Embassy involved twenty-six male and female hostages of varying nationalities being held in a large building of over fifty rooms, all accessible to the terrorists. At Spaghetti House and at Balcombe Street the criminals were both fewer and more closely confined. Third, the combined operations by police, military and other services were by far and away more extensive than anything seen previously in London or elsewhere in Britain, needing the close and often direct involvement of the British Government and foreign embassies. Fourth, political and international issues were from the start at the forefront of all events both inside and outside the Embassy, and directly affected both the conduct of the terrorists and the conduct of police operations. Finally, the terrorists were prepared not only to kill their hostages but also to die themselves for their beliefs. It was this kamikaze attitude that prompted the name which the six terrorists gave themselves: 'The Group of the Martyr'.

The title has its origins over a thousand years ago in a rebellion in the Persian Empire. A province known today as Kerbela sought independence from the Imperial Caliph and a revolt was raised by the grandson of the Prophet Mohammed. A battle was fought on the banks of the Euphrates; the rebellion was crushed and the young leader killed. From that day the Moslems of the area honoured the memory of his martyrdom and in 680 AD created the title 'Group of the Martyr' for use by future revolutionaries.

Readiness for martyrdom was also to be found amongst a few of the hostages. Time is important in this type of situation. The theory is that if negotiations can be drawn out, terrorists and hostages will build up a relationship where each has an increasing respect and concern for the other. Known in professional police circles as 'The Stockholm syndrome', the strategy was in this particular circumstance of less value: the unusual ingredients present within the Iranian Embassy led later to the coining of another phrase: 'The London syndrome'.

How had six highly dedicated and well-trained men come together? What was the cause for which they were prepared to die? To find the answer we need to go back to 1979 with the fall of the Shah in Iran and the seizure of power by the Ayatollah Khomeini.

The six Arabs in question were dedicated to obtaining independence for Khuzestan, a province in southwest Iran, rich in oil. They knew that autonomy for the province would never be granted by the Ayatollah and that under his rule they would be marked men. They fled to Iraq where they made careful plans to seize the Iranian Embassy in London and to take hostages.

Their purpose was to secure worldwide publicity for the needs of Khuzestan and to compel the Iranian authorities to release 'political' prisoners. If needs be they were prepared to kill hostages to achieve that aim. The plan envisaged that the British Government, faced with progressive slaughter of hostages, would provide safe passage and an aircraft for the terrorists when they were ready to leave Britain. I am no politician and would hardly claim to be an expert on international affairs but, if I were, I would certainly want to look very closely at the involvement of Iraq in all this.

During March and April 1980 seven Arabs made their way in

two groups from the Middle East to London. They were found rooms in Earls Court and somehow obtained two Polish sub-machine guns, four pistols, ammunition, hand grenades and explosives. I do not know how they came by their weapons but the suspicion remains with me that the most likely channel was the diplomatic bag with its privileged passage through customs. The seventh man was not directly involved in the attack and need not concern us here.

The scene was set for the plan to be put into operation, but there was one actor – who was to play a lead in the drama to follow – already on stage: Police Constable 469'K' Trevor James Lock, age forty-one, with fifteen years' service in the Metropolitan Police. From January 1980 Lock had been attached to the Diplomatic Protection Group, which has a special responsibility for protecting diplomats and embassies in the metropolis.

Early on the morning of Wednesday, 30 April, Constable Lock reported for duty; he was posted to the protection of the Iranian Embassy and issued with a .38 Smith and Wesson revolver and ammunition. He loaded the revolver and placed it in the holster in his belt – out of sight under his uniform jacket. He then took up post at the Embassy.

Shortly after eleven o'clock Constable Lock was standing in the rain outside the Embassy when a member of the staff offered him a cup of coffee. Moving inside the porch of the building, he shut the front door. Almost immediately two BBC reporters – Simeon Harris and Chris Cramer – arrived for a routine visit to the Embassy, followed by the postman. Lock checked a parcel in the morning mail and then turned to resume duty outside. Just then an Arab wearing jeans and an anorak pushed his way in and pulled out a revolver. A struggle between the two men followed and the Aram fell back off balance. As he did so,. five other Arabs entered the Embassy, carrying firearms. Automatic weapons were fired and pieces of glass flew into Lock's face and eyes. He and the others were forced back inside the Embassy. The alarm connecting the Embassy to New Scotland Yard was sounded and within minutes armed police officers had surrounded the building and cordoned off the area.

Inside, the terrorists held twenty-six hostages. Mainly Iranians, they also included an Indian, a Pakistani, a Syrian and four British citizens in addition to Trevor Lock. The siege had begun, and the theatre tickets which Lock had bought to take his wife to the show 'Ipi Tombi' that evening were going to be of no use to him, for he was about to play a part which would make his name known throughout Britain and beyond.

At the time I was on a short holiday in Scotland, spending the day on the upper reaches of the River Clyde. The amount of holiday a Commissioner of Police can take in any year tends to be curtailed at the best of times by pressure of events and responsibilities but, for me in particular, holidays seemed to act as a magnet for trouble. Twice before, family holidays had been interrupted by dramatic events in London. Taking leave had become a jinx and the Assistant Commissioners had learned to expect the worst when I went away.

I was back in London within hours and on arrival I went straight to the forward operational control established near the Embassy. I was to spend much of the next week there. At the control, I was met and briefed by Wilford Gibson, the Assistant Commissioner in charge of uniform operations, with him were Deputy Assistant Commissioner Peter Neivens, my Director of Information who had the world press to handle, and John Dellow, the Deputy Assistant Commissioner who, with Deputy Assistant Commissioner Edgar Maybanks, was handling the operation on the ground. Contingency plans had been drawn up in respect of all London's embassies and high commissions and, although the circumstances at the Iranian Embassy had a number of exceptional features, I found the plans were working well.

Police marksmen had been moved into various positions. Un-armed police had been brought up to keep the public at a safe distance from the arc of fire of the terrorists in the Embassy, and away from the effects of any explosion should the terrorists carry out their threat to blow up the building. In other words a 'sterile area' had been created.

The Chief Superintendent of the Diplomatic Protection Group, Roger Bromley, had approached the Embassy and made contact with the terrorists. They had shouted their demands which were:

The release within twenty-four hours of ninety-one prisoners held in Iran.

The recognition of the national rights of the Iranians and the end to a liquidation campaign and daily mass exterminations.

The provision of an aircraft to transport the hostages and the terrorists from England after their demands had been met.

The demands concluded with a warning that any police interference would endanger the lives of the hostages and was accompanied by a threat to blow up the building.

The massive build-up of police capability and resources at the scene continued. Forward and rear controls had been established. Inner and outer cordons sealed off the Embassy. Trained and skilled negotiators were present, as well as an officer with close knowledge of Arabian affairs, and interpreters of the Arabic and Farsi languages.

Because of the political character of the terrorists' demands a Home Office official was at the operational control as the Government liaison officer, an arrangement that was to continue throughout the siege. A psychiatrist – Professor John Gunn, who was retained by the Metropolitan Police to advise on such operations – was to play a valuable part in the days which followed. Doctors were also available. Communication experts in large numbers made all the necessary links, including one directly with the Cabinet Office Briefing Room.

In support were police and civilian staff from many branches of the Metropolitan Police. Police dogs, including specially trained dogs, were on hand. A large vehicle park was set up and traffic diversions put in. Lastly, but by no means least, the Metropolitan Police catering service came to provide food for large numbers round the clock. During the six days of the siege tens of thousands of meals and snacks were provided by the catering service together with untold gallons of tea, coffee and soft drinks.

Most significantly of all, as events turned out, the Special Air Service had been placed on alert and were soon to come onto the scene.

The police had to cope with other problems quite apart from those within the Embassy. The alarm sounded in the nearby Brazilian Embassy, but this was found to be false. A bomb threat was made against Iran Airlines in Piccadilly. Requests were received for police protection at the Iranian Consulate and the Iranian Education Office, both of which are in Kensington. Residents in adjoining embassies and houses and those working nearby had to be evacuated.

The siege attracted political demonstrators who created further problems for the police. At about noon on the first day of the siege Iranian demonstrators congregated at the police cordons around the Embassy to voice their allegiance with their comrades being held hostage. As their numbers grew so did the noise, including religious chanting, and from time to time violence broke out. Several arrests were made and one police officer suffered a fractured leg. The establishment of a separate police command point and deployment of considerable police manpower enabled the demonstrators to be marshalled. A policy was adopted of allowing demonstrators to leave the area but not to return. This led to protests from Iranians throughout the world. Another important consideration was the need to avoid anything which might affect the well-being of the American hostages then being held in Iran. A demonstration by the Iranians led to a counter-demonstration by citizens of the United States who were in London. The presence of the Iranians lasted throughout the siege, and included one lady, certainly among the most noisy and in possession of what appeared to be a cast iron constitution, who arrived very early on 30 April and was the last to leave on 5 May. The noise made by the demonstrators was a nuisance but we were able to make use of it to our operational advantage.

From the forward control outside the Embassy I went to see William Whitelaw, the Home Secretary and Douglas Hurd, the Minister of State at the Foreign Office. I explained what had happened, what action we had taken, and what demands were being made by the terrorists. I said that I needed to know what line the Cabinet would take in response to the terrorists' demands. In other words, would the British Government agree to all or part of the demands of the terrorists? I said plainly that in my view the right course was one of no concession. Indeed I do not believe that there are any circumstances in which I would have advised a British Government otherwise. Various scenarios can be envisaged where those under threat may be royalty or VIPs but the basic issue remains: to capitulate or to stand firm. If terrorists are in no doubt that the authorities in Britain will stand firm, then we may well deflect rather than attract terrorism to our shores. A decision by Cabinet was needed at this early stage because the conduct of further police operations depended very largely on the line the Government was going to adopt.

The Home Secretary attended a Cabinet meeting shortly after my visit and within a short time gave me the answer I wanted to hear: the Cabinet were unanimous that none of the terrorists' demands should be met. He added that the Prime Minister particularly wished me to know that I had her personal support and that she wished me well. I could not have asked for a more prompt or more clear-cut response.

Once we knew that there would be no capitulation by HM Government to the terrorists' demands, our strategy was based on attempting to talk the terrorists into surrender without violence or bloodshed on either side. Our tactics were shaped by this strategy and we knew that it was likely to take time. Only if this strategy failed or looked like failing was it in my mind to recommend that the SAS be committed to an assault on the Embassy.

Through the remaining days of the siege police worked patiently to bring it to a peaceful conclusion. The key men in this were the officers who acted as negotiators with the terrorists. The role of negotiator is an exceedingly difficult one. There is little or nothing on which to negotiate because the only issue which is acceptable is the release of all the hostages and the unconditional surrender of the terrorists. Somehow the negotiators had to make bricks out of straw, and lead the terrorists to believe that a settlement of their case was being pursued. Above all, a negotiator has to seek protraction of time, defusion of tension and the establishment of a working relationship with the terrorists.

Our negotiators did not fail us. They had the most exacting task and were subjected to every form of frustration and vexation, but they were superb. The contribution they made was incalculable. Subsequently we were all thrilled and overwhelmed by the success of the SAS, but 'they also serve who only stand and wait', and the negotiators certainly did this. Indeed it was they who provided the time for the SAS to develop and practise their assault plan, without which the storming of the Embassy would have been entirely 'hit-or-miss' and could have been disastrous.

The negotiators sought in particular to get on good terms with the terrorists. Efforts were continually made to secure an 'honourable solution', that is to say one where all lives would be saved while the terrorists did not lose face. A key aspect of this would be publicity for the terrorists' demands, linked with demonstration of the reasonableness of those demands being underlined by surrender to London's police, with their reputation for peaceful methods. The negotiators also exerted pressure on the besieged terrorists by dwelling on the condition of some hostages who showed signs of illness, which resulted in the release of five hostages during the siege.

In all this painfully slow work, the police controllers and negotiators sought first to isolate the terrorists. This was an extremely difficult task as they were lodged in an embassy which had over fifty rooms, and was fitted with telephones, telex, television and radios. One of the many telephones continued to work for a while, which only handicapped further the task of the police.

Backing up the work of the police control was the Cabinet Office Briefing Room (COBRA), staffed by civil servants and others. To say it is not a front line organization is to detract in no way from its importance. We put a number of requests back to COBRA and on some of them – like the request for the help by foreign ambassadors – they took their time in replying, which was both frustrating to us and raised the level of tension within the Embassy. But it, too, helped to protract negotiations.

There is no police officer on the staff of COBRA and it has been suggested that COBRA would work more effectively if a senior officer was present. I do not see it that way. COBRA is conveying to the operational commander political decisions of the Government; in addition it has an advisory role to play. In coming to a political decision, ministers need to have a police view and this is obtained from the Commissioner. As to advice, any suggestions from COBRA will have to be weighed by the operational police commander in the light of the prevailing circumstances. If a senior police officer was a member of COBRA, making an input to their advice, this could compromise or hamper the role of the operational commander who has to make the decisions.

All these things and more were going on outside the Embassy, but what was happening inside? It would have been helpful to know the full answer at the time. We were building up information but much of the detail was only learned subsequently from the redoubtable Trevor Lock.

Lock showed remarkable coolness and skill in retaining his revolver. When the terrorists first seized the Embassy and all who were in it, Lock had various notebooks and documents in the right hand patch pocket of his raincoat, over his gun. All hostages were searched by the terrorists and when Lock's turn came he noticed that the hands of the Arab in question were shaking as if he was nervous. The Arab patted Lock's sides, felt the books and said, 'What's these?' Lock pulled up the pockets of his coat without removing the contents and said, 'Books, maps.' The Arab then left him alone. Thereafter, throughout the days of the siege, Lock lived mainly on dried biscuits and water to avoid as far as possible having to go to the lavatory. Any such visit was under very close guard and if Lock had removed his clothing, the gun would almost certainly have been spotted.

After the search, Lock joined the other hostages in one of the rooms of the Embassy; among them was the Iranian Chargé d'Affaires of the Embassy, Dr Afrouz, who had injuries to his face. The women hostages were separated from the men, and they began crying and wailing. One of the women told Lock that she was pregnant; she began lying on the floor making noises and movements as if she was having contractions. Lock urged the terrorists to secure the attendance of a doctor for the woman and the Chargé d'Affaires, but it was not until the fourth day of the siege that she was released. In all, five hostages were released, one on the first day, one on the second day, two on the fourth day and one on the fifth day.

Lock noticed throughout the siege that the trigger hammers of the guns carried by the terrorists were pulled back, and that one of them held a green grenade with his first finger on the ring and with the lever in the palm of his hand. He began to build up a rapport with the BBC men – Cramer and Harris – and also with a Syrian called Mustapha Karkouti, who could speak Persian and Arabic as well as English.

The first night, the Iranian hostages held a prayer session before sleeping on the floor guarded by terrorists. Lock stayed in a chair where he could be seen by the hostages, in order to calm them as well as to earn the respect of the terrorists. He was seeking, too, to identify the position in the building of each terrorist.

Lock was frequently disturbed: the terrorists were nervous of an attack from outside and took alarm at any noise. Early in the morning a terrorist came and sat by Lock.

'Are you hungry?' he asked.

'No.'

'Are you tired?'

'A little.'

'Why not lie down with the rest?'

'Because I am a policeman and must make sure that everyone else is OK.'

'Do you want anything to eat?'

'No.'

'We are very sorry about your face; do you want anything?'

'No, I will be OK.'

As morning came, each Iranian hostage put a small piece of paper on the floor, placed his or her forehead on it, and began saying prayers. During this second day the BBC man, Chris Cramer, began to develop stomach pains to an extent that he was writhing on the floor holding his sides and shaking. This caused a good deal of commotion and the terrorists finally decided to release him. Although Cramer by this time was shouting and screaming with pain, the leading terrorist, known as Salim, suspected trickery by the police and ordered Lock, the other BBC man Simeon Harris, and the Embassy chauffeur, Morris, to sit on the floor under guard with their legs crossed and their hands behind their heads. Salim's parting words were, 'If the police are up to something I will shout to him [the guard] to shoot you.'

Cramer was safely released and a prayer session followed together with a long debate in Persian between the terrorists and the Iranian hostages on the politics of their country. The authorities in Iran were informed about the obvious grievances and demands of the hostages. It became obvious that the Iranian Government was not interested, and this led to further wailing by the Iranian hostages and increased the nervousness of the terrorists.

By the third day Lock had appeared several times at a window of the Embassy to convey messages, one of which was that the hostages would like to speak to Tony Crabb, a BBC executive, and this was arranged. Lock sought time and time again to persuade the terrorists to surrender, urging them not to shoot any hostages. 'The police will not attack as long as you do not hurt or kill any hostage,' he told them. 'They will wait outside for ten years if they have to, if it would mean a peaceful end to the siege, with no bloodshed.'

By the fourth day tension within the Embassy had greatly increased, partly because of dissatisfaction by the terrorists with the broadcast of their demands. It was Lock's task to explain this through an open window to the police officers outside, and while he did so two pistols were poking into the small of his back. The requested broadcast was made in full on the BBC World Service, and tension within the Embassy relaxed, the Iranian hostages weeping openly. It had been a good day, with two hostages released.

In a noteworthy conversation with one of the terrorists that day, Trevor Lock said, 'I'm curious. When you first came into the porch where I was standing and things happened the way they did, what

157

would have happened if I had been standing outside the building as I normally would have been?'

'Don't ask me,' the terrorist replied. 'You are now my friend.'

Another day came and hopes that the ordeal might soon be at an end were shared by terrorists and hostages alike. But the terrorist leader, Salim, began to write slogans in Persian, Arabic and in English on the walls of an Embassy room, some of which read: 'Arabistans fight for freedom' and 'Down with the Ayatollah'. This last slogan caused particular resentment to one or two hostages. One man called Lavasani argued vehemently and later viciously with Salim. The terrorist cocked his machine pistol and pointed it at Lavasani. Trevor Lock put himself between them, but Lavasani continued to speak provocatively. Lock first told him to stop talking and, when this request had no effect, threatened to hit him if he continued as he was putting the lives of all the hostages at risk. In English Lavasani replied, 'I promise I will say no more, but only for the policeman as I respect him.'

Things quietened down a little but arguments amongst the terrorists continued, indicating that they were under great tension. Lavasani remained a man marked for the attention and hatred of the terrorists – hatred which he returned in good measure, regarding himself as a fanatic and, if necessary, a martyr for the cause of the Ayatollah.

The terrorists had asked for the ambassadors of several Arab countries to come to the Embassy to negotiate a settlement between the British Government and the terrorists – on terms acceptable to the latter, including safe and free air transport out of the United Kingdom. Police negotiations led to one more hostage being released – it was Lock's companion, Mustapha Karkouti, the Syrian. But, as each hour passed, tension again began to mount.

Finally Salim said, 'We are not spending another night here – we have had enough; the police will not allow the ambassadors to come and we are going to kill a hostage.' Lock was taken to the telephone linked to the police control and told by the terrorists to describe what he saw: Lavasani's hands being tied with wire flex and then attached by more flex to the banister of nearby stairs. Lavasani was blindfolded, but looked calm and more than ready to meet his death. Before being led away, Trevor Lock begged for Lavasani's life but a few minutes later he heard three shots.

Trevor Lock was taken downstairs and saw a red carpet raised over what appeared to be the shape of a body. He sought to lift up the carpet but was told to leave it alone. On instructions from the terrorists he spoke by telephone to police control to say that a hostage – Lavasani – had been killed. At about 6.45 p.m. the body of the dead hostage was put outside the front door of the Embassy. At the same time Salim told the police over the telephone that they were shortly going to kill another hostage.

What followed is now well known.

Let me return first, however, to how matters were developing at the forward police control outside the Embassy. There the closing stages of the siege had been anxious and frustrating. The terrorists had made repeated threats to the hostages and these all had to be taken seriously. It had become increasingly necessary to reassess what developments would justify military intervention. A mass breakout from the Embassy was one possibility. My view was that should there be good evidence that two hostages had been murdered, a military assault should be made on the Embassy as quickly as possible in order to save the lives of the remaining hostages. I put this to the Home Secretary and he agreed in principle.

In consequence, the SAS began to finalize their plans and preparations for such an eventuality. A mock-up of the Embassy was prepared by our Architects' Branch at New Scotland Yard on which the SAS began to train for an assault, should it prove necessary.

The police negotiators had continued with their patient task of keeping in contact with the terrorists and seeking their surrender, but the turning point came when we heard three shots which, as we now know, killed Lavasani, followed by the terrorists' assertion (through PC Lock) that a hostage had been shot and that further executions would follow. Other information available to us tended to support this.

A little earlier I had sent a letter under my signature, in English and in Farsi, into the Embassy addressed to the terrorists. It read as follows:

> I think it is right that I should explain to you clearly and in writing the way in which my police officers are dealing with the taking of the hostages in the Iranian Embassy.
>
> I am responsible for preserving the peace and enforcing the law in London and I do this independently of politicians and Government. I and my officers deeply wish to work to a peaceful solution of what has occurred. We fully understand how both the hostages and those who hold them feel threatened and frightened. You are cut off from your families and friends. But you need not feel frightened or threatened by the police. It is not our way in Britain to resort to violence against those who are peaceful.
>
> You have nothing to fear from my officers provided you do not harm those in your care. I firmly hope that we can now bring this incident to a close peacefully and calmly.
>
> David McNee

This offered a 'way out' for the terrorists but the offer drew no response.

The help of the Muslim Imam of the Central London Mosque was sought and he spoke to the terrorists to try and persuade them not to do anything to harm the hostages or themselves, but this too was of no avail.

At 5 p.m. on 5 May, the Commander of the SAS reported that his troops were at ten minutes' readiness for a full assault. At 5.05 p.m. snippets of the terrorists' conversation were heard, as follows:

> 'We do something before sunset.'
> 'Kill two or three or four.'
> 'Kill all by 10 p.m.'

We also believed that the windows and doors of the Embassy were being barricaded.

When the body of the dead hostage, Lavasani, was recovered from the front door of the Embassy shortly before 7 p.m., examination showed that death had occurred some hours previously. This seemed to suggest that the first three shots heard shortly after noon had killed him and that later shots, heard at 6.42 p.m., had possibly killed one or more others. As threats had been made to kill a further hostage at 7.15 p.m., we concluded that there was a high probability that at least two hostages had already been killed and that the terrorists were ready to kill the remainder.

Urgent action was required and I sought immediate discussion with the Home Secretary. The questions in my mind were, how does one decide when police operations are unlikely to achieve the safe release of the hostages and capture of the terrorists?

Is a serious threat to cause grave injury or death to a hostage or hostages sufficient? Is one death too many? With twenty-six hostages would two deaths be a more realistic figure to justify military assault, with all the uncertainty as to its consequences? Whatever option you select the commodity at stake is human life, someone's husband, wife, son, daughter, father or mother. My conclusion now was that the siege could be brought to an end and the safety of the hostages secured best by military force and that such action should be taken forthwith. I said as much to the Home Secretary. He authorized the commitment of the SAS, saying that the precise timing of the assault was to be a matter for the police forward control outside the Embassy in consultation with the military Commander.

The SAS would be acting not as in war but in support of the police and, like the police, they were answerable to the law and the courts for their actions. It will be recalled that during subsequent proceedings at a coroner's court looking into the deaths of the terrorists, officers of the SAS were summoned by the coroner to give evidence and did so.

I discussed the position with the officer commanding the SAS and agreed the final details. I remember earlier watching with amazement his apparent appetite as he ate a large meal of stew while the events of the day were developing. I also recall my last words to him: 'Don't forget that Trevor Lock is in there in uniform.'

The actual sequence of events went as follows:

6.42 p.m.	Two shots followed by a third were heard.
6.46 p.m.	The body of a man was pushed outside the front door of the Embassy and recovered by police.
6.56 p.m.	I spoke to the Home Secretary and secured his agreement to deployment of the SAS.
7.07 p.m.	I handed formal control of the incident to the SAS.
7.24 p.m.	The SAS launched their attack on the Embassy.
7.40 p.m.	I spoke to the Home Secretary to report the successful outcome of the attack, including the safe recovery of Trevor Lock.

But let me leave the description of the final moments to Trevor Lock:

He [the terrorist] banged against the office door which opened and as we went through it his machine pistol flew out of his hand, fell on the floor and skidded halfway along the office, i.e. about eight feet. We both then ended up on the floor in the office. He rolled over onto his front and tried to crawl towards the gun. I laid across his back, put my left arm around his throat and pulled his head back. He was kicking and struggling. I said, 'You caused this. I gave you an alternative but you wouldn't take it, you bastard.'

'It was not me, it was the others,' he replied. I then drew my gun from the holster, forced the muzzle in his right ear and said, 'It's down to you. You're the leader, aren't you? They would have done as you told them.' He then said, 'Don't hurt me, don't hurt me.'

I took my gun and pointed it under his chin. Then I saw what looked like to be lemons rolling beside me – they exploded and I was thrown off the terrorist. My eyes were watering and I could hardly breathe; through the haze I saw the terrorist move towards the machine pistol. I leapt on top of him. At this stage his hand was about four inches from the gun. I was shouting at him and then the door burst open and I heard someone shout, 'Trevor, move over!' I rolled over to my right away from the terrorist and then heard rapid gunfire. I looked to my left and the terrorist was lying there, apparently lifeless. I saw a man dressed all in black wearing a gas mask who shouted, 'Make for the corridor!' I climbed over a desk and leant through the window. I took my hat off with my left hand as I still had my gun in my right, and heard a voice from outside say, 'Trevor, get down.' This I did until I heard another voice in the office say, 'Trevor, this way.' I ran through the door to be picked up by two men under the armpits and passed from one pair of men to another all the way down the stairs to the ground floor and let out through the back door. My gun was taken from me by someone – at no time had I discharged my firearm. I was then taken to a field ambulance where I was examined, before being transported away from the scene.

These words tell the drama of the end of the siege more effectively than any I could find. I can perhaps best add as light relief a sentence or two on what was happening to me at the same time. After committing the SAS, I knew that within ten minutes very forceful action would take place. I was in a forward control about three houses away from the Iranian Embassy. I had been told that there would be a small explosion, but in fact I heard a bang which almost lifted me off my feet (and that at my weight is saying something!). As I looked toward the Embassy, the smell of CS gas was so strong that my eyes were much affected, and anyone looking at me at the time might have thought I was crying. The flames that burst from the windows of the Embassy led me to think that my career might also be going up in smoke. A few minutes later came the wonderful news that nearly all the hostages were freed. Trevor Lock was unharmed. The SAS had come through with only minor injuries. At 7.50 p.m. the military Commander returned control to the police and the operation was brought to a conclusion with all the hostages being taken for care and treatment to the Metropolitan Police nursing home at Hendon.

It appeared to have been a successful military operation. But I remember looking at John Dellow's face at the moment the SAS were committed to the assault and seeing there sadness and disappointment that all the days of patient negotiation by the police to secure the release of the hostages and to save the lives of the terrorists had not finally won through; that aggression was now to take over.

Was the operation in fact as successful as it seemed? On the debit side were the deaths of two innocent people as well as of five terrorists, and an embassy set on fire. Against this, twenty-four hostages had been brought to safety together with Constable Lock. But of much greater importance was the fact that despite all their threats and violence, the terrorists had succeeded in none of their aims and the policy of the British Government of making no concessions to terrorists had been wholly upheld. The world publicity given to this and the five days' events had ensured that this policy, and the firmness of the police and military in carrying it out, would be well noted by all who might be planning future terrorist acts. It was also more likely, as has indeed proved the case in, for example, Spain and Italy, that other governments would follow a similar policy.

Two final stories are perhaps worth telling. The first is that when the decision to deploy the SAS was taken, it was vital to ascertain the location of the terrorists and hostages as accurately as possible. To this end Salim was kept in conversation on the telephone. He was highly suspicious and kept insisting that he could hear noises. The negotiator knew it was essential to hold Salim on the telephone and, just as the first of the controlled explosions to gain entry to the Embassy occurred, the negotiator was saying, 'No, Salim, there is nothing suspicious, nothing to worry about.'

The second incident could only happen in Britain, with its attention to protocol and propriety. As the SAS launched their assault and the Embassy burst into flames an envelope came into police hands. It was addressed to the Iranian Embassy and it was from the Foreign and Commonwealth Office asking that the Embassy flag should be lowered at half mast in respect of the death of President Tito:

> Her Majesty's Vice-Marshal of the Diplomatic Corps presents his compliments to Their Excellencies the High Commissioners and Ambassadors and to the Acting High Commissioners and Ambassadors and to the Acting High Commissioners and

Chargés d'Affaires and has the honour to inform them that Her Majesty the Queen has commanded that flags be flown at half mast from 8.00 a.m. to sunset tomorrow, Tuesday, 6 May owing to the death of His Excellency the President of the Socialist Federal Republic of Yugoslavia.

Her Majesty's Vice-Marshal of the Diplomatic Corps takes this opportunity of renewing to Their Excellencies the High Commissioners and Ambassadors and to the Acting High Commissioners and Chargés d'Affaires the assurance of his highest consideration.

In reporting to the House of Commons on 6 May, the Home Secretary said:

I know that the House will wish to join me in congratulating the Metropolitan Police on an operation that they carried out with skill, care and determination. Their conduct throughout was an example of the highest standards of the British police. The success of the final assault and rescue is an outstanding tribute to the professionalism and bravery of the SAS. I am sure that the House, and, indeed, the country, will wish to join the Government in giving thanks to all those involved – police, military or civilian.

The following day 142 Members of Parliament of all parties signed a Motion for the House of Commons on the following lines:

That this House congratulates the Home Secretary and the Commissioner of Police of the Metropolis on their decisiveness and resolution which so successfully brought to an end the Princes Gate Siege, while securing the release of the hostages; places on record its gratitude to the men of the Special Air Service on their exemplary courage and expertise; commands the gallantry and devotion to duty of the men and women of the Metropolitan Police, especially PC Trevor Lock, and expresses the hope that the President and Government of Iran will now move with similar resolve and speed to secure the release of the United States diplomatic hostages illegally detained in Iran.

How did I see my personal role as Commissioner throughout these dramatic and onerous days? First let me make the point that although the siege had a number of very special features, it had to be

approached in the same way as any other police task. As I said in the
first of only two statements to the media:

> All my officers engaged in this incident are concerned to do
> what we always try to do – resolve the situation without loss of
> life and uphold the law. It is not the time to go into great detail –
> we must show patience and perseverance, that is what we
> propose to do.

Patience and perseverance were indeed two qualities which I had
personally to exercise. My instinct was to take charge of the tactical
operations and this was a feeling difficult to quell. But it had to be
done in order to retain objectivity in making a continuous assessment of the operation and the participants – including police
commanders. Further, while the incident was a centrepiece, there
was still a force to be run. Although the siege was naturally the focus
of attention, everyday policing of the metropolis had to continue
and be supervised.

I met twice daily with my Deputy and four Assistant Commissioners to consider overall strategy, and this was done in close
co-operation with the Deputy Assistant Commissioners – Dellow
and Maybanks – in charge of the operation. It was important to
withdraw the Deputy Assistant Commissioners from the front line –
if only to another room – during these consultations to assist in
objectivity. An Assistant Commissioner was given a 24-hour responsibility in turn for giving all support and guidance to the
Deputy Assistant Commissioner in charge. I also visited the scene
twice daily to bring myself up to date with developments and to
maintain morale.

It was particularly important for me to identify signs of stress,
for the pressures and strain were not only to be found within the
Embassy; they were very much at work on operational police
officers and negotiators. If such signs were identified, it was essential that the officer concerned was withdrawn from further direct
participation in dealing with the siege.

I did not appear daily on television or radio, nor deal with the
press; this was a task for the operational head and for the Director

of Information at New Scotland Yard. My personal involvement with the media was reserved until the end – this would have been the case whatever the outcome.

Lastly, police responsibilities have to be exercised within the policy of HM Government. To this end it is for the Commissioner to deal directly with ministers and secure a clear, concise statement of policy, having given them a precise and unambiguous statement of the facts. It was my good fortune to be working with Mr Whitelaw as Home Secretary for from him, from the first day to the last, I got all the support and guidance on ministerial policy which was required. This greatly facilitated the operational task of the police.

During my thirty-six years' police service I met many courageous men but few have been the equal of Police Constable Trevor Lock. As soon as it was known that Trevor Lock was safe, Mrs Lock was told and taken to New Scotland Yard where she joined her husband. That was a meeting for which I and the whole force had prayed, and I confess that there were tears in my eyes when they met. Later, they were taken to the Howard Hotel and accommodated there under the name of Duffy – the name of the then head of the Anti-Terrorist Squad. This was a device to protect the Locks for twenty-four hours from press interference and publicity. The next day Lock was 'debriefed', as the saying goes, and in the months which followed he was honoured by the Queen (with the award of the George Medal), by the City of London (with the granting of the Freedom of the City) and indeed by the nation at large.

As regards my opinion of Lock's conduct as a police officer during the siege, I can only repeat my words to the world press when we met them together at the time: 'You write about bravery, now look at it.'

8

Crime

ON MY ARRIVAL at the Yard I had promised to try and make the streets of London safer and to give greater protection to the homes of Londoners.

Grand objectives! Particularly in view of the almost universal trends in rising crime, violence, vandalism and general hooliganism. Nevertheless, thoughout my time as Commissioner it remained my overriding aim, despite all the demands of public events and major disorders.

'Offences reported to the police' and 'clear up' rates (i.e. the number of crimes reported to the police which are solved) are notoriously poor guides to the actual level of criminal activity in an area, and to the extent to which the police are dealing successfully with crime. Nevertheless they are the only regular information we have. The crime figures for 1978, my first full year, showed a decrease from the 1977 figures: the first such decrease in eight years. In 1979 there was a further decline, including a small decline in serious crime. During my last two full years, 1980 and 1981, the number of reported crimes rose again as they had done since the 1950s. This increase has to be put in context. First, in the years 1980 and 1981 there were greater increases in the level of reported crime for the rest of England and Wales than in London. In 1980 reported crime in the metropolis increased by five per cent and in 1981 there was an eight per cent increase; the respective percentage increases in the rest of England and Wales were six and eleven per cent.

If you look further afield the comparison is even more striking, as the increase in crime was worldwide. From fairly extensive visits to Europe and America I know that major increases in crime are certainly not 'a British malaise', but are to be found everywhere.

'Clear up' rates for crimes generally are lower in the metropolis than in the rest of England and Wales. But this too has to be put in context. First, it is important to recognize that the Metropolitan Police follows to the letter the rules laid down by the Home Office for the recording of crime statistics. Indeed the Statistical Adviser to the force is seconded to the force by the Home Office. Comparison of 'clear up' rates between forces is a crude measure. The disparities that exist themselves call for further inquiry. This is very much an area to which the Home Office Inspectorate of Constabulary should give urgent attention. For my part, service in different forces leaves me in no doubt that the Metropolitan Police is no less efficient in dealing with crime than any other force – rather the reverse. Comment about police performance as measured by 'clear up' rate, if it is to make sense, must examine those cases where police can have a major impact by detection. Where this applies as in, for example, murder, assault and fraud, the detection rate of reported crime is high. The bulk of London's crime is made up of burglary and motor vehicle crimes, which is largely opportunist, and these types of crimes do not readily lend themselves to detection methods. To deal with these, the emphasis has to be on crime prevention.

Second, London is a great international city: vast industrial, commercial and individual wealth lies within its boundaries. The scale of everything – population, immigrants, visitors, tourists, vehicles, buildings, commerce, entertainment and so on – is far greater than anywhere else in the UK. One consequence is that the metropolis is also a great centre for criminals and the commission of crime, particularly serious crime which can have links with other countries. The complexity and extensiveness of criminal activity is also greater – and I say that as a detective with long experience in Glasgow.

Because of these and other factors the detection of crime in the metropolis can be complex, protracted and difficult. Detectives are not able to rely as readily as elsewhere on knowing and questioning *local* suspects and criminals. Crime in one area of London is frequently committed by persons who have come from an altogether different part of the metropolis, or from outside.

An analysis of crimes detected by police in the metropolis shows that over the last ten years the actual number has remained largely the same, although this number has progressively become a small percentage of an increasing total. Why should this be, when numbers in the force rose by 4,000 between 1979 and 1982? The answers lie in two main factors: economic constraints and increasing demands. The need for economies resulted in a reduction in the numbers of hours worked by each officer – less overtime. The number of calls for police assistance, the number of crimes, the number of public order incidents all kept rising. The net effect was that we were no better off.

It is not often that I have been in total agreement with the public utterances of Jim Anderton, Chief Constable of Greater Manchester, and still less often with those of John Alderson, former Chief Constable of Devon and Cornwall. When addressing the Manchester Statistical Society, Anderton said rhetorically: 'What precisely do the statistics tell us about the state of criminality in the nation and what do they suggest should be done about it? Very little, is the answer I would give you.' In his annual report for 1980 John Alderson wrote: '. . . it would not be right to rely too heavily on the statistics of reported crime as an accurate measurement of police efficiency in preventing crime, since extra activity and presence of police provide added opportunity for public reportage of crime.' Agreed.

The argument is sometimes put forward that to deal with the prime aims of reducing and preventing crime the police service should not be side-tracked by other duties. They should not waste time on dealing with such minor matters as, say, lost or found property, domestic disputes, assistance to persons locked out of their cars or houses. The argument has even been extended to say that police should not give more than cursory attention to burglaries and thefts where the losses are negligible and the likelihood of detection minimal. This approach to crime has been

170

formalized in the United States. It is called 'case screening' and theorists claim it is successful and that detectives are more purposively employed.

I remain sceptical about this, as I do of much of the fine-sounding theory coming from America where the crime situation in big cities is, by our standards, absolutely appalling. I understand that the Metropolitan Police may be committed to such an approach in the future. If so, I wish the force success, and will watch the outcome with interest. Something similar, but on a more limited scale, was tried in experiments by specialist burglary squads whilst I was Commissioner, but the initial visit to the scene and the approach by police to the victim was retained as the focal point of the method. The police need the confidence and support of the public. Nothing wins this more fully than help and reassurance given by police officers to the victims of crime. Any burglary or theft, however small the loss, is important to the victim, who in many cases may suffer an emotional shock. Prompt and sympathetic action by police is essential. If public confidence is to be retained it is incumbent on the police to provide a broad-based service.

I decided that the best prospect of preventing crime and making London safer lay in getting more police officers on the streets. As I have said, the strength of the Metropolitan Police rose during the time I was Commissioner from around 22,500 to 26,500. During the same period the numbers in the CID increased from 3,202 to 3,438. But you do not recruit young men and women one day and then turn them out the next day onto the streets as competent police constables or detectives. It takes two years to complete the *basic* training of new recruits and much longer to make a good detective. Thus, Londoners will only benefit over the next five years or longer from the greater numbers of officers.

Linked with the increase in recruits, I also maintained an unremitting drive during my time as Commissioner to put and keep more and more officers where they were wanted – on the streets. My most senior officers knew that they had little prospect of gaining my consent to an increase in the strength of a headquarters branch unless there were exceptional reasons for it, since it would entail withdrawing officers from ordinary duty. I made sure that all local commanders knew my wish to see as many officers as possible out of offices, out of stations, out of cars, and on to foot patrol. The force was reorganized gradually to release 1,000 officers for ordinary police duties. 'Panda' cars were withdrawn from central London so that patrolling could be done on foot. Technology such as computerization of message systems and management information systems, was introduced to improve the police presence on the streets and provide an efficient response.

However, 26,500 officers cannot keep a constant vigil on a police area of 800 square miles with a resident population of seven million, and a constant flow of visitors. It was essential to identify priorities.

One of my priorities was to take action against armed robbers. Firearms were being used with a level of impunity hitherto unknown and the danger to employees and the public, inside and outside the premises being robbed, was very real.

Events during the last five years – not only in London but throughout Britain – involving use of guns by police, television programmes showing police fire power, and violent crimes causing death or serious injury to police officers, have led to a debate on whether the British policeman should still be the traditional 'unarmed bobby'. It is regrettably no longer true that London's police all go about their business unarmed. Most do, but a number do not and the question has rightly been asked whether this is really necessary. In trying to answer this question, some commentators have looked at the number of reported crimes involving firearms and the number of occasions these firearms were discharged. Others have looked at the number of offences where the firearms were real as against those where the weapons used proved to be air weapons or imitation guns. Such assessments however are only a part of the picture.

In essence the reasons for police officers being armed are:

(a) the increase in threats to royalty and VIPs (witness attacks on President Reagan, the Pope, the blanks fired at the Queen, and the shooting of the Israeli Ambassador).

(b) increased terrorism and threats of terrorism.

(c) the use of firearms by criminals in robberies.

(d) a general increase in violence involving, at times, firearms.

The consequences of the above need little explanation. Protection duties clearly require officers to be armed. Likewise, officers dealing with the suppression and detection of armed robbery cannot be left defenceless. There were many cases during my Commissionership of police officers being severely wounded and even killed by armed criminals which remain with me, but none so personal or grievous as the deaths of Francis O'Neill* and Ken Howorth and the maiming of Philip Olds. O'Neill was stabbed to death by an addict trying to obtain drugs on a false prescription; Howorth, a Bomb Disposal Officer, was killed while dismantling an IRA bomb in a Wimpy Bar in Oxford Street; Philip Olds was shot in the course of an armed robbery, and is now paralysed from the waist down.

Violence shows no sign of diminishing. Until it does the extent to which police officers need to be armed will not be reduced. It remains highly unlikely, however, that most Londoners will notice any move away from the very important tradition of their bobbies as a whole not carrying arms, or that they will ever come face to face with an armed police officer. The day of officers openly carrying weapons on a regular basis is still, happily, not a reality.

To return to armed robberies, the money stolen was often used for further criminal activity. From the mid 1970s there was increasing evidence that criminals known to be concerned with armed robberies were becoming deeply involved in drug trafficking. There was a two-way traffic; either money obtained from illegal drug trading was being used to finance and mount armed robberies, or money from robberies was being used for purchasing drugs. In either case the return on capital was certainly greater than that available to honest citizens from legitimate investment.

* see Appendix II

There appeared to be no shortage of people willing to act as couriers for drug dealers. Cannabis and cocaine were the predominant drugs, but the much more dangerous narcotic, heroin, was also on the scene. Two major fields of criminal activity, armed robbery and drug trafficking, had come closer together and the threat they represented had to be faced. The criminal network was supplied with information on a wide scale, was well-planned and well-directed. But there was a weak link. The drug pusher or drug addict is a type of individual who, when cornered, is often ready and willing to implicate others in the hope of obtaining a lighter sentence for himself. The murky world of drug abuse does not always readily share the bond of silence which is so much a way of life of other criminals. Drug cases have always produced a supply of informants on a wide scale, and soon the robbery ranks were breached.

The wall of silence was first broken in the case of 'Bertie' Smalls. The facts of this case are that on 10 August 1972 an armed robbery was made on a branch of Barclays Bank in Wembley, and over £130,000 in bank notes was stolen. In December of the same year, Flying Squad officers of the Metropolitan Police arrested Bertie Smalls in Northampton for the offence. Soon after his arrest, he indicated that he was willing to provide information, if it would be to his benefit, implicating other criminals in other offences. The police made no response but in March 1973, during committal proceedings against him, Smalls made a renewed approach through his solicitor. Discussions which followed between the Director of Public Prosecutions, the police and Smalls' solicitor resulted in Smalls turning Queen's Evidence and naming thirty-two other bank robbers, the majority of whom were later prosecuted and convicted. No criminal has ever informed on such a scale before. The case led to the coining of the term 'supergrass'.

The term 'supergrass' is of course journalese. The official police term, which is not without humour, is 'resident informant', so called because the criminal who has been charged and is willing to give information is remanded with a condition of residence acceptable to police – normally a police station.

Purging the soul is not new, nor is the role of informants. To 'grass' is old slang for the giving away of information on fellow criminals, but the scale of the information being provided was unprecedented. The openness of the 'supergrasses' provided a challenge for the police and the judicial system.

These men – for to date no woman has claimed a place in such company – are usually well-established, professional criminals. The offences involved are usually serious crimes such as armed robberies or burglaries of high-value property. When arrested, the offenders give detailed information not only about their own involvement but also about that of their associates. They are motivated largely by a desire to reduce the punishment for their crimes and, very occasionally, it is a matter of revenge. It is not a genuine desire to see the law enforced.

As I have said, the first 'supergrass' case – that of Bertie Smalls, came before the courts in 1973, but the total immunity afforded to Smalls attracted a great deal of adverse comment in Parliament and elsewhere, and no future case was handled in the same way. Instead it was left to the courts to impose sentences reflecting the value of the information provided and thereby encourage other informants.

A test of the new procedure came when one 'supergrass', Charlie Lowe, was unimpressed by a sentence of eleven and a half years passed by the court, even though he had disclosed a great deal of information against his associates. He appealed and his sentence was reduced to five years with Mr Justice Roskill saying, 'It was in the public's interest that persons such as this should be encouraged to give information to police in order that others may be brought to justice.'

It needs to be emphasized that it is not the police who decide whether a 'supergrass' can be used in court – that is a decision for the Director of Public Prosecutions. Properly used, the 'supergrass' system is an effective weapon for dealing with serious crimes already committed. By securing the arrest and conviction of major criminals, and often violent criminals at that, further offences by these men are prevented.

There was criticism that because the system is historic, police resources are diverted from concentrating on *current* crimes and gaining information to prevent future crimes. Such criticism is not really valid because current crime nearly always is involved and the targets are professional thieves who are constantly criminally active.

The morality of the system has also come under fire and such criticism undoubtedly has substance. There must be a possibility of a criminal engaged in the commission of crime believing that if arrested all he need do is turn 'supergrass' and thereby obtain a greatly reduced sentence, with possibly the fruits of his crime (stolen money, property, investments, etc.) also remaining intact. But there is no evidence that the 'supergrass' system is being used to an extent that crime is thereby being encouraged, nor that it has led to an increase in police corruption. The reality of both possibilities has to be clearly recognized and guarded against, and for this reason alone decisions about the control and use of the resident informant system are made at a high level and in close consultation with the prosecuting authority. Monitoring the system in a particular case is also maintained at the same level.

The Metropolitan Police pioneered the use of resident informants in this country and a number of the problems and difficulties which have arisen have been resolved not only by careful planning but also by ad hoc solutions. Always paramount is the requirement to keep within the law. In the United States the resident informant system is well established with accepted procedures and special facilities. Unlike the case in this country, immunity from prosecution is granted.

Safeguarding the 'supergrass' and his family is of course essential. The requirement may include providing new National Health and Insurance numbers, a new driving licence, a new passport, as well as re-housing the whole family. It is far from straightforward because now such documents as, for example, a new birth or marriage certificate or taxation forms are not issued at a drop of a hat. The Government could play a part by passing legislation making provision for such measures. Ad hoc arrangements allow for flexibility but are not desirable in the long term. The benefits of the resident informant system outweigh the disadvantages but it must be properly handled. If the Government is serious about preventing and controlling crime – particularly serious crime – then special provision for informers must be part of the package.

The action taken against armed robbery was very successful, but when you eliminate one problem, criminal activity soon finds other outlets. Banks became much safer places, aided by the preventive measures installed by the banking institutions, but cash in transit became a target, as did building societies, post offices and off-licence premises. There was no respite for the Central Robbery Squad or the police on the streets.

What of the other end of the spectrum of crime, in other words, crimes on the street and burglary? Both were and are highly prevalent. Street crime, usually lumped together today under the name of 'mugging', is not new to the streets of London. Footpads, pickpockets and purse snatchers have been with us for centuries. In recent years the crime of 'mugging' has caught the headlines because of the involvement of young black people, and it has provided fruitful material for attention by the media, right wing and left wing extremists, and by black people complaining of an excessively high level of policing in their areas. It is difficult to assess the precise extent to which black people are *actually* involved. My belief is that the numbers are very small measured against the numbers of the black community in the metropolis as a whole. But equally there is no denying that in a great number of cases the victims describe their attacker as black. This is one area where the black community must help put the record straight by condemning the erring minority in their midst.

The fear of 'mugging' certainly prevents people, and especially the elderly and infirm, from going out of their homes as freely and as often as they wish. The extent to which people are frightened and distressed is very real, although it is not always related to the actual level of crime. A variety of initiatives to change this position were undertaken by commanders of the districts with a high incidence of street crimes. Areas and individuals were identified for special attention and specific patrols were introduced but, despite these and other efforts, this insidious crime continued apace.

The other great scourge of our cities is burglary, and indeed there is a close relationship between burglary and street crime, for those engaged in street crime readily turn their hand to burglary, or have already done so. Effective police action against street crimes drives the perpetrators to other forms of crime. Displacement of crime to other forms of offences is an ever-present problem for the police. Once again, this is why breaking the upward spiral of crime and securing a general improvement requires action by the public as a whole and not just by police alone.

Dealing with burglary is a far tougher proposition for police than dealing with street crime, for it is much more diverse in time, location and offender, and the number of criminals involved is much greater.

I have already explained how thousands more policemen were recruited or released for beat patrol on the streets, which is the best deterrent of all. Behind them a variety of 'burglary squads' were set up, some to concentrate on burglaries where detection had the best chance of success, and a more limited police response allocated to other cases. Letters were sent to householders to explain the police approach and, when arrests were made, interrogation was intense to ascertain if the arrested person had also been responsible for other offences. As back-up, a computer was used experimentally to improve the storage, analysis and retrieval of information for detectives.

London detectives are increasingly over-burdened with the size of the burglary problem, and in consequence their 'cutting edge' is blunted. In view of the number of burglaries I found it difficult to see how to relieve this burden. I continue to reject any suggestion that there should be, as in some American police forces, a 'graduated response', i.e. giving very restricted attention to burglaries involving little or no loss or damage. Likelihood of detection was the only criterion for differing police response. Some relief could be found through reducing the paperwork and records; my experience as a detective had often been that the higher the level of paper, the lower the level of success in finding the offender. Hence the trials with a Crime Reporting Information System, which in essense is a high-sounding name for the computerization of the details of criminal investigations. The system is designed for long term benefits but I believe it to be essential to meet the policing demands of this decade and beyond. At the time of my retirement a decision on the future use of the system was awaited from the Home Office.

What is required above all is public and political drive. The same attention and all necessary finance should be given to dealing with the problem of burglaries as is given to dealing with public disorders. As we all know, burglary is an everyday, persistent and prevalent offence, which threatens each one of us every day and night. It is time that it was treated by Government and all concerned with the highest priority.

A first requirement is to see that the police are fully equipped to deal with the problem. For the impact of policing on burglary and street crime depends very largely on the powers of the police to stop and search persons, to obtain warrants for the searching of houses and premises and to interrogate suspected persons. These are the vulnerable areas for the criminal. The need here seems clear. The public expects the police to prevent, investigate and detect crime. But the police cannot do this in a way which is satisfactory to themselves or the public while the criminal law is imprecise and ambiguous. There is a need for clearly defined, readily understandable police powers which equip officers to do the job that society expects of them. More than ever before, the protection of the public from the criminal requires a system of justice as effective in securing the conviction of the guilty as it is in securing the acquittal of the innocent.

You might think all that to be no more than common sense; but when I put forward proposals on such basis to the Royal Commission on Police Powers and Criminal Procedure, comments like these appeared in the press at the time: 'Much too hard a Hammer' (the *Observer*); 'MPs fury over the Hammer' (the *Daily Express*). Harriet Harman, the Legal Officer of the National Council for Civil Liberties and now a Labour Member of Parliament wrote in *The*

Times to suggest that the proposals I made 'could destroy the consensus on which British policing is traditionally based.' I wholeheartedly disagree: the confidence of the public in the police depends as much on effectiveness as on a comforting attitude and a smiling, kindly face.

In the past, the police in England and Wales have been dealing with a population which, in the main, was ignorant of its civil rights. Because Parliament had become very reluctant to face up to the necessity of giving the police adequate powers to deal with crime, officers have been expected to rely upon this ignorance when making the necessary inquiries and tests for the solving of crime. The judiciary have accepted this position. As recently as 1970 Lord Denning, in his judgment in *Ghani v Jones* (1970) 1 Q.B. 693, said:

> No magistrate – nor judge even – has any power to issue a search warrant for murder. He can issue a search warrant for stolen goods and for some statutory offences such as coinage. But not for murder. Not to dig for the body. Nor to look for the axe, the gun or the poison dregs. The police have to get the consent of the householder to enter if they can; or, if not, do it by stealth or by force. Somehow they seem to manage. No decent person refuses them permission. If he does, he is probably implicated in some way or other. So the police risk an action for trespass. It is not much risk.

Parliament has been willing to give very wide powers to police to deal with cruelty to animals, taking of birds' eggs and similar offences, subjects which are popular with the press and the general public, but has given no such wide powers to police to deal with violence or threatened violence to the public. The effect of this is that many police officers have, early in their career, learned to use methods bordering on trickery or stealth in their investigations. They have frequently risked civil actions when doing so, but until the last decade the number of civil actions brought against police officers was extremely small. One fears that sometimes so-called pious perjury of this nature from junior officers can lead to even more serious perjury on other matters later in their careers. I consider it quite wrong that police officers – to use the words of Lord Denning – should be expected by stealth or by force, and at the risk of an action for trespass, to exercise necessary powers in the investigation of crime.

The paramount duty of any Commissioner of Police is to ensure that his officers are men of the highest integrity. A requirement to use stealth or force illegally is obviously a powerful embarrassment to any Commissioner who is seeking to achieve this objective. I took the view that I should be considering not just the situation in London as it was at the time of my report to the Royal Commission, but as it was likely to be over the next few decades. The general public is far more conscious of its rights but seemingly more apathetic about its responsibilities. The greatest growth in work in my Solicitors' Department was then on the civil side. Actions against my officers and myself arising out of arrests, searches etc. had risen from 16 in 1967 to 182 in 1982. There are a number of reasons for this increase, one of which no doubt is a greater knowledge by individuals of their rights and of the high monetary awards sometimes made by civil courts, together with the monitoring activities of professional bodies concerned with individual rights and of the media. It is probably no mere coincidence that the standard of proof in a civil court is less than in a criminal court. None of this is wrong, but it is now increasingly clear that the days when investigating officers could expect to bluff their way into obtaining consent to take body samples, or enter premises, were numbered.

It is, of course, a matter for society at large to determine what kind of police service it wants and what reasonable constraints must be placed, in the interests of civil liberty, on police action.

At the same time society should understand that measures introduced to protect the freedom and rights of the individual citizen can also lessen the chances of criminals being caught and convicted. That in turn increases the risk of further rises in crime. Society must also realize that it is not right to expect police to obtain the necessary powers by stealth and force. All the necessary powers must be clearly within the law. No one, least of all I, disputes the need to safeguard the individual's civil liberties, but we must always seek to ensure that the scales of justice are correctly balanced. If not, other fundamental rights such as the right to live peaceably in the security of one's home and the right to go about one's business unmolested, may be seriously threatened. This was my message and I asked the Royal Commission to give the police the powers and facilities necessary to do their job in the public interest.

The recommendations which followed could fill a book. These are just those dealing with the most controversial subject: police powers of search and other powers of obtaining evidence:

(a) Power for police to stop, search and detain persons and their vehicles in a public place for articles which may cause injury to the person or damage to property.

(b) Power for police to seize property found in a public place and believed to be of evidential value.

(c) Power for police to search a member of the public and his possessions in a public place where, by reason of such persons present at a particular location, an officer believes that such search might assist in the prevention of a serious crime dangerous to the public.

(d) Power for police to set up road blocks in certain circumstances.

(e) Power for police to apply for a warrant to search for evidence of an offence.

(f) Power for police to apply for an order under the Bankers' Book Evidence Act 1879 at any stage in their investigation and that such an order should relate to all records held by a bank and further that the definition of 'bank' should be widened.

(g) The clarification and widening of the power of search on arrest.

(h) The clarification of the use of necessary force when a power of search exists.

(i) Power for police to apply to a judge of the High Court for a fingerprinting order for persons or category of persons in a particular area.

(j) Power for police to obtain names and addresses of witnesses.

(k) That the powers and principles which a member of a police force possesses by virtue of Section 19(1) of the Police Act 1964 shall extend to any place or area outside England and Wales over which any court in England and Wales has or is deemed to have jurisdiction.

These proposals do not seem to me to be either Draconian or unreasonable. Certainly if the police had such powers, honest citizens would be much better protected against criminals. But I am not hopeful, for already a Conservative Government, elected in part on a law and order ticket, has taken away the powers of the police to stop and search suspected persons and this does not give confidence that other powers which the police require will be provided.

The Bill introduced into Parliament in 1983 would not have given the police more powers; not much more would have been achieved than maintaining the status quo. Some of the present rules on police procedures would have been made clearer and checks on the police would have increased. What would certainly be required of the police would be more paperwork, and increased employment of officers within police stations and thus less on the streets. I saw little in the provisions which would help the people of London to feel better protected against criminals.

Constitutionally the Bill was lost because of the Dissolution of Parliament prior to the General Election. The real failure lay in the fact that the Government did not market its product effectively.

The Courts, lawyers and judicial system also have a great part to play in the drive against the criminal and in making London a safer place. Robert Mark has said much on this that is very relevant. I add two points only which cause me great concern.

The first is that the legal aid system is being abused. Straightforward cases where the facts are clear and the guilt of the offender indisputable are prolonged before the courts without good reason. In consequence the work of the courts becomes congested, witnesses become dissatisfied, and police officers are taken away from their ordinary duties. The fault, and the remedy, lies with the legal profession. A great many detectives are tied up in crown courts every day and contested cases seem to take longer and longer since the advent of the legal aid system.

Second, the way in which civilian prosecution witnesses are treated by defence lawyers can be outrageous. Such treatment is impolite and objectionable, and at times downright disgraceful. This, linked with frustration at being kept hanging about for hours if not days at courts, where facilities for witnesses are more often than not quite shocking, is coming close to making the present judicial system unworkable. Once a member of the public has become involved in a case which involves attendance at court as a witness, it is highly likely that the experience will lead him or her to determine never to agree to be a witness again. Courts tend to be operated for the convenience of the judiciary, lawyers and defendants – in that order – with witnesses being the losers in every respect. The general public is becoming increasingly aware of this, and only the criminal stands to benefit.

I have not been able to say much in this chapter for anyone's comfort, least of all my own. What prospect lies ahead for us and our country? When I was Commissioner I took time off to address a congregation at St George's Tron Church in Glasgow where I worshipped for many years, and where I am still an Elder. My words were:

> As we look into the future and project the dramatic increase of the past twenty years into the next twenty years, one could be forgiven for smiling under a sense of hopelessness. Even those of us who are considered old by our children may yet have to live in a time where burglary, theft, vandalism, murder, assault and rape is at least twice as prevalent as it is today. Crime definitions and patterns may change but total numbers will still increase.

I was called 'a prophet of doom' for my pains, but unless each of us sets standards in the future which are higher than in the past, is anyone saying that my forecast will be wrong?

We all remember Dixon of Dock Green, a famous television London policeman created by a great and much loved actor – Jack Warner. During my time as Commissioner Jack Warner died, and Dixon died with him. The memory of him and of the actor whose skill created him was marked by the attendance of Metropolitan Police officers at the funeral and memorial service. I wrote to Mrs Warner at the time and she replied:

> Thank you so very much for your kind letter. I cannot tell you how proud I was, as I know Jack would have been, to have such a wonderful group of police officers at his funeral.
>
> The flowers in the shape of a 'Blue Lamp' were beautiful. What a lovely idea.
>
> I thought you might like to have the enclosed little tribute to Jack by his sister Elsie (Waters).

The little tribute read:

> Dear old Dixon's gone
> He's taken his final call.
> The Golden Gates just opened wide
> When he said 'Evenin' All'.

Dixon of Dock Green has been replaced on the television screen and in some people's eyes by Reagan of 'The Sweeney' but the public with whom the 'Sweeney' deal are not the people among whom Dixon lived and on whom he could rely. Of course neither picture is wholly accurate, but this could be a reflection of how times and crimes have changed. It could be that if we each try to do a little better, and especially to help others including the police, times may change for the better. This picture is too naïve and simple to be pursued if only for the reason that there is no turning back the clock, but the essence of the requirement is to maintain the traditional role and image of the British 'bobby'. As regards what I said at St George's Tron about the future, there is an alternative prospect within our grasp if we care to take it. There is no reason why the level of crime should not be greatly reduced but it will require much effort by all.

For a start, each one of us must accept that it is right to keep the law and wrong to break it. But there is more to it than that. Goodness and honesty are right, evil and dishonesty are wrong. We cannot have it both ways. We cannot expect others to lead honest lives and then indulge in small dishonesties ourselves. We cannot expect others to speak the truth while we tell lies, or expect others to be decent while we engage in indecent living. Truth is not divisible and neither is honesty. It is by the living of our daily lives that we are judged, and no more so than by young people, who see quickly through humbug and hypocrisy. We need to set high standards of behaviour, to be honest with each other in our dealings, whether large or small. The extent to which each one of us does so will determine how free we are in the future from crime and violence.

9

Corruption and Countryman

OPERATION COUNTRYMAN! What an evocative, emotional phrase that has become. What a lot has been written and spoken about it in newspapers, plays and television programmes, and much of it wide of the mark. And just to put the record straight right at the start, it was not the Metropolitan Police who gave the investigation this alleged derogatory name; it was the investigators' own choice.

I will try to give the facts as briefly and clearly as I can, for they speak for themselves. We need to look first at the earlier background to corruption in the Metropolitan Police. In 1970 Frank Williamson, one of HM Inspectors of Constabulary with a special responsibility for crime, was appointed in an advisory role to oversee an inquiry into alleged corruption in the Metropolitan Police, known as 'the *Times* inquiry' because that newspaper raised the allegations. There is little doubt that Williamson was obstructed in his task and that he had justifiable cause for complaint. Thereafter he took opportunities to appear on television or use other means to speak of the obstruction he had met and to create the impression that the Metropolitan Police would always close ranks to an outside inquiry. More about Frank Williamson later.

In July 1978 Metropolitan Police officers identified what appeared to be a corrupt association between armed robbers and officers in the City of London Police. This was reported to the City of London Police and their first reaction was to ask New Scotland Yard to conduct an investigation into the allegations. Shortly afterwards further information was obtained, which led the Metropolitan Police to conclude that it would be preferable for the investigation to be conducted by officers from a force outside London. Peter Marshall, Commissioner of the City of London Police, asked the advice of the Home Office, and it was eventually suggested that the investigation should be undertaken by Leonard Burt, then an Assistant Chief Constable of the Dorset Police. His Chief Constable, Arthur Hambleton, agreed.

I was not consulted at the time by the Home Office or anyone else about the appointment, there being no reason for doing so at that stage. I knew nothing of Burt's qualifications as an investigator, but I had no reason to doubt his professionalism. He was appointed under Section 49 of the Police Act 1964, and his terms of reference were set by the City of London Police to investigate a number of specific complaints relating to alleged malpractice by City of London officers in connection with certain serious incidents. When it appeared after a few weeks that Metropolitan Police officers might possibly be involved, Pat Kavanagh, Deputy Commissioner, asked Burt to extend his enquiries to the Metropolitan Police to investigate those allegations.

In the Metropolitan Police the Deputy Commissioner is responsible for organizing the investigation of complaints against officers of the force and disciplinary proceedings, with the Commissioner as the appellate authority. What had happened in 1970 was much in Kavanagh's mind. He was determined that the Metropolitan Police should not again be accused of interfering with or obstructing an independent inquiry.

The team were initially accommodated in Camberwell Police Station, but they alleged an attempt had been made to interfere with their records and asked to be moved to a location outside the Metropolitan Police District. It was never confirmed, but I did not then, nor do I now, doubt their word. If they had lied about that they would have had to be playing a very deep game indeed. To my mind, however, the right action would have been to increase the security of the office to preserve the confidentiality of their documents and records and stay put. There would have been advantages, both in terms of cost and investigation, for the team to remain.

Nevertheless, their feelings were important to the success of the investigation and so, with the co-operation of Sir Peter Matthews, the Chief Constable of Surrey, the team was moved to Godalming Police Station. Although this accorded with the team's wishes the arrangement led to wasted time, officers now having to travel to and from London. They also worked a short week, returning to their homes on Friday afternoons and spending Monday mornings travelling back to Godalming.

Burt for some time made no reports to New Scotland Yard about the inquiries he was making and Kavanagh, sensitive to the possibility that action on his part might be interpreted as interference, decided not to ask about progress.

Initially the Countryman team concentrated on collecting oral information by conversations with criminals, including some 'supergrasses'. In general, written statements were not taken, and later some of those concerned would not confirm in writing what they were supposed to have said – something which detectives with long experience of criminal investigations did not find surprising.

From the start the inquiry attracted enormous publicity – not all of it accurate. Consequently, the team received many direct complaints against the police which were unconnected with the incidents under investigation. For some reason best known to himself Burt did not refer these complaints to the police forces concerned for separate investigation, but decided to keep them within the Countryman team.

Burt encouraged the team to see themselves as being some general anti-corruption squad dedicated to cleaning up the Metropolitan Police. What happened, of course, is that the team was overwhelmed with work. With Arthur Hambleton's support Burt tried to resolve that workload problem not by limiting the scope of his inquiries to those allegations we had asked him to look into but by asking for his team to be increased from thirty officers to over eighty officers. Once again, the spectre of interference guided our decision and the request was met in full. Officers from provincial forces all over the south were seconded to the investigating team.

The team continued to cast their net wide, so as to cover

complaints received from all quarters instead of getting on with the job they had been given to do. The result was that their efforts were dissipated.

All sorts of tittle-tattle by criminals, by associates of criminals, or by disgruntled complainants was listened to and acted upon. Some of the allegations may have been made in good faith but much of the information was from people with axes to grind, either with animosity towards particular police officers or with hope of obtaining early release from prison or some other benefit. It needs to be remembered that evidence from convicted persons requires corroboration if it is to be given much weight by a court.

As the information began to pile up, the team asked for a computer to store it and for ease of retrieval. My experience is that effective investigation is best made by keeping your information as tight as possible, with a small and closely knit squad only having access to it. But once again, because of the wish to let the Countryman team go the way of its own choosing, provision of the computer, like provision of the increased manpower and the specially located headquarters, was agreed. The cost now looked like mounting into millions of pounds but although we blanched we did not demur. 'Spare the rod and spoil the child' was an adage we might have remembered with advantage.

All this, I should add, was of course done in consultation and agreement with the Home Office and with the knowledge of the Home Secretary. Home Office officials were involved with the inquiry to an unprecedented extent.

Anxieties, however, were beginning to be expressed. Months passed without any apparent positive progress. In July 1979 Sir Thomas Hetherington, the Director of Public Prosecutions, called to see me and Pat Kavanagh to say he was worried about the length of time the inquiry was taking and to express doubts about the expertise of the team. We told him that we too had doubts, but had no desire to give grounds for any interference.

We had offered to take weight off the Countryman team by accepting responsibility for any complaints and information unrelated to the inquiry which they cared to pass to us. We were told that this would not be done as the complaints and information had been passed to the team in confidence. It seemed that the Countryman team did not trust the Attorney General or the Director of Public Prosecutions, let alone the Deputy Commissioner and the Assistant Commissioner in charge of the CID at New Scotland Yard.

Progress with the inquiry did not improve, and in October 1979 Pat Kavanagh saw Arthur Hambleton and Len Burt and told them that although fourteen months had passed since the start of the inquiry, he did not know what they had achieved or where they were going. Burt countered by blaming the Director of Public Prosecutions for delay in making a decision on a report submitted to him by the team twenty-four weeks previously. I was later told that the delay was due to the inadequacy of the report. Burt resented the suggestion that he was hoarding information and launching in-quiries that were far beyond his original brief.

Pat Kavanagh reminded Burt that although he was seeking to help, not hinder him, as Deputy Commissioner he was entitled to be kept informed of matters affecting the discipline and reputation of the force. Arthur Hambleton saw the substance of this and agreed that the Deputy Commissioner should be regularly kept up to date.

A month later, however, there was still no information. By now I had reached the end of my patience and I wrote personally to Arthur Hambleton in strong terms to complain that we did not know what allegations had been made against Metropolitan Police officers or what had been done about them. I emphasized that I was not seeking to interfere with the inquiry, nor to be provided with day to day information, but I could not wholly abdicate responsibility for allegations made against officers of my force and for its good conduct generally. I had also more than once made it very plain to both Hambleton and Burt and to the general public that if there was any obstruction to their investigation, they should get in touch with me direct and I would deal with it.

In answer to my letter Arthur Hambleton came to see me at New Scotland Yard in November 1979. The Director of Public Prosecu-tions and Pat Kavanagh were also present. We were joined later by Burt. Hambleton brought part of the information I had sought with him, and he promised the rest in a few days and regular updating thereafter. He told us that Burt had been ill but that he was now fully recovered. At the meeting it was agreed that the Countryman team would not take on any additional inquiries without prior consultation. The Director also offered to provide a member of his staff full time for the team, and this exceptional and helpful offer, was accepted. Within less than two weeks a report appeared in *The Sunday Times* saying that Burt was angry about the obstacles being placed in the way of his investigation by Metropolitan Police officers and by the Director of Public Prosecutions.

I do not know whether Burt was angry, but I know I was. I had a press release prepared denying that the inquiry was being obstructed. Before releasing it I sent a copy to Burt and to the Director. A meeting was called by Pat Kavanagh at New Scotland Yard which was attended by Arthur Hambleton, the Director of Public Prosecutions, and Ernie Bright, Assistant Commissioner of the City of London Police. The four of them prepared a detailed press statement which was released by the Dorset Police Force that same day under Len Burt's name:

OPERATION COUNTRYMAN

1 This press statement is issued to explain the current position and to correct some of the misleading reports which have appeared in recent weeks about Operation Countryman.

2 In August 1978, HM Chief Inspector of Constabulary, following a request by the Commissioner of the City of London Police, asked the Chief Constable of Dorset to provide a senior officer to investigate alleged irregularities by detectives of the City of London Force. At the same time, the Deputy Commissioner of the Metropolitan Police asked that associated allegations about Metropolitan Police officers be included in the investigation. I, Leonard Burt, the Assistant Chief Constable of Dorset, was appointed with a number of detectives.

3 As the inquiry progressed, it became necessary to augment the team and a total of eighty detectives with supporting clerical staff are now engaged. This does not mean that the allegations against police officers received by Operation Countryman have dramatically increased; indeed some of the complaints received have been investigated and proved unfounded.

4 Five officers of the Metropolitan Police have been suspended from duty and files have been submitted to the Director of Public Prosecutions for proceedings against four of these officers. A City of London officer has been charged, appeared at court and will be dealt with in the future.

5 During the whole of the inquiry, constant consultations have taken place with the staff of the Director of Public Prosecutions and on several occasions I have sought the advice of the Director. Additionally, on 2 occasions, advice has been obtained from the Attorney General and the Director jointly.

6 Suggestions that the Countryman investigations have been obstructed are completely without truth. I and my officers have received the fullest co-operation and every assistance from the Director and the two Commissioners. In particular, the Director has acceded to a request I made concerning the giving of certain limited undertakings to persons helping our inquiries, and I unhesitatingly accept that, when criminal proceedings against police officers are being considered, there can be no departure from the evidential requirements which apply to civilian suspects.

7 Recently, the Director of Public Prosecutions has made available a senior member of his Legal Staff to advise me and my senior officers, and he now occupies an office at Godalming Police Station in the Countryman suite.

8 My detectives are working extremely hard; they are dedicated and have the will to succeed; they are undaunted by some reports that have appeared in the press and other media. Events in the future will prove that the Countryman team has been more than adequate for its task and that any difficulties they have encountered have been overcome.

193

9 This statement has been seen by the Commissioners of the Metropolitan and City of London Police and the Director of Public Prosecutions.

L BURT
Assistant Chief Constable of Dorset
7 December 1979

The claim made much later by Arthur Hambleton in a television interview that the Countryman inquiry would have folded up if he had not agreed to the statement was nonsense. To my knowledge the meeting went off without any acrimony. Certainly Hambleton never complained to me that he had been put under pressure to agree to the release.

After the meeting, Pat Kavanagh told me Hambleton had alleged that Don Neesham, Commander of the Flying Squad, had been unhelpful to the Countryman team. No firm evidence was produced to support the allegation – only the thought that Neesham was being over-protective of the men under his command. In order once again to avoid any accusation of obstruction to the Countryman inquiry, it was decided to move Neesham to other duties. When told of this, however, he exercised his right to retire on pension.

During these months Pat Kavanagh and I visited the headquarters of the Countryman team at Godalming to talk with them and see what and how well they were doing.

I was not impressed. It seemed to me that the name of any police officer mentioned to members of the Countryman team, in conversations with criminals and others, was being fed into the computer. Wholly innocent officers were accordingly going into the pool of suspects, often only on the word of rogues. Far too much attention was being given to compiling a mass of intelligence, much of it of doubtful quality, and I was convinced that the team were being sidetracked from their primary objective. No arrests after many months of inquiry was not my idea of success.

More time passed. The only development was Arthur Hambleton's announcement that he would be retiring on 29 February 1980.

He agreed that it would be advantageous for another Chief Constable to take over responsibility for the Countryman inquiry and Sir Peter Matthews, Chief Constable of Surrey, was asked to take it on. Len Burt was to continue to head the investigation until he returned to his force on 1 May 1980, by which time it was thought that the back of the job would be broken.

In the remaining months Arthur Hambleton seemed bent on conducting a private war directed almost exclusively against the Director of Public Prosecutions and the Attorney General. This came to a head when the Countryman team at last made their first arrest – of a Detective Inspector of the City of London Police on a charge unconnected with the main Countryman inquiry. The proceedings were brought in an extraordinary way in that the Director was bypassed by Burt's officers who were represented by a Dorset county solicitor and brought the case before a court in Hertfordshire. The magistrates granted an application for the accused officer to be remanded in police custody for three days and he was taken to Dorset.

It was an ill-judged, ill-prepared move, and on 18 February 1980 a representative of the Director of Public Prosecutions had to attend court to announce that the prosecution would be withdrawn due to inadequate evidence. Hambleton was furious, claiming that the whole Countryman investigation would be discredited. The Metropolitan Police was astonished at the way established procedures had been ignored and at the disregard of the Director, and was also somewhat surprised that there were no apparent consequences. Such unprofessional conduct by Metropolitan Police detectives would have brought coals of fire upon their heads both from within the force and from the legal pundits of the media. There not unnaturally followed some talk amongst Metropolitan CID officers of double standards. Was the Countryman team exempt from the normal rules applying to police proceedings? The whole incident certainly did nothing to enhance the good standing of the team.

Some extraordinary meetings followed. At the Home Office in February, Hambleton went so far as saying that the Director was

195

not helping the Countryman team and indeed actually obstructing it. The examples he cited were neither convincing nor constructive. In an outburst he said that he had no confidence in the Director and that he would not continue to work with the Director's representative, who had been specially appointed to work full-time at the Countryman headquarters at Godalming.

A little later in the month we were told that Burt had ordered the Director's representative to leave the Godalming headquarters but he had not done so. The man was being ostracized. The Attorney General quickly arranged a meeting with the Director, Hambleton and Sir Peter Matthews. Since we were not directly involved with what was being discussed, the Metropolitan Police was not represented at the meeting, but certainly none of this was for the good of the inquiry.

Once Hambleton had gone and Burt had returned to Dorset, progress began to be made again. Peter Matthews as the Chief Constable in charge quickly sought to confine the inquiry to its original terms of reference and passed extraneous matters to the Complaint Investigation Bureau (CIB) of the Metropolitan Police or to the City of London Police. He also sought the assistance of Deputy Assistant Commissioner Steventon, who had long experience of dealing with crime and criminals in the Metropolitan Police, and an outstanding record when head of CIB and elsewhere in making effective inquiries into allegations of police misconduct.

Eight Metropolitan Police officers were eventually prosecuted: none was convicted by the courts. Two were subsequently dismissed in consequence of disciplinary proceedings taken within the Metropolitan Police, and one resigned. On 30 June 1982 Metropolitan Police involvement in the Countryman inquiry ceased.

These are the facts and they make a sad record. Operation Countryman was not effective.

Just how ineffective the inquiry was becomes all too clear when we compare it with another major inquiry which had many similar features. In 1973 allegations were made of corruption in the Metropolitan Police in connection with the distribution and sale of obscene publications in the West End of London – it became known as the Humphreys Inquiry because the allegations were made by James Humphreys, a notorious criminal, who fled the country when wanted on a warrant for serious offences under the Obscene Publications Act. Gilbert Kelland, later my Assistant Commissioner in charge of the CID, was then a Deputy Assistant Commissioner. He was appointed in April 1973 under Section 49 of the Police Act 1964, to investigate the allegations by James Humphreys. Seventy-four police officers of all ranks from Constable to Commander were identified as probably being involved in the allegations. Kelland's inquiry team never exceeded at any one time a maximum of eight personally selected officers. The inquiry was exceedingly difficult and complex, but by pursuing relentlessly the primary objects of the investigation, the outcome by 1977 was that fifteen officers were prosecuted and thirteen convicted. The ranks of the officers convicted were: two former Commanders, one Detective Chief Superintendent, one Detective Chief Inspector, five Detective Inspectors, two Detective Sergeants, two Detective Constables.

An appeal by one of the Commanders was allowed on the grounds of a misdirection by the trial judge. Nine other officers were found guilty of disciplinary offences and dismissed or required to resign. Twelve officers retired voluntarily; twenty-eight officers left the force on pension. At the end of the inquiry only twelve of the seventy-four officers on whom the investigation concentrated remained in the force.

Kelland's investigation was a model of how such an inquiry should be conducted. The results refute utterly the notion that the Metropolitan Police cannot be relied upon to investigate properly allegations against its own. The facts of the investigation are well known to the media and political commentators, but are seldom mentioned by them when commenting on allegations that the Metropolitan Police cannot be trusted to conduct internal criminal or disciplinary inquiries.

The results are in stark contrast to the failure of the Countryman team to obtain the conviction in court of a single Metropolitan Police officer. In further contrast, three senior officers on the

Countryman list of suspects were separately investigated by the Complaints Investigation Bureau of the Metropolitan Police in regard to other offences and this led to proceedings and convictions in court of two of the officers.

The success of the Kelland inquiry shows the falseness of another frequently made assertion, that for a major investigation to be effective it must be conducted by a senior officer from an outside force. The reverse is true. Kelland is in no doubt that he was able to direct the Humphreys Inquiry more effectively because he had many years' previous police experience in various ranks in the West End, and a close knowledge of the work of the Metropolitan Police. He and his team were aware of how corruption can operate within such an environment. Kelland also had the benefit of extensive contacts throughout the force, and he knew in particular which officers were of strong character, integrity and good repute. Information vital to the success of the inquiry was given to him because of his high reputation in the force and because of the good relationship he had with officers who had served under him in the past. The same was true of the specially selected members of his team.

It is very much Gilbert Kelland's view that a major and complex inquiry within the Metropolitan Police is likely to be more success-ful if carried out by experienced officers selected from within the force. This had been borne out by an earlier investigation in the 1970s by Commander Clarkson, a CID officer in Metropolitan Police, into allegations against Drug Squad officers after a team led by an Assistant Chief Constable of Lancashire had failed to lead to successful court proceedings. Clarkson was appointed to deal with any possible disciplinary (not criminal) proceedings but he un-covered evidence of a criminal conspiracy resulting in a Detective Chief Inspector and junior detectives standing trial at the Old Bailey. Members of Parliament and others became obsessed by the words 'independent inquiry' and ignored the *practical* considera-tions and past results of how best to deal with allegations of corruption.

Let me say a word too about the allegation of so called 'obstruc-tion' by Metropolitan Police officers to the Countryman inquiry.

First, what was meant by it? Only vague, general allegations were made, and the obstruction was never specified. Although Arthur Hambleton said on television, long after the Countryman inquiry was over, that the team was obstructed, at no time during the investigation did he communicate this to me, despite a number of personal pleas that I should be told immediately of any such difficulty.

Can it be that some Metropolitan Police officers were cautious in answering questions put to them by Countryman officers? As Kelland would tell you, those who are guilty or who have something to hide do not usually blurt out the truth when asked. You have to dig and delve to find evidence from elsewhere. When Kelland's team found obstruction of this kind or any other, they overcame it.

I still find it puzzling that a Chief Constable with a great many years' service in that rank can personally agree to issue from his own headquarters a statement to the effect that the Countryman inquiry was not being obstructed by the Metropolitan Police and yet, more than two years later, go public on television to say that he issued the statement knowing that it was false.

Lastly, the attack by the Countryman team on the Director of Public Prosecutions and his staff seems to me to be one of the worst features of the entire Countryman saga. Under the Attorney General, the Director is in his post to advise and assist the police in the prosecution of serious criminal cases. He and his staff are not only skilled in interpreting and applying the criminal law, they also develop a finely tuned understanding and appreciation of what is required to secure a conviction. Hambleton's distrust of both the Attorney General and the Director was extraordinary and unprecedented. There seems to have been no good reason for it.

Perhaps if the Countryman team had given the Director and his staff more of their trust, and taken the Deputy Commissioner more into their confidence, they might have been more successful. I am not naïve enough to suppose that the person who holds the post of Director of Public Prosecutions or the members of his staff are necessarily free from the weaknesses that affect other mortals. But if I had been in Arthur Hambleton's shoes and suspected that the

Director or his staff were being obstructive I would have assembled the evidence to support my case and gone directly to see the Home Secretary or the Attorney General.

Other voices sounded in support of Hambleton's allegations. The issue of police corruption or, more specifically, Metropolitan Police corruption was taken up by Liberal MPs David Steel and Stephen Ross. Ross, who is Member for the Isle of Wight, gave the impression that he had personal information from prisoners in Parkhurst Prison supporting the allegations against Metropolitan Police officers. I have been told that shortly before the matter was raised in the House of Commons Mr Ross had a meeting – ironically held in the old Metropolitan Police building on the Embankment – with certain journalists who told him about Countryman and their own inquiries.

Around this time John Alderson, former Chief Constable of Devon and Cornwall, was seen in the House of Lords with his Liberal Party associates. John Alderson also gave a television interview in a programme devoted to the Countryman investigation. Yet he played no part in the Countryman inquiry. He had no direct knowledge of its conduct. Two officers only from his force were in the Countryman team and then only for a matter of months. At no time did he talk to me about the conduct or progress of the inquiry. Nevertheless he saw fit to appear on television and make the suggestion that corruption in the Metropolitan Police was institutionalized. He had left the Metropolitan Police in the early 1970s. Where was his evidence for this? He certainly never raised the matter publicly when he was an Assistant Commissioner in the force. And that was at a time when Bob Mark was in need of support in his determination to deal with corruption.

Then there is Frank Williamson, a former Inspector of Constabulary who, it seems is always ready to speak to the media against London policemen, long after leaving the police service. I mentioned earlier Williamson's lack of success with an inquiry into the Metropolitan Police in 1970. When in 1977 I was named as successor to Robert Mark, Williamson got in touch with me and suggested that we might meet for lunch. I readily agreed and

Williamson travelled north from his Cheshire home while I travelled south from Glasgow. My Deputy in Strathclyde, Elphie Dalglish, went with me and we all met in a pleasant hotel in Cumbria for lunch. Williamson talked at length about his inquiry into the allegations put forward by *The Times* against the Metropolitan Police officers – and about corruption in the Metropolitan Police generally. I was grateful to him for taking the trouble to meet me in this way and found our talk very helpful. Both Elphie and I however were concerned that Frank Williamson seemed to have become obsessed with two things: corruption generally, and his failure to get to grips with the job given him by the Home Secretary in 1970 to press home the *Times* inquiry to a successful conclusion.

I know how he must have felt, for police corruption has always been a matter of concern to me. Nothing does more to undermine the police service than a corrupt police officer. There is only one way to deal with it ruthlessly. But it is not always a simple matter and when you cannot get to the heart of corruption it is frustrating in the extreme. As the Home Office adviser Williamson had direct access to the Home Secretary and to the Permanent Undersecretary of State of the Home Office whenever he needed it. If at any time he was anxious about how the inquiry was proceeding he could have discussed it with them. He had a direct and close link with Robert Mark who was both an old friend and at the time Deputy Commissioner of the Metropolitan Police. Moreover if Williamson had been dissatisfied with the progress of the inquiry he could always have threatened to resign. This would really have put the cat among the pigeons, particularly as one of Britain's national newspapers had an extremely close interest in the matter. So far as I know, he made no such move. But months later, when major changes were being made in the senior posts of the Metropolitan Police, when Robert Mark was about to become Commissioner with an expressed commitment to turn back the tide of corruption and when a real watershed had been reached in the affairs of the Metropolitan Police, Williamson threw his hand in and resigned.

Robert Mark speaks about this in his autobiography.

Frank Williamson, who had served with me in the Manchester force before becoming Chief Constable of Carlisle and then of Cumbria, had suffered every conceivable frustration during the long drawn out *Times* inquiry. He was thoroughly disillusioned and depressed by continual disagreement with, and obstruction by, policemen who did not share his very high standard of personal and professional integrity. He therefore decided to resign notwithstanding the utmost persuasion by Philip Allen, Jimmy Waddell and 'Jimmy' James, now the Receiver for the Metropolitan Police, not to leave the service to which he had devoted his life, as his father before him. I did my best to persuade him.

He had considerable experience, exceptional ability and unquestioned integrity, and his continued potential value to the police service was considerable. Moreover, all his battles were on the point of being won. He knew that the old guard were on the point of being swept away and that all the reforms he had in mind were in the immediate offing. But he had had enough, and it says much of the conditions under which we laboured that a man of his calibre had reached such a point. He left the service at the end of the year, an honourable man unable to accept any longer the frustration and difficulties of the ideals of the police service in which he deeply believed.

Fair enough, but not so fair to keep bobbing in and out of retirement to attack those who were trying to succeed where he failed. When we met over lunch a few months before I became Commissioner, and Williamson told me what he thought was the situation in the Metropolitan Police, he provided me with a large grey envelope, which I still have. In it were papers setting out his thoughts on the *Times* inquiry and his recommendations for changes in the CID of the Metropolitan Police.

The more important of the latter were:

(a) The need to bring some experienced officers from provincial forces into senior posts in the CID.

(b) Appoint uniform officers to senior posts in the CID.

(c) Monitor more closely the handling of criminal information.

(d) Review the organization and work of the Flying Squad and other specialist branches of the CID.

(e) Improve the standing of the Fraud Squad.

(f) Review and improve the role of the CID Training School.

(g) Involve uniform officers in the investigation of crime.

(h) Control more closely claims for overtime working and for expenses.

(i) Supervise more closely the role and rewards of information.

They were helpful recommendations. If Frank Williamson had cared to check when I had been Commissioner for a few years he would have found that each had been acted upon. Some had already been implemented before I became Commissioner.

The Kelland inquiry into the Humphreys allegations was in its final stages as I became Commissioner. In some ways it marked a watershed in the history of the Metropolitan Police; and I made use of it. I recommended Kelland's appointment as Assistant Commissioner and put him in charge of the CID in August 1977. He then, with my approval, made major changes to the senior posts in his department, restructured the Central Drug Squad, and reorganized the Flying Squad. Away from headquarters or divisions, at my personal instigation, all officers including the CID were brought under the command – for the first time – of the uniformed head of the division.

The changes had the support of the mass of the CID. They were backed by the knowledge of a hard line being taken against unprofessional conduct. Retribution would be exacted for corruption. The writing was on the wall and it remained there. During the years which followed further measures were introduced:

(a) No officer was allowed to meet any person on bail or against whom criminal proceedings were pending without special permission. The Metropolitan Police was almost the only force having this restriction, designed to avoid such meetings being used to suborn policemen.

(b) New procedures were brought in to prevent malpractice in the recording of contemporaneous notes of police interviews.

(c) Officers employed on special duties where big money could be on offer to tempt the potentially corrupt were transferred to more routine duties after strictly limited periods. This covered employment in such squads as had dealings with vice, pornography, or West End clubs.

(d) A Force Inspectorate was set up, under a Deputy Assistant Commissioner who reported directly to the Deputy Commissioner, with copies of the reports also going to the Home Office. The Inspectorate was required to give special attention to the more sensitive areas of police work and these were inspected with greater frequency than more routine duties. It proved to be a most effective organization, largely because special care was taken to ensure that the Inspectorate was led by a Deputy Assistant Commissioner of wide experience and high ability, supported by good quality police and civil staff.

(e) Officers were forbidden to supply information to courts about past assistance given by prisoners, except in oral evidence or with prior authority.

(f) Strengthened and stricter central controls were introduced over the payment of money to informants.

(g) The Complaints Investigation Bureau (formerly A10) with special responsibility for inquiries into corruption was reorganized and strengthened.

(h) If any officer, however junior, had any disquiet about what was going on, encouragement was given for him to approach the Bureau direct.

This was not window dressing. While after months of effort the Countryman inquiry had managed only eight prosecutions against Metropolitan Police officers, all unsuccessful, the Metropolitan Police itself took action leading to over 100 officers being dismissed or required to resign.

In the five years before I was appointed, convictions (which is my measure of success) of Metropolitan Police officers on criminal charges were 52.7%, 50%, 60.9%, 53.4% and 42.3% of the cases brought to the courts. During the five years from 1977 they were 68.3%, 86.5%, 69.4%, 70.6% and 62.5%. These figures speak for themselves. Indeed the comment has been made that in Scotland Yard all the howitzers are pointing inwards and all the pea-shooters outward. It is not true, but I understand the point being made. The importance of taking the firmest line can hardly be over-emphasized. In a publication on corruption issued by the Police Foundation of the United States, Herman Goldstein wrote:

> Of all the problems involved in the complex business of policing, few are more fundamental than corruption. When corruption exists in a police agency, the potential for dealing with a multitude of other problems is severely diminished. This is true because two factors that are essential elements of any program to improve the quality of police service are seriously eroded. First, public confidence in the police is undermined. Second, the police administrator's ability to direct and control his personnel is substantially reduced.

I would go along with that. Corruption in a police force is like sin in society at large. You will never wholly eradicate it for it is embedded in the greed and selfishness of human nature. Often the laws which Parliament makes and expects the police to enforce make corruption more likely. The law regarding the control of pornography is an example because it is imprecise and therefore leaves much to police discrimination, with consequent increased scope for corruption. Corruption is not institutionalized in the Metropolitan Police, as some so glibly allege, but like any other large organization dishonesty will flourish if given the chance – as perhaps newspapers, television companies, business firms and other bodies have found within their own ranks. In recognition of this you have always to be vigilant, know and understand the problems, reduce temptation, not put officers at risk more than need be, deal quickly with any early signs and suspicions, and be ruthless in your determination to get rid of those who succumb.

When I took up the post as Commissioner the disclosures of corruption in senior ranks by the Kelland inquiry were still being made known. Another inquiry into allegations of corruption at senior levels in the force was being held by the then Chief Constable of Kent. The reputation of the CID was shaken. Morale in the force generally was low, partly because of discontent over police pay and conditions of work. Many of the excellent proposals, like interchange between CID and uniform branch, proposed by Robert Mark, had still to be fully effected.

When I left nearly six years later there had been many changes for the better. If you listen to programmes on Countryman and to retired senior officers who failed to press home their own inquiries when in the police service you might think otherwise – but you would be wrong. As regards the machinery for investigating complaints against police officers, let me just say this. First, it needs always to be appreciated that some complaints can never be satisfactorily resolved because the case is the word of one person, the complainant, against another, the police officer, with little else to corroborate either story. No machinery, however carefully constructed, can find a way through that dilemma. Second, I agree strongly with Robert Mark that the investigation of complaints must be left in the hands of the police and discipline in the hands of chief officers of police who are best placed by far to identify and deal with officers in their forces who step out of line. If you transfer these responsibilities in part or wholly to civil bodies the practical result (however worthy the principles involved) will be that corrupt officers will be more likely and not less likely to avoid being nailed for their wrong doing and thereby remain within the police service.

An increasing complexity of procedures is not likely to satisfy those who have valid complaint What is needed is early contact by a senior officer with a complainant, a professional investigation giving weight to all the evidence, and as prompt a report as possible. With, of course, close supervision and direction by Deputy Chief Constables of investigations and discipline, linked with effective action where necessary by the office of the Director of Public Prosecutions.

10

The End of it All

GRUNWICK, LEWISHAM, SOUTHALL, the Iranian Embassy siege, Brixton – after coming through all this and a lot more, I had hopes that my last year as Commissioner might be spent in calmer waters.

Calmer waters? 1982 turned out to be the most turbulent time of my entire service. One man alone made certain of that – Michael Fagan – the man who sat on the end of the Queen's bed on 9 July 1982. What a dreadful event, what criticisms it brought on the force and what coals of fire it heaped upon my head. Fires which were stoked further by the disclosures about Commander Trestrail and, in a different context, by Mr David Steel MP and the Liberal Party through their deliberate and unjustified revival at the same time of allegations made in Operation Countryman.

1982 seemed determined to put me in competition with the prophet Job by subjecting me to successive tribulations, none of which was of my making. The year had begun badly by the announcement of my retirement in March shortly after the release of statistics which showed a steep rise in crime in the country as a whole, and following controversy over the issue of the involvement of young black people in London's street crime. There were suggestions that I was retiring prematurely and under something of a cloud. Nothing was further from the truth.

When I was appointed Commissioner in March 1977 I was aged fifty-two and Merlyn Rees had written to me as Home Secretary specifically to say that as I would not reach the age of sixty until 1985, a term of as much as eight years for so exacting an appointment would not necessarily be in the interest of the police service or of the individual concerned.

He therefore proposed that my appointment should be made on the understanding that the length of my tenure of office should be reviewed on both sides after five years. I wrote to agree with this sensible proposition. At the time Merlyn Rees asked me not to make this understanding public but, naturally, towards the end of the five-year period William Whitelaw, who was by then Home Secretary, began to consider what future arrangements should be made. After what I am sure must have been careful consideration, he personally asked me to continue serving for a further three years, until the end of 1984. So much for any suggestion that I was persuaded to retire early because of rising crime or other events. It was a firm and specific offer. I asked for time to consider it.

In fact I spent several weeks giving the matter a great deal of thought because the decision was clearly one of importance not just to me, but to the policing of the metropolis, to the force, to my successor and to my family. My first reaction was one of satisfaction; such a major extension of service was after all an unequivocal expression of confidence in me as Commissioner. I had also found my years as Commissioner rewarding, and thought I had been able to contribute to the improved management of the force and to the policing of London. There were, too, a number of initiatives – for example providing and making the best use of a greater police presence on the streets – which I would have liked more time to bring to completion. There were other projects which I still had in mind to launch. But first thoughts are not always the best ones and continued reflection led me to the conclusion that five years was probably long enough for any Commissioner to serve in modern times. I am making no complaint, but the wear and tear of the job, mentally and physically, is very considerable. You are never free of it, not even on holiday, as I well know from being recalled to London on a number of occasions.

There is no closed season or summer recess for a Commissioner of Police: August, February or any month is as onerous as any other time. I was aware of the toll taken of me, and it was only sensible to recognize, not only in my own interest but also in the interest of the force, what three more years would do.

I thought also of the need to bring to bear on the policing of London new ideas, new initiatives, new attitudes and new energy, and perhaps after five years it would be better if these were to come from a new Commissioner than from me. Further to all this, it was inevitable that 1983 or early 1984 would see a general election. This could mean a change of government or a change of ministers within a continuing Conservative Government. I thought it best for the policing of London, and most fair to my successor, that a new Commissioner should have a few months to settle in before facing such events, rather than take on the post in the immediate aftermath of a general election.

Lastly, but of particular relevance as regards the force, was that my Deputy, Pat Kavanagh, would be retiring in March 1983 and it would be important for my successor to have a few months 'running in' with him rather than have a simultaneous double change at the top of the Met. I finally took the decision, not without a heavy heart, that to serve for five years was probably best, and accordingly wrote to the Home Office at the end of August 1981 to give my reasons.

William Whitelaw was good enough to understand and respect the considerations which had led me to my decision and he did not press me to depart from it. When later my decision became known, I was heartened to receive a letter from Robert Mark in most generous terms saying how he wholly shared my opinion that five years was the right length of time to serve as Commissioner. I did, however, agree readily with William Whitelaw that I should not go on the very day – 12 March 1982 – that my five years' service as Commissioner were complete but for general convenience serve for a few extra months, until midnight on 1 October 1982.

I can now ruefully reflect on the fact that if I had left office on 12 March 1982 I would have been reclining in retirement when Michael Fagan entered the Queen's bedchamber, when Commander Trestrail confessed to what he had been doing, and when the media revived again the pressures of Operation Countryman. There is more than a touch of irony there.

Events began to go awry fairly early in 1982. When I agreed with the Home Secretary that I would serve until late in 1982 we had also agreed that it would be sensible and in the best interests of the force for no announcement of my forthcoming retirement to be made until the early summer of that year. Indeed my intention was known at the time only to the most senior officials of the Home Office, to my Deputy, to my staff officer, to my family and to one or two others.

The confidence was well kept until March 1982 when John Newing, a Commander at New Scotland Yard, received a telephone call from Ken Hyder of *Labour Weekly*. Hyder asked who was going to be the next Commissioner, and seemed to be exceptionally well-informed on what had been going on between the Home Office and myself. It was very clear from what he said that he knew there was a memorandum in the Home Office putting forward names for appointment as Commissioner in consequence of my forthcoming retirement in a few months' time, and that he was using his knowledge of the existence of this memorandum to fish for further information. He got nothing from the Commander and certainly no indication that I might be contemplating retirement. Newing was my former staff officer and immediately after this telephone conversation he came to see me. I in turn spoke to Robert Andrew, head of the Police Department at the Home Office, and we agreed that there was no alternative but to bring forward the announcement of my retirement, planned for later in the year. Any other course would have been impossible because the existence of the Home Office memorandum in question could not be denied, and a reply of 'no comment' or something similar to questions from Fleet Street would have indicated at once that something was in the air.

Thus in March 1982 it was made public that I would be retiring within the year. It was coincidence that the announcement came out shortly after the controversy which had been stirred up by the publication of statistics concerning the involvement of black people in 'mugging' crime. My departure had nothing at all to do with this.

Events thereafter proceeded fairly smoothly for a few months, and perhaps I could make the point here that policing of London in 1982 in fact went extremely well, although little publicity was given to the success of the Metropolitan Police in achieving this. Although it was a long fine summer for the most part, there were no race riots in Brixton or other localities, and generally, as Lord Scarman has remarked, notable progress was made in improving relations between the police and ethnic minorities. The police Commanders of areas which had been the scene of disorders in 1981 had done sterling work. Their officers had responded well to their directions, and it paid off. None of the gloomy predictions of the dire consequences of a long hot summer had been fulfilled.

The Notting Hill Carnival also took place over three days wholly without violence, and indeed without almost any incident at all to spoil its enjoyment. In 1976, the year before I became Commissioner, there had been serious rioting during the days of the carnival. Each subsequent year had brought an improvement and the 1982 Carnival was the best ever. The potential for hooliganism and rioting was there as in previous years (as misbehaviour of crowds at one football match after another demonstrated) but it was contained by good co-operation with the Carnival organizers and by good policing. It is a sad reflection that it is only when events like the Carnival go awry that they get publicity; when policing goes well, nothing much is said.

This would have been a good note to end on, but it was not to be; Michael Fagan and the events at Buckingham Palace in July were to intervene.

As in most things, the issues involved were far more complex than appeared at the time. Indeed, it was in the interest of the Home Office and Buckingham Palace officials that the whole story was not told.

In August 1979 Lord Mountbatten was murdered in southern Ireland and this obviously raised the whole question of the level of protection to be afforded to the Royal Family. With the agreement of the Home Office and the Palace I appointed a working party under Assistant Commissioner John Wilson and Deputy Assistant Commissioner John Dellow to review current policy and practice for protecting the Royal Family and their residences, and to make recommendations for their improvement.

The working party reported in September 1979. Many recommendations were made for improving the protection of each member of the Royal Family and the security of their homes. These were sensible recommendations which had my approval. But it was not always possible to bring them into effect with the urgency I wished to see because of considerations raised by officials of the Royal Household and by those of the Home Office and of the Property Services Agency of the Department of the Environment (who are responsible for the royal residences) and by their opposition to some of the recommendations.

I accept of course that it is always necessary to balance security requirements against the important need of members of the Royal Family to have privacy in their lives. But my point is that if the Commissioner is not able, for good reason or otherwise, to impose what he regards as operational requirements, how can he be regarded as having ultimate responsibility for the safeguarding and security of Buckingham Palace and other royal residences?

The most serious illustration of the difficulties which arose for me relates to the recommendation in the report by Wilson and Dellow that all aspects of protection of the Royal Family and their homes should be brought together under one command and that this command would thereby have total responsibility and authority for all aspects of royal protection. This recommendation had my full approval and was put to the Royal Household and to the Home Office for agreement. At first all went reasonably well. Deputy Assistant Commissioner Helm was appointed to have overall responsibility for royal protection, but officials of the Royal Household reserved their acceptance of the appointment and the Home Office indicated that the appointment was essentially a temporary matter, with preference being given in due course to an officer of lower rank taking over the post.

Difficulties increased when Helm resigned six months later for personal reasons. This led to the Home Office emphasizing their contention that a post for a Deputy Assistant Commissioner having overall responsibility for protection of the Royal Family was not necessary, and that it should suffice to have another Commander working alongside the Queen's Police Officer, Commander Trestrail. You can imagine my anger after the Fagan incident at one recommendation made to me by the Home Office, that a Deputy Assistant Commissioner should be put in charge of Protection at Buckingham Palace. A good instance of running with the hare and hunting with the hounds!

In the early part of 1980, progress towards a unified command had ceased and it required my personal intervention in the spring of 1981 to get the question of a unified command structure re-opened. There was still little or no progress. When a report by the Force Inspectorate relating to this issue was sent to the Home Office in June 1981, it took them two months to reply and then only to suggest a meeting. Even this did not take place until October when it was agreed that further amalgamation of responsibility outlined at the meeting should proceed.

Progress continued to be woefully slow. When, in early 1982, Wilford Gibson, the Assistant Commissioner with overall responsibility under me for royal protection, met the Master of the Royal Household in an effort to get on with rationalization of policing of royal palaces, he was greeted with the comment that care must be taken that what was proposed was not change for change's sake, and that it would in any case all need further consideration and consultation within the Royal Household. It was not until April that a further meeting could be arranged with a Royal Household official and again this was inconclusive, with more time slipping away until Sir Brian Cubbon, the Home Office Permanent Secretary, wrote on 6 July to press the matter on the Household officials. A day later a member of Cubbon's staff wrote to the Yard to apologize for the time that it had taken to reach this point and to express hope that the necessary meeting with the Royal Household officials would not now be long delayed. Alas, it was too late. For on Friday, 9 July Michael Fagan entered the Queen's bedroom.

The first very senior police officer to be informed of Fagan's intrusion was Deputy Assistant Commissioner John Radley, who quite rightly reported by telephone to Brian Cubbon at the Home Office. This was on the morning of Friday, 9 July. But the Home Office did not inform the Home Secretary until the following Monday. At the time John Radley was told I was on my way to Tooting Police Station. On arrival I was greeted with a message to get in touch with New Scotland Yard immediately. I had received many messages in the past to contact the Yard 'as soon as possible', but never before had my office asked me to drop everything in order to get in touch. Clearly something was very wrong. I lost no time and was given the unbelievable news by Assistant Commissioner Gilbert Kelland. Within hours I had appointed John Dellow, by then Assistant Commissioner 'B' Department, to examine and report as a matter or urgency on what had happened. I made it plain that he was to recommend what immediate action needed to be taken to improve security at the Palace, and also to report on the longer term requirements for protecting the Royal Family and their residences.

I was stunned by a confusion of feelings. A sickening sinking in the pit of the stomach, disbelief linked with dismay, mixed with a sense of shame that we, the Metropolitan Police, had failed to protect Her Majesty. Anger too, and growing by the minute, since what had happened was an outrage.

We now know that soon after half past six on the morning of 9 July Fagan climbed the railings of Buckingham Palace without setting off any alarm. As he walked to the Palace itself, another security alarm failed to work. He first entered the Stamp Room of the building and activated an alarm; nobody responded to it. If there had not been this failure of duty all that followed might well have been avoided. He left the Stamp Room through the window by which he had entered and then re-entered the Palace again through an unfastened window of the office of the Master of the Royal Household. He went through the state apartments, where he passed a cleaner without challenge even though she noticed that he was scruffily dressed and barefooted. He sat on one of the thrones in the state rooms before entering the Queen's private apartments.

There Fagan went into the dog room. Unfortunately the dogs

were already out on a morning walk. He broke a glass ashtray and, holding a piece of it, entered the Queen's bedroom where Her Majesty was asleep. He drew back the curtains and spoke to the Queen who by then was awake. Her Majesty kept Fagan in conversation and attempted to summon assistance by pressing a bell push. When this had no result, the Queen spoke on her telephone to the Palace switchboard. The operator passed on a message to the police room that the Queen wanted a police officer to attend her bedroom. Apparently it was ten minutes before a constable came to the room. Meanwhile, but not as a result of any of the Queen's telephone calls, a maid and soon afterwards a footman came to the Queen's apartment and took Fagan away.

It was a disgraceful sequence of failures. One alarm beam had been easily evaded. Another had not worked. There had been no response to the third which had been treated as a false alarm. None of the Queen's calls for assistance had brought the response it should have done from the duty sergeant in the Palace. In addition, Fagan had been seen acting suspiciously near the railings of the Palace grounds by a police officer who was going off duty and on his way home by motorcycle. He reported what he had seen to a police constable in the Queen's gardens who in turn passed on the information by personal radio to the police room in the Palace. A superficial search only was carried out. The officer who had spotted Fagan did not challenge him or seek to keep him in sight.

As soon as the news broke, a great hubbub arose. There was a series of conferences with the Home Office and Palace officials leading to the Home Secretary making his first statement to the House of Commons on Monday, 12 July. It was not well received. The House reacted unfavourably to the Home Secretary's bland assurances that security at the Palace had been improved only shortly before Fagan's entry. This inevitably led to the comment that if these improvements had enabled a man to enter the Queen's bedroom, how bad was security before? There was also an unfavourable reaction in the House to the Home Secretary in person and this spread outwards in widening circles to the media, with a clamour for 'heads to roll', and the higher the person whose head was to roll the better. Pressure was exerted in particular by right wing Conservatives for both Whitelaw and me to resign.

The pressure did not come only from the House of Commons and the press. On Tuesday, 13 July I was visited by Sir Brian Cubbon. Brian was never a man readily at ease and as he came into the room this characteristic was more evident than usual. He sat down. After a brief exchange of small talk, he suggested out of the blue that I might wish to consider resigning, making comparison with the recent resignation of Lord Carrington over the Argentinian invasion of the Falkland Islands. My reply was a brief but emphatic no. I pointed out that the instructions issued on my behalf were right, that no Commissioner could be held personally responsible for operational negligence on the part of officers of junior rank and that in part the incident was a consequence of lack of co-operation from officials of government departments and of the Royal Household. Cubbon pressed for my resignation and when I refused, he said, 'Surely you do not wish to see the Home Secretary resign?' I did not and said so.

The thought struck me that perhaps Cubbon had been sent on his mission by the Home Secretary – or, if not actually sent, had at least come to ask me to retire with the knowledge of the Home Secretary. I asked him if this were so. He replied that the Home Secretary was not aware that he had come to see me. If true, that made his visit in a way even worse. It was both improper and impertinent for a civil servant, however senior, to ask for my resignation without direction from the Home Secretary.

When I saw William Whitelaw later the same morning, he said that he understood Cubbon had come to see me. He, however, made no direct request for my resignation, and I saw no case for offering it. I had done all I could as Commissioner to provide for the security of Buckingham Palace. I had been prevented by Royal Household officials and by officials of the Home Office and Department of the Environment from introducing the security measures I wished to see taken. This apart, the failure to protect the Monarch arose from negligence on the part of two or three officers of the rank of Constable and Sergeant. No vigilance on my part could have prevented that. Further, there was no direct comparison with the resignation of Lord Carrington over advice given to Government about the possible invasion by Argentina of the Falkland Islands.

None of these considerations, however, did anything to stop the calls day after day in one way or another for Whitelaw's head or mine. Faced with this kind of clamour and criticism, much of it unjustified or inaccurate, a great sense of isolation descends upon you. No one wants to get involved in case you are a loser. A further statement was made in the House by the Home Secretary. There was little in it for the Metropolitan Police or David McNee. I got greater comfort and support from the Prime Minister, who made the telling point that you do not sack the general because a sentry falls asleep at his post.

It would have been satisfying to speak out at the time, if only to defend the Metropolitan Police by showing that responsibility for security at the Palace had never been the sole responsibility of the force; that it was shared with officials of the Royal Household, the Home Office and the Department of the Environment. But it would have been wrong to try to shift the responsibility from where it rightly belonged. The operational policing of the Palace was the responsibility of the Metropolitan Police. We had failed in that task. Again, it would not have been fair to have spoken out at the time because the junior police officers concerned with the operational failures were facing disciplinary charges. Until the facts on which these charges were based had been fully investigated it would have been wrong for me to apportion blame.

The operational requirements never could have been fully met. Buckingham Palace is a family home, and round-the-clock guards carrying arms and patrolling the corridors would have been a great intrusion on the privacy of the Queen and her family. Moreover Fagan entered the Queen's bedroom after the police officer on night duty in her apartments had finished his shift. The security arrangements then operating to meet the wishes of the Royal Household were that this officer was not replaced by another police officer but by a Household footman. At the time of the break-in, the footman was out exercising the Queen's dogs and this was the reason there was no response to Her Majesty's bell push alarms. If a day duty police officer had been present, Fagan would have been stopped.

None of this could have been said at the time without attracting headlines such as: 'McNee blames his men before disciplinary charges are heard', 'McNee says Palace security has always been inadequate', 'McNee accuses Palace and Government for Delay in Security Measures'. There was nothing for it but to keep calm and ride the storm out. It was the lowest point of my entire career. But a great many letters of sympathy and support were sent to me. That helped. And British humour was never far away: a widow of seventy said that she did not understand what all the fuss was about – she had been hoping to see a man sitting on her bed ever since her husband died twenty years previously.

By the end of that week I was going to need a sense of humour. at 6 p.m. on Friday, 16 July, Sir Philip Moore, Private Secretary to the Queen, called on the telephone to ask if he could see me at Buckingham Palace. When I saw him, Sir Philip told me that the previous Wednesday he had met with a journalist on the *Sun* who had informed him that a male prostitute was alleging he regularly associated with Commander Trestrail, the Queen's Police Officer. This was another tremendous shock to the system. There had never been any suspicion or the slightest indication of any homosexual attitudes by Trestrail. 'What are you going to do about it?' Sir Philip concluded. 'Leave it with me,' I replied. 'Obviously he can't stay with the Queen any longer.' I learnt with some irritation that Sir Philip had passed the same information much earlier in the day to Brian Cubbon. No one at the Home Office, however, had seen fit to make it known to me or to the Home Secretary. I found that quite inexplicable.

It was about 7 p.m. when I returned to New Scotland Yard. I acted swiftly, calling in Gilbert Kelland and instructing him to investigate the allegation. Later the same evening Kelvin Mackenzie, the Editor of the *Sun*, came into the Yard and I heard the story again from him. Kelvin Mackenzie and his staff gave the Metropolitan Police every assistance, providing detailed information, including the telephone number of the male prostitute. They helped to bring this sad and unhappy matter to a quick conclusion.

Early on the following day, Gilbert Kelland phoned me at home to say the male prostitute had been traced and was at New Scotland Yard for questioning. His final comment was 'It's a true bill'; detective talk for saying that the allegation was true. I told Kelland to see Trestrail and added that I was on my way immediately to the Yard.

Soon after midday I was told that Trestrail had admitted a relationship with the male prostitute over a number of years and had resigned from the force. It was a dreadful ending to a career of high service to the Royal Family and a tragedy for the man. We all felt this intensely and I went to see Trestrail before he left the Yard. He was greatly distressed, saying that it was all his fault and how deeply sorry he was for so grievously embarrassing the Queen and the Metropolitan Police. As I said goodbye I wished him well for the future and I was joined in this by Sir Philip Moore, who was also present. A few days later Trestrail sent me a letter in words characteristic of him. He thanked me for my kindness and compassion on that black Saturday, saying he would never forget my farewell to him. He recognized that he would have to learn to live with the shame and disgrace which had befallen him, but prayed that he had not done too much damage to the reputation of the force that he had been proud to work for and which had been so very generous to him. That same Saturday I had also asked Robert Andrew of the Home Office Police Department to come to New Scotland Yard where I told him all the facts. For some reason which I still do not understand today, the Home Office did not report any of this to the Home Secretary until he arrived at Queen Anne's Gate the following Monday.

On that Monday there were meetings in the Home Secretary's room during which a statement was prepared for him to make in the House of Commons. Once again, it was very clear that the Metropolitan Police was expected to bear the brunt of public criticism for the breach of security at Buckingham Palace followed by the Trestrail disclosures. No government department nor the Security Service was going to accept the slightest responsibility for any tardiness in making preparations for the protection of the Royal Family, for the security clearance given to Trestrail by positive vetting or for anything else that had happened. The Home Secretary's statements in the House of Commons towards the end of July were made with this well in mind. Again there were no words of support or defence for the Metropolitan Police. Nor during this time did I receive any contact from the Home Office.

The policy and guidelines for positive vetting are set up by the Government. The investigation into background and character of people selected for positive vetting is undertaken by Government officials from the Ministry of Defence. If the person under investigation is a Metropolitan Police officer, the Commissioner is told whether or not the officer is cleared on security grounds, but he is told nothing else.

For years government policy had been for positive vetting to be limited to persons who have frequent and regular access to documents classified as Top Secret. Trestrail did not come into this category and so had not been positively vetted. In 1982, however, Gilbert Kelland took the view that the government guidelines were too restrictive and on his own initiative directed that Trestrail should be vetted. The vetting was undertaken by two Ministry of Defence officials who found nothing to lead them to conclude that Trestrail had character defects or other problems. Trestrail had served as a protection officer for the Royal Family under four Commissioners. He was appointed in 1966 by Sir Joseph Simpson to be protection officer to the Duke of Edinburgh, and had later been moved to the top post of The Queen's Police Officer. He had served as a royalty protection officer under Sir Joseph Simpson, Sir John Waldron, Sir Robert Mark and myself.

So far as I am aware, none of us had any reason for thinking that he was not well suited for the work. On the contrary, his record of service had been outstanding; he had an eye-catching personality and an impeccable demeanour. I can also say without hesitation that officers who served with Michael Trestrail during his career showed an extremely high regard for him. Police officers have their personal and family background rigorously investigated when first recruited. Each officer is also reported on annually and at length by his supervisory officers. No report on Trestrail ever cast doubt on his conduct or personal standards.

The concluding remarks in the report of Lord Bridge of Harwich, who was appointed by the Home Secretary to look into the whole affair, bear repeating:

> Almost without exception, those who knew Commander Trestrail expressed to me their personal regret that his distinguished career should have had to end so unhappily and their sympathy with him in the ordeal to which he was subjected by the singularly unpleasant publicity which the circumstances of his resignation attracted. I share those sentiments.*[a]

And so do I.

After the disclosures about Michael Trestrail I had decided that all officers engaged on royal protection duties would be positively vetted. Lord Bridge saw this as an understandable reaction on my part to public concern. Nevertheless he did not regard it as justifiable given the criterion against which it was decided when police officers should be positively vetted: 'actual or potential access to highly secret intelligence or counter-intelligence information'.*[b] Lord Bridge thought it an imprecise definition which ought to be amended to give more positive guidance. But as he observed, '. . . PV procedures are not, and cannot be, infallible. In Trestrail's case they were carried out efficiently and thoroughly. The failure to discover Trestrail's homosexual activities attracts no blame.'*[c]

When I learnt of Michael Fagan's intrusion into the Queen's

---

* The quotes are taken from:
'Report of an Inquiry by the Rt Hon Lord Bridge of Harwich into the appointment as the Queen's Police Officer, and the activities, of Commander Trestrail; to determine whether security was breached or put at risk, and advise whether in consequence any change in security arrangements is necessary or desirable.'
Order by the House of Commons printed 24 November 1982 HC59 HMSO

[a] paragraph 10
[b] paragraph 9.6
[c] paragraph 9.9

bedroom, I sent a letter of apology to Her Majesty on behalf of the Metropolitan Police for the dereliction of duty which had led to the intrusion of her privacy. Some weeks later there was one of the usual summer garden parties at Buckingham Palace. In the garden is a marquee specially reserved for members of the Royal Family, members of the Government, diplomats and distinguished visitors from overseas. While taking tea it is customary for the Monarch to converse with such ambassadors and High Commissioners as may be present and with overseas visitors.

At the garden party which I attended a message was sent to me that the Queen would like me to join her and, as I got up, the Court official said that the invitation also extended to my wife. We made our way to where the Queen stood and, after putting us at our ease, she asked the Queen Mother to join us. All this was done in full view of the large crowd watching with interest from outside the marquee. From this and the Queen's conversation I am in no doubt that she was indicating in her own inimitable way her support for the Metropolitan Police. It was the generosity of that gesture that helped me to ride out the storm of public criticism.

There was no support among the press or politicians, for 'when the hunt is on, all dogs bark'. The reaction of the editors of some national newspapers was hostile; the *Daily Mail* set the pace in its demands for the resignation of the Home Secretary and myself. It was even alleged that some encouragement was given to certain newspapers to press for my resignation. Support for the Metropolitan Police from the Home Secretary was minimal, in significant contrast to the way he had quickly spoken in Parliament in total support of his civil servants, when they were under fire for not reporting the Fagan incident to him straight away. It certainly differed markedly from an incident which occurred shortly after World War II, when an intruder got into the room of the Queen Mother. The papers show that the principal action of the Home Office then was for a strong letter of support to be sent by the Permanent Secretary to the Commissioner.

Roy Hattersley, as the Opposition spokesman for Home Affairs, also showed his calibre by expressing severe criticism of the

Metropolitan Police while displaying at the same time little real knowledge of the organization, or its needs and problems. He suggested, for example, dividing the Metropolitan Police District into a number of separate police forces, overlooking the obvious fact that London is an urban metropolis and not a county.

I was not however wholly without support. I was well supported by my senior officers at New Scotland Yard, all but one of whom urged me to stay as Commissioner. Later, on 28 July, when the Home Secretary met representatives of the Association of London Boroughs (who provide much of the finance for the Metropolitan Police), the Chairman, Mr Peter Bowness and the Vice Chairman, Mr Roy Shaw, who come from opposing political parties asked that it should be put formally on record that the Association had full confidence in the Metropolitan Police and in its Commissioner.

And so the barking slowly diminished. Any police officer from Constable to Commissioner knows well enough that throughout his service he is going to be the target for complaints and criticisms, some of which may be undeserved. This is now an unavoidable fact of life for police officers. In the last month or so before my retirement I had lunch with the editor of a national newspaper which had published a great deal of adverse comment about me and the Metropolitan Police during the height of the Palace incidents. I reminded him of this in a friendly way during the course of our meal. His reply was to say that I surely did not take any notice of the criticism and adverse comments made about me, especially the suggestion that I should resign, because none of it was really meant. Well, maybe so, but if anyone is going to write personal untruths and cruel words which are not meant, they should bear in mind the effect it may be having on individual lives. Goodness knows that my hide is thick enough, but there is also the effect that non-stop and mainly unjustified criticism, much of it personal, had on my wife and members of my family.

Newspapers, however, can make handsome amends. Close to my retirement, *The Times* published a leader under the heading, 'No Mean Man from No Mean City'. It set out fully in factual and complimentary terms my achievements during the years I had been

Commissioner. During the same week, the *Daily Mail*, which had been the newspaper most severe in its attacks on me, published the following leader:

Farewell To a Great Police Chief

After the scandal of the intruder at Buckingham Palace, our advice in this column was that Metropolitan Police Commissioner Sir David McNee should resign.

Our argument was that this was appropriate not because it was his fault but that, given his pending retirement in October anyway, his resignation would have a symbolic value in bringing home to every member of the force the vital importance of protecting the Sovereign. In retrospect we were wrong. Sir David was not in any realistic sense responsible for Palace security because the royal household arrangements had been something of a law unto themselves and it is only since the incident that a unified system of protection became possible. Moreover, it would have been a tremendous shame if he had appeared to retire in any degree under a cloud.

For he, on the contrary, deserves our thanks for noble service in a demanding job at a testing time. He is a good, honest man who has had to contend with a great deal of evil political pressure.

Significantly, the highlights of his period of office have been the Grunwick picket line, the Iranian Embassy siege and the Brixton riots. These episodes typify the growing lawlessness he has had to deal with, reflected also in rising crime figures. Yet this was not the fault of the police: the wave of violence and crime is common to the whole Western world.

He has been quietly improving his force, increasing numbers and efficiency and, especially, moving 1,500 police officers from behind desks on to the beat.

Despite the many unfounded allegations emanating from Operation Countryman, he has acted firmly against corruption and in his term of office he sacked nearly twice as many officers as did Sir Robert Mark.

Although less extrovert than his predecessor, he has done much for the public image of the police and has exerted much effort to improve community relations.

Perhaps inevitably, after the Brixton riots, there was a bad period for the police. The Left-wing press, Parliamentary committees and the race relations industry went to town with criticisms of the 'sus' laws, the Special Patrol Group and Operation Swamp, in Brixton. The Scarman Report seemed like a culmination of the process of criticizing and restraining the police in the performance of their duties.

Sir David acted boldly by announcing in March that more than half the robberies and violent thefts which occurred in 1981 were committed by coloured assailants. This appears from the latest sharp fall in these crimes to have produced a very positive response from the black community, the vast majority of whom, as Sir David has always emphasized, are law-abiding.

At all events, Sir David leaves to his successor a police force in good shape and good heart to meet successfully the challenges of the next five years.

11

And So to Bed

AND SO TO BED . . . well, not quite, because I still intend to be active and, hopefully, useful in one way or another. After being Commissioner there is naturally a sense of relief at the shedding of the responsibilities and daily burdens but the normality of earlier years has also gone for ever. Wherever you go you are recognized, what you did and what you failed to do is public knowledge and with you for the rest of your life.

What thoughts from those years remain with me? The answer is 'many' and of course it is inevitable that I continue to reflect on the major issues with which I was involved, particularly as there is more time now for such reflection. What then are these major issues and what are my concluding thoughts?

'Accountability' – that remains probably the most currently debated subject in regard to the police service, even if it is not the most important. Not much debated by police officers, I should add, who are preoccupied with meeting the increasing demands of their work. But much debated by central and local politicians, political commentators, and the media.

It is not, however, just a fashionable debating topic. It is much more serious than that, for the question to be determined in essence is, who is to control policing and, particularly, who is to control the Metropolitan Police?

From much of what is said and written, one might think that as matters now stand the Metropolitan Police is operating without any accountability. This is a totally false picture for, if you will forgive the phrase, the force is accountable up to the eye-balls.

The Metropolitan Police is accountable in a host of ways:

To the law, and in particular to any Acts which Parliament may see fit to enact.

To the courts, with many cases being examined first by the Director of Public Prosecutions and thereafter going before magistrates' and crown courts where barristers argue the correctness or otherwise of police action.

To a very senior member of the Cabinet who is the police authority of the force, and who is aided in the exercise of this responsibility by a major department of state.

To Parliament, by means of an annual report which the Commissioner presents through the Home Secretary. Any one of over 600 Members of Parliament also may question the policies and procedures of the force, particularly if he or she is a Member for a London constituency.

To the Public Accounts Committee of Parliament who may review the expenditure of the force.

To elected representatives and officials of the London boroughs and other local authorities of the Metropolitan Police District who may question and seek information on the policing of the metropolis.

To the Director of Public Prosecutions and the Police Complaints Board in regard to complaints against police officers.

To the many thousands of people, amongst whom are listed MPs, local councillors, lawyers, who write for information to New Scotland Yard and their local police stations.

Above all this, is trial by the media: 'Accountability' by another name.

On reflection there is a level of accountability with greater influence over police affairs than even the press; greater in respect of the Met than of other police forces. That is the day-to-day (almost hour-to-hour) working relationship that exists between New Scotland Yard and the Home Office, which exercises a close scrutiny of all that the force undertakes. There are other checks and balances. For example the Metropolitan Police has regular liaison with organizations such as the Commission for Racial Equality and the Inner London Education Authority; such links often have a very positive effect upon policing policies.

I think the Metropolitan Police is one of the most accountable organizations in society today, and rightly so. Let those who consider otherwise look first at themselves, which not surprisingly leads me to the Greater London Council.

As Commissioner, my introduction to the debate over accountability began with the publication in July 1978 of the Marshall Inquiry Report which was sponsored by the GLC. As I recall, I received a copy of this Report with a letter from Sir James Swaffield, Chief Executive of the GLC, indicating that his chairman, Sir Horace Cutler, was looking for a meeting with the Home Secretary and myself to discuss that part of the report which concluded:

> The sections of the Metropolitan Police which operate on a national basis should be detached from those which provide police service for London.
>
> Closer links should be established through a police committee which would approve the police force budget and have a voice in the appointment of the Commissioner, but not operational control of the force.*

Sir Horace was looking to the GLC to join the Home Office and the Commissioner to form a triumvirate overseeing policing policy. It was at one time suggested that Mr Brooke-Partridge should be given the responsibility of being the liaison officer between the GLC and the Metropolitan Police. I can still clearly recall attending a concert at the Royal Festival Hall, sponsored by the GLC, at which Margaret Thatcher and Denis Thatcher were the guests of honour. It was before she became Prime Minister. Sir Horace spent much of the evening making overtures to me about his proposals for the Met

* Paragraph 13.1

228

and the recommendations of the Marshall Report. I gave him short shrift. Our conversation took place in the company and hearing of our guests of honour and there was no doubt that the proposals fell on deaf ears.

In my view the aim of the GLC was then and still is to clarify a role for itself as the strategic planning authority for Greater London, but it has no statutory responsibility for the police and I see no reason for this to change. The task of levying the finances of the force is the responsibility of the Receiver for the Metropolitan Police District in conjunction with the London boroughs, the Home Office and Parliament. Operational responsibility lies with the Commissioner and I can see no case for the GLC joining the Home Secretary as Police Authority. Certainly a local voice is necessary, but this comes properly not from the GLC but from the London boroughs centrally through their Association and locally by close contact with the District Police Commanders.

On a number of occasions I proposed to the Home Secretary that there should be formal arrangements for regular consultation between the Home Secretary, the Commissioner and the London boroughs. Not only was the London Boroughs Association strongly in favour of this being set up, but my suggestion was also accepted by Mr Whitelaw. I was angry that he decided to defer announcing the establishment of such a consultative group for the Metropolitan Police until after I had left the force.

Lord Scarman made similar recommendations in his Report on the Brixton disorders, but he made no proposal for any modification or change in the position of the Home Secretary as Police Authority for the force. This, together with his views on what form local consultation should take, brought criticism from left wing politicians of the GLC since it was not in line with their demands. What Ken Livingstone and Paul Boateng seek is clear; they made no secret of it in their manifesto:

> A Labour controlled GLC will invite boroughs to join in establishing a police committee to monitor the work of the police force as a prelude to their gaining power to control the police . . .

and later:

> A Labour GLC will campaign for a Police Authority consisting
> solely of elected members of the GLC and London boroughs to
> have control of the Metropolitan and City Police. This author-
> ity to have power to appoint all officers to the rank of Chief
> Superintendent and above, to scrutinize the day to day affairs
> of the force and to allocate the resources to the various police
> functions . . .

I agree with Lord Scarman that the Metropolitan Police ought to be
well informed of the needs and demands of its local communities.
And for the GLC to criticize the Metropolitan Police – as it has done
in its paper on accountability – for its centralized bureaucracy is a
classic case of the pot calling the kettle black. Police officers in
London often told me that in their view only the present Conservative Government stands in the way of constitutional changes in the
present arrangements for control of the Metropolitan Police, and
that the return to power of a Socialist or Liberal/SDP Government
would lead to such changes. If this should come about, the operational independence of the force will be affected whatever affirma-
tions are made to the contrary. For example, direct control over
promotion and over the allocation of police resources will in
practice put control over operational policing in the hands of the
political authority, which is precisely what the Police Act 1964
seeks to avoid, and for very good reason.

It is also interesting that from what is being said by GLC leaders,
it appears that once the national functions of the Metropolitan
Police have been hived off to central government, the force would be
allowed to remain unchanged. In other words, the proposal by Roy
Hattersley that the large force should be split up into smaller units is
not part of the GLC's plans. But then how could it be? To do so
would be to divest the GLC of the power it is seeking.

I would add one further comment – apart from the ribald one
that to have had Ken Livingstone as head of my Police Authority
would certainly have been interesting for us both. It is that if for the
future the long-established relationship between the Commissioner

and Home Secretary is to function with the greatest efficiency it is necessary for the Home Office to act more competently than in recent years. It is not satisfactory, for example, for the Home Office only to exercise a *post facto* role or to come forward when things go well, as in the Iranian siege, but to take a step sharply backwards when affairs go amiss, as with the security of Buckingham Palace.

A tendency by Home Office civil servants to exercise control over police operations, such as has developed in recent years, is also unwelcome, as is the inclination to resolve, or at least defer, problems by setting up a committee of inquiry or review body of some sort.

It is not for me to tell the Home Office what should be its business although I am not above having a try. But I would suggest that much of the trouble in which the Department has been in over the last two or three years has been brought about by its uncertain approach to law and order.

Let me give an example. The Home Office has been repeatedly embarrassed in recent years by Chief Constables 'going public' and speaking out on all manner of issues. Much of this has been ill-judged and the Home Office has been critical of the Chief Constables concerned. But should not the Home Office rather be critical of its own failure in this field? Is it not that Chief Constables have had to speak out on behalf of the police and police problems because the Home Office has not represented police interests adequately and provided the proper material and advice for the Home Secretary to fulfil his role as spokesman for the police service?

Paul Johnson put this well in an article in the *Daily Mail* of 31 March 1982:

> But if Chief Constables are now in the arena of debate, it is the politicians who have dragged them there. Nor do I blame solely the Livingstones. Much of the responsibility lies with Conservative ministers, and in particular with those at the Home Office, for failing to provide our Chief Constables and the police as a whole with the vigorous, loyal, detailed and continuous defence which the vicious attacks on them make necessary.

So much for accountability, although no doubt the debate will go on. What about the organization and size of the force? After years in command, what are my thoughts now.

26,500 police officers and 15,000 civilians responsible for an area the size of Greater London is obviously a very large command. Over the years, thought has been given to whether it could be sub-divided. But one has only to think of the problems of controlling the flow of traffic through London, or preventing and detecting crime in London, to take but two examples, to see how difficult dividing overall operational command would be. Not that Roy Hattersley saw any such difficulty when he referred to the inability of the Metropolitan Police successfully to discharge all the duties imposed upon it: 'It is too large, it attempts too many diverse tasks, it is badly managed, and it has no effective authority to control its actions.' I remember thinking when reading those words that, considering the state of the Labour Party at the time he spoke, he should look to the beam in his own eye.

Nevertheless, the proposal to create eight super districts was on the table when I took up appointment as Commissioner, and creating a public furore and undermining confidence all round.

I also gave much thought to whether power was excessively concentrated at the centre, i.e. at New Scotland Yard, with four functional and competing departments, each operating under an Assistant Commissioner. Would it be better to alter the structure by establishing four territorial commands, covering in total the whole of the metropolis, with only policy makers at the centre?

In brief it would mean that four Assistant Commissioners would each be given more or less the same responsibilities for a separate part of the metropolis. The Metropolitan Police District is already divided into four areas of comparable size and complexity, with a Deputy Assistant Commissioner allocated to each area. If Assistant Commissioners were given responsibility for total policing of the areas (virtually as chief officers of police), controlled, co-ordinated and assisted by the Commissioner and headquarters support branches, would the problems of the force become more manageable?

Maybe and maybe not; but even if the former proved to be the case, would it have been worth all the turmoil and disarray, within and without the force, which would have been caused in the period of transition, a period which could well extend over several years?

It is this which you have always to bear in mind as Commissioner: the effect which any measure will have on the morale and efficiency of the rank and file of the force and thereby on the service rendered to the public. The touchstone of good policing in London in the end is not whether the force headquarters is organized in this way or that, but how well more than 20,000 police sergeants and constables, uniform and detective, conduct themselves and serve the public.

The question of morale within the police service as within any organization has to be a major concern for the man at the top. An unhappy, dispirited, discontented work force will not give the kind of performance required. It was for this reason – and also I have no doubt because of my wish to remain in touch with the men and women who actually do the job on the streets – that from the very start I tried to increase contact between top management within the force and the Federation and Superintendents' Association. I encouraged a greater degree of informal contact as well as increasing the formal arrangements for discussions between management and the staff associations. We did not always agree, but the readiness of Jim Jardine, John Newman, Harry Slipper, Steve Barrett and their colleagues to disagree was itself a healthy sign. They were great characters whose company I always enjoyed. The way they fêted me on my departure perhaps suggests that feeling was not purely one-sided.

The existing organization at New Scotland Yard has stood the test of time and works well. Unlike what has happened in government departments and public bodies, New Scotland Yard has had the same number of Assistant Commissioners and police departments for decades, despite the great increase in police work in London. There is no certainty that change will lead to a better service to the public – and that is what counts – and every likelihood that the process of change would be prolonged and disturbing.

My last thoughts, like my first, were that it was best to leave well alone.

Having said that, I tried never to be complacent about how London was being policed, never to fall into a belief that all was well and that there was no room for improvement. 'The price of peace is eternal vigilance', and the organization and methods or the force must always be under review.

I believe in practising what I preach. I initiated a major review of all training and recruitment; organizational changes which released larger number of officers for police duty; a review of all the civil support branches; a drawing together of the considerable efforts of the force under the collective heading of 'Community Relations'; and an examination in depth by the Policy Studies Institute of the relations between the Metropolitan Police and all sections of the general public.

Another concluding, albeit obvious, thought is that the people will only continue to hold the police in high regard if police officers, at all levels, deal promptly and forcibly with corruption in whatever form it takes, set high standards in public and private life, and exercise propriety in what they say and how they conduct themselves.

It is sometimes said that the public wish to see standards maintained by police officers which they as private citizens do not maintain themselves. That may seem a little unfair and in many ways it is. But it is a high compliment, and an indication of the high regard in which the police service is held.

More than enough has already been said and written about corruption, and my final word is only to hope that the public, leaders of public life and the media will recognize what immense efforts have been made over the last ten years under both Robert Mark and myself to deal with corruption in the Metropolitan Police whenever and wherever it was found. I am in no doubt that the force is all the better for these efforts and that new standards have been set. A special tribute is due to the contribution by Bob Mark. He was a distinguished Commissioner but nowhere more so than in his dealing with corruption. By his initiative, energy and courage the evils of police corruption were faced without compromise, and the insidious tide turned back.

I am less confident about the current level of public support for the police. As elsewhere, police officers in London need to know that they have the confidence of the public. You cannot have an effective police service without public support, and it is for this very reason that some will seek to undermine it. If I were to name whom I put in this particular category I might be in deep trouble, but I got the impression that many of them were based in London.

A matter of considerable concern to me is that, despite the consistent high rating achieved by the police service in successive public opinion polls, confidence amongst those who exercise influence in public life, including those in the professional classes, seems not what it used to be. If I am right about this, then an immediate priority for the future must be the restoration of their greater trust and support. This will inevitably be a slow, uphill task, achievable only (and I repeat myself again) by the application of professional standards at every level within the service.

It will also be necessary for the police service to improve its performance in the sphere of public communication. Chief officers need to reflect carefully how they can best contribute to this; confidence and trust do not result from outbursts by individual officers.

When he was Commissioner, Robert Mark made splendid use of television. Following him and knowing that this was not my forte, I deliberately restricted the number of appearances I made. I chose to operate in a different manner, and established a personal relationship with all the editors of major newspapers. I gave hundreds of speeches and lectures; some were serious, some light-hearted, but each made a point or two about some aspect of policing and its social impact. The course I chose was more laborious, but it underlines how important it is for each chief officer to choose the way which is most suited to him personally.

Effective communication, however, like police community relations, requires co-operation. I remain unconvinced that the media is always sufficiently balanced in its approach to the problems of policing. Somewhere along the way I got the reputation of being media-shy; I suspect some even regarded me as anti-press. This no doubt stemmed from my policy of infrequent television appearances and refusing many of the seemingly never-ending demands of the media for interviews. But the plain fact is that I did make a number of appearances on both television and radio. Once the guest of Terry Wogan and twice the guest of Jimmy Young – it falls to very few to achieve such heights. I hope I got my priorities right. I wrote several articles for and was interviewed several times by the press; even the First Lady of Fleet Street – Jean Rook – managed to storm the barricades outside my office on the eighth floor of New Scotland Yard.

Certainly I did not get off on the right foot with the BBC. Desmond Wilcox and Eddie Mirzoeff had been granted extensive facilities by Bob Mark to do a programme about New Scotland Yard and the Metropolitan Police. It was completed and put together before my arrival and broadcast on 21 June 1977. I was invited a few days after my appointment to attend a preview of the programme. It portrayed the Metropolitan Police and New Scotland Yard in 'big brother' terms, concentrating upon record keeping, surveillance, Crime Squad activity, police use of firearms and the policing of demonstrations.

I felt that the programme gave a distorted view of police work; it lacked balance. I commented on this and asked why there was nothing about other aspects of police work. For example, they had spent two days researching the programme with the then head of the Community Relations Branch – Bob Bryan. I asked where his contribution was. The excuse I was given for the fact that he himself was not on film was that he had not been sufficiently articulate. Now at one time or another I may have accused Bob Bryan of all manner of things but being inarticulate would certainly not have been one of them. I was confronted in general by the ultra-sensitive reaction all too common in media people when they are criticized – defensiveness; a trait frequently attributed by the press and others to police officers. A lively discussion was brought to an early

236

conclusion when I left rather abruptly to keep an appointment with my daughter. It was a genuine reason for leaving but afterwards I saw that I may have been thought to have walked out. To be truthful that thought disturbed me hardly at all.

Then there was our attempt to introduce some contractual control over material filmed by the BBC as a result of facilities granted by us for proposed programmes. The quest for this arose from a desire to protect people's privacy and confidentiality in respect of a programme that the BBC wanted to make about missing persons. It was in my view a justifiable objective – not only to protect persons filmed at the time but also subsequently. All too often film from the cutting-room floor – and excerpts from broadcast programmes – finds a way into other, subsequent and often unconnected programmes. There has to be some protection against this kind of misuse – and organizations as well as individuals are entitled to expect protection. Some measure of control by organizations over the use of material which television companies or their employees acquire as the result of permission given and facilities granted by the organizations is not an unreasonable demand.

We failed to achieve our contractual objective and eventually settled for the usual BBC letter of intent. The wrangle, however, attracted some publicity and, coming at the same time as the Law and Order series of films, seemed to become confused and connected with the criticism those programmes attracted from some quarters of the service. It might be surprising to some people that I never publicly expressed any view on T. F. Newman's highly partial portrayals of the criminal justice system, for the impression was fostered within the media that they were causing me great concern. The same could be said of Newman's scripts, which suggested a criminal justice system riddled with corruption. The dramatic distortions of these portrayals really warranted no public comment – from me, at least. It was largely the combination of these things, I believe, that contributed to the view that McNee was at odds with the media.

Press, radio and television, particularly the last, are now most powerful institutions in our midst. They are largely free to exercise their power as they wish, and able to castigate those who refuse to play ball with them. In the main they exercise responsibility, but when they do not the Press Council is a toothless watchdog.

The police are often much indebted to the media for their help in particular cases, like the voluntary maintenance of a news black-out on a kidnapping. But my comments here do not relate to individual cases but to the role of the men and women of the media as major opinion-makers in a world where I am not convinced that they always fully appreciate the social and political effects of what they do.

To my mind there is an excessive interest in conflict and contention, with an inclination toward criticism, much of which undermines the public institutions and standards on which the stability of our lives is based. Linked with this is the aforementioned tendency by all forms of the media to react strongly to criticisms of themselves.

The reporting of police matters has changed over the past few years. No one is more aware of it than the old style crime reporters, whom I knew well throughout my police service. Where the focus was once upon crime, criminals and major investigations, today the media concentrates more on social issues affected by policing methods and the approach is often a critical one. Concern is with the right of the individual rather than with some wider public good as in the past. This may be a healthy approach but it needs to be kept in perspective and we must have regard to its direct and indirect effects on our society.

I am reminded of a conversation I had with Griffin Bell, the Attorney General of the United States of America during part of the time when Jimmy Carter was President. He identified the immediate priorities for his country as an improvement in the quality of life, and greater freedom from crime in particular, rather than continuing with predominant emphasis upon the rights of the individual which had been the approach to criminal justice in the United States since World War II. He was quite outspoken in identifying a clear public desire for a return to greater stability and a revival of traditional virtues, including patriotism.

There is, of course, a need for balance in all this but we need to be careful that an obsession with the need to protect the innocent and preserve the rights of individuals does not allow the guilty to go increasingly free.

While speaking of the United States, I am sure that in Britain we should not go overboard in our policing with the use of technology as some American police forces have done. As a chief officer I introduced advanced command systems, extensive computerization of records, the first police helicopter unit in London, and a wide range of advanced technical equipment for criminal observation and detection, but I was insistent on the need to keep all this firmly in its place.

I visited major police forces in all parts of the world as often as I could because I believe firmly in the need to learn from others; I went to Europe, the United States, Canada, the Far East and Australia. One lesson I learnt from these travels, and particularly from visiting the United States, alerted me to the danger of relying too heavily on technology in seeking solutions to problems of policing. Technology complements human skills, knowledge and understanding but can never be a substitute for them, for policing is essentially concerned with human behaviour and relationships.

From the 1960s onwards successive governments have injected increasing technological aid into the police service. Panda cars, computers, personal radios and much else – all aimed largely at offsetting deficiencies in police manpower, which until the last year or so have been considerable. The aim was to deploy and use more effectively such strengths and resources as were available. What was not foreseen was the unintended consequences of these large technological inputs.

The advent of the panda car, introduced to improve mobility and speed of response, lessened daily contact between police officers and members of the public with consequent deterioration in their relations.

The police national computer (costing many millions of pounds) provided easy access to information previously kept on manual files. A clear improvement in operational effectiveness, the computer has reduced the time a police officer takes to make checks on people whom he stops and the time that suspects are detained on the streets or in cars. This is to the benefit of civil liberty; and I should add that information is much more secure when stored on computers than on a multitude of pieces of paper on files. But an over-reliance on computerized information has brought about an accompanying loss in the ability of police officers to test a person's explanation of his movements or presence in suspicious circumstances by indulging in small talk and conversation; or maybe the ready availability of centralized information and direction has fostered the reluctance of some officers to do this. Whatever the reason, the subtlety of street interviews, which were commonplace when I was on the beat, has diminished.

The greatest change in policing, however, has been brought about by the wide introduction of the personal radio. There is no disputing it has brought great benefits. But it has also taken the attention of police officers away from what is going on around them. Too often I have seen a constable looking down at the ground listening to what is being said from a central police station rather than looking around him to see what is actually going on.

Paradoxically, the personal radio has made police officers less self-reliant, less reliant on obtaining support from the local community, and more reliant on their colleagues, not only for advice but for physical support in dealing with an incident. In my day as a patrolling officer, discretion and caution were essential for survival. It paid well to build up local contacts and to get to know people on your beat, for you never knew when you were going to need their help. Technological improvements in communication sadly have led to a reduction in the traditional close relationship between the police and the people, which historically has distinguished policing in Britain from that in any other country of the world.

Just in case these comments make me appear to be something out of the Stone Age, let me just say again that no chief officer of police introduced more technological aids than I did — I just believe that technology has to be kept firmly in harness and not allowed to undermine the traditional basis of what makes a good police officer. As in everything else, the right balance is necessary. It was partly with these unintended consequences in mind that I initiated the review of training, for it seemed to me that there was a need to get back to the basics of policing.

As I come to the end of my concluding thoughts I ask, what are we really seeking in our policing? I think it is peace on the streets, security in our homes and safety for our families. For the last forty years there has been a deterioration in this country and all over the world. To put matters right will be a joint enterprise, for if the police service is to cope with crime, it needs and must have the involvement and active help of all law-abiding citizens. The underlying message of Lord Scarman's Report on the Brixton disorders is that policing is far too important to be left to the police service alone.

It is a fact that the policing can be affected by decisions taken elsewhere in the criminal justice system. One illustration of this is the abolition of capital punishment. As Commissioner it was always a topic I steered well clear of. To have or not to have capital punishment is a political decision for Parliament; it is not a matter in my view for public comment by serving police officers who should hold the ring, not step within it. But now I have retired I feel less reticent. I may be accused of taking a very simplistic view of a complex issue but I grew up and served as a policeman in one of the toughest cities in the world, yet during the years when capital punishment was in force I rarely encountered cases of armed crime.

When I look back on my early years I remember how the villains of Glasgow were intimidated by the threat of the gallows. The shadow of Tyburn hovered in the background, tempering the violence of men who would otherwise not have thought twice about using a firearm. The character of evil has not changed since then but the fear of punishment certainly has.

Potential killers no longer worry about the ultimate penalty. The prospect for the taking of life is eight or nine years in prison if they behave themselves. Nowadays criminals are using firearms more and more. The fact that the death toll is not higher owes more to the skill of the surgeon than it does to the charity of the criminal. Lives are put in jeopardy by violent men who no longer gamble their liberty against the highest stakes. Reintroducing the death penalty in 1983 would have changed the nature of that gamble; by its very existence hanging would have served as a deterrent unmatched by any present circumstance.

Any future debate about the principle of the death penalty has to be separated from the debate about the practice – about who should face it and who should not. I believe those considerations should be left for the judiciary. It would be wrong at any time to restore the death penalty in such a way that society is faced with some of the obvious dilemmas it confronted before. I do not believe that we should say that a specific offence – the killing of a police officer, for instance, or the murder of a prison officer – merits the death penalty. Such classification is neither desirable nor helpful. Discretion has to be the key word. And that should rest with the judges, who can consider all the facts – the background of the accused and the circumstances of the crime – before passing sentence.

There is another area which we need to look at with a fresh eye: how to evaluate police performance. As a chief officer of police I was always ready to highlight reductions in crime as a measure of police effectiveness. The trouble is, that particular sword cuts two ways – and recent trends in crime have been upwards. The crime rate is a social trend and is affected by other social trends such as the rate of unemployment, homelessness and the incidence of poverty. Individual crimes are the consequence of human behaviour and much of that behaviour, although technically contravening criminal law, is never reported to the police. Lack of confidence in the police may suppress the crime rate; increased confidence may inflate it. Arrests and detentions also depend to some extent upon public co-operation which is itself a function of the level of public confidence in the police. Clearly, therefore, there are dangers in assessing police performance in terms of the number of reported crimes or clear-up rates. We cannot discount changes in the rates entirely, but they need careful interpretation and are certainly not a sufficient measure of police effectiveness.

Rapid response to public calls for police assistance is important, but more as an indication of police ability to respond quickly than as a crime prevention exercise, since most calls are made after the event – and often well after. Over the years, I have become increasingly convinced that police performance needs to be measured on two fronts: efficiency and effectiveness. Police efficiency is evaluated in much the same way as any other public agency – in terms of its decision-making processes, its ability to marshal resources, its internal communications system, its budgetary control procedures. Police effectiveness may be indicated by changes for the better in the crime rate, but a much more appropriate measure is the extent of public satisfaction with its police force; and that is a reflection of the way police officers deal with people. Unprofessional conduct in any form is likely to be the greatest enemy of effectiveness.

I am in no doubt that the police service in the years to come will continue to play its part. It will also remain under continuing examination. No part of the police service is or will be free from such examination; its policies, practices, procedures and priorities will all come under scrutiny.

So should the attitudes, standards and support of the general public be under examination. I do not want to labour the point, but let me just say this: it is not order that threatens our homes and country – it is disorder. It is not law which threatens our well-being and safety – it is lawlessness. It is not the police who are a threat to the country's peace and prosperity – it is the criminal, the anarchist, the extremist and the terrorist.

Riots will come again as they have done from time to time over many years and, as in the past, the police will be in the middle seeking to hold the balance between liberty and enforcement of the law. On the day of my arrival at New Scotland Yard, I said that in my view the main problem which I would be facing as Commissioner would be that of race and the conflicts which racial issues bring for policing. Nothing which occurred during my time as

243

Commissioner led me to deviate from that view and I think that it will be the principal problem to be faced by my successor, and probably too by his successor.

The right policing approach will remain impartial enforcement of the law, and not, as I found in other countries, determining police priorities by what is politically expedient. The police must of course remain sensitive to the needs and feelings of all who make up a local community, but not at the expense of applying the rule of law, fairly and consistently, without regard to a man or woman's social position, politics, creed, race or colour. There is also a strong responsibility for black people to respond to an increasingly forthcoming and constructive approach to racial issues by the police. They too must show a willingness to understand the tasks and difficulties of the police.

I am sometimes asked about the pressures of the job of being Commissioner of Police. Well, make no mistake, they are immense. The Commissioner is, as I quoted earlier, 'More exposed to criticism and the vicissitudes of fortune than any other member of the public service.' In exercising the responsibilities of the post, there is not only never a break but also the fact that storm clouds, when they come, all seem to come together. Policing is about men and women, and there is always scope for misunderstanding, misjudgment, mistakes and irrationality on both sides. At any time you may, for instance, be having a quiet meal at home with your wife when any one of your 26,500 officers or any one of London's seven million people or a foreign visitor may be doing something foolish which within hours will bring very great problems indeed for you as Commissioner. Ignorance may be bliss, but you are not allowed to remain in ignorance for long.

There is also a constant concern, indeed an anxiety, that your views and requirements, particularly on how to deal with sensitive issues, are adequately communicated and understood at all levels and particularly at the level of constable. This is a problem faced by all commanders and managers but it is acute when the total organization exceeds over 40,000 police and civil staff spread over a wide and densely populated area and dealing face to face with the public in a wide range of tasks. Of course I worried, of course I got tired, but I always slept well and came to each day refreshed, ready and indeed enthusiastic for what it might bring.

I sometimes reflect that many unexpected turns of event had brought me to the post of Commissioner. If World War II had not taken me into the Royal Navy, I might still be working in a bank; if my last ship had not collided with another I would have sailed to the Pacific rather than obtained early release from the Navy to join the police. If I had not, unwillingly, gone to the Dunbartonshire Constabulary, I might have remained a senior detective in Glasgow; if it had not been for an accident I would not have acted as chief there which in turn led me to the top post in Glasgow. The timing of local government reorganization created the large regional force of Strathclyde and this in turn gave me experience which led to New Scotland Yard and the metropolis.

Yes, the pressures grew at each rung of the ladder, and never more so than at the last rung to Commissioner. At the start of my story I wrote of the strong Christian faith of my mother and father, how they and my church instilled that faith in me. The simple and truthful answer to how pressures affected me is that this faith and commitment, shared with a closely knit family, sustained me always but particularly when faced by great crises in the policing of London or by weeks and weeks of criticism from press and all sectors of the media. Indeed, in the service of Our Lord 'is perfect freedom'.

I remain optimistic about the future. When the year 2000 arrives, I may not be around to greet it (although I am always hopeful) and there will of course have been changes in policing methods and technology, but I believe that fundamentally the police service will be little different from today. The service will continue to operate within a democratic framework, standing firmly within the community on the twin pillars of public confidence and co-operation.

Above all, and this is the note on which I wish to end, British police officers will remain steadfast servants of the public, providing militants do not destroy public confidence in them or their confidence in themselves. I am indeed thankful to all the police officers with whom I have served in many different ranks and posts. I remember them all with high respect for their courage and loyalty, with gratitude for their humanity and patience in dealing with the public, and with affection for their unfailing humour. I will always hold particular memories of four courageous men. Trevor Lock and Philip Olds who are still with us, although Philip is severely disabled; and Kenneth Howorth and Frank O'Neill who gave their lives in defence of us all. I take away with me the memory of Metropolitan Police officers bravely holding the line with courage and efficiency during periods of great disorder and drama, and undertaking the equally important duties of policing by night and day the streets of London.

We all owe them more than we know.

APPENDIX I

Letter from David Lane, Chairman of the Commission for Racial Equality:

17 March 1982

re: CRIME STATISTICS

A copy of the full text of your press release and accompanying statistical tables, published on 10 March, has only reached me this week. Having read them, I am extremely concerned over the balance of the presentation and that the purpose of the colour-breakdown of 'robbery and other violent theft' does not seem to have been convincingly explained.

As you know, and as we made clear in our immediate public comments on 10 March, we are not opposed to crime statistics being analysed on a comprehensive basis and the results being published with careful explanation. From previous discussions I assume that your main purpose in making the colour-breakdown was to enlist public support, especially among the coloured community, with regard to street crime, in tackling what everyone agrees is a serious situation.

However, in the picture as it was presented, attention came to be focused almost entirely on the coloured element in 'robbery and other violent theft'; there seems to have been no clear appeal for public support and little reference to other aspects of the crime scene, including the growth of racially-motivated attacks *against* coloured people. Not surprisingly, the result was very crude reporting in some newspapers, which must have given readers the impression of a general high criminality among coloured people. I fear that the prospect of greater support from the minority communities may even have been lessened, not increased, because many will feel that publication of the statistics has been 'slanted'. The reaction of Courtney Laws in Brixton was significant.

It does appear strange, given the sensitivity of this whole subject and its relevance to race relations, that the intention to publish a partial colour-breakdown was not mentioned when some of us met Pat Kavanagh and his colleagues late last month while you were abroad, and that no one in the Commission was alerted or consulted before 10 March. I very much hope that on any such occasion in future we shall be given an opportunity of discussion with Scotland Yard before publication.

I am sending a copy of this letter to the Home Secretary.

David Lane

PS   Enclosed is the text of the comment I made on 10 March in answer to media enquiries.

My reply outlined the object of the release and gave voice to subsequent reservations as to its effect.

8 April 1982

I am replying to your letter of 17 March 1982. The sole – not simply the main – purpose of giving the figures in relation to street crime broken down by the skin colour of the assailant (as identified by the victim) was, as you suggest, to enlist public support, especially among the black community, to help us tackle a very serious problem. It was our intention to lay out the facts of a situation that was already being fuelled by rumour and extremism, in order to shed some much-needed light upon an extremely emotive and sensitive issue.

I stand by that decision since I believe, quite firmly, that if the problem of street crime and the involvement of young black people in it is to be resolved it has to be opened up to public debate. At no time, though, has it ever been suggested by the Metropolitan Police that black people are inherently more criminal than white people. Indeed Mr Kelland went out of his way to stress that the vast majority of black people are respectable, law-abiding citizens. I enclose for your information copies of Mr Kelland's opening address, his reply to Peter Burden of the *Daily Mail* and his discussion of the statistical chart relating to the offences of 'Robbery and other Violent Thefts'. You can thus see what was said as opposed to what was reported.

Nevertheless, I accept that some of the reporting of the issue has, regrettably, fostered an impression of black criminality. This was certainly not our intention since we are looking for the support of the black community, not its censure.

Some of the criticism that has been levelled at us has focused on the fact that street crime is a relatively small proportion of the overall crime figures but the issue of violent street crime really goes beyond mere numbers. It has a profound effect upon a community. It generates an atmosphere of fear and apprehension and undermines the quality of life in our inner cities. Moreover in London the fact that so many victims are identifying their attackers as black is a dimension that disrupts the social fabric yet further. It helps to generate racial hatred. Currently we may be witnessing a reflection of that in a number of incidents and attacks which have an obvious racial basis.

By exposing the facts to public debate we were hoping it would be made plain that black communities are as strongly in favour of law and order as any other section of society. Unequivocal statements demonstrating this would do a great deal to draw the teeth of those extremists who are actively opposed to racial harmony and equality.

It is apparent from some of the comment that has ensued that our aim has not been realized; at least, not to the extent we were hoping for. The issue has become blurred in the welter of criticism that has been directed at us for presenting the crime figures in the way we did. The responsibility for that presentation is mine and, as you know, it has had the support of the Home Secretary in the House, but I suspect that however the problem had been presented there would have been those who would have misinterpreted police motives — in some cases deliberately.

Interestingly, since the publication of the figures and the widespread publicity they received, it seems there have been significant decreases in street crime in some parts of London. I am having that reported effect monitored as closely as possible.

Meanwhile I hope that I can count upon your support to convince people of our good intention and thereby help us to tackle the serious problem of street crime.

David McNee

APPENDIX II

EULOGY DELIVERED BY THE COMMISSIONER AT
THE FUNERAL OF
POLICE CONSTABLE FRANCIS JOSEPH O'NEILL

'All it needs for evil to triumph
is for good men to do nothing'

Francis Joseph O'Neill was a good man. He did not stand aside. He acted. He did so in a way that characterized his police service. It was not done in pursuit of personal ambition, but in the service of others.

He was a dedicated police officer, whose quiet, determined approach to his work epitomizes all that is the strength of the police service; the unarmed constable striving selflessly to uphold the law.

On Saturday, 25 October 1980, Constable O'Neill responded to a call for assistance as he had done many times in the past. All police officers do so in the knowledge of the price which may have to be paid in a world which is becoming ever more violent. Only the few are called upon to pay the price in full.

A police officer must strive to attain a higher standard of duty, must endure a greater degree of self-sacrifice than the ordinary citizen. That is the nature of the British police service and, while it remains so, the confidence and the esteem of the public at large will be secure.

In doing his duty, in making the ultimate sacrifice, Constable O'Neill acted in the finest traditions of the police service. His actions are a testament to the ideals of our policing system, which he staunchly upheld.

At this time our thoughts are principally with the family of

Constable O'Neill. No words can adequately describe the grief that they are suffering; no words can sufficiently provide the comfort that they need.

In time,

> Out of the darkness there will be light;
> Out of the frailty there will be strength; and
> Out of the sorrow there will be happiness.

Of that I am certain.

The light, the strength and the happiness for the family will be found in the strong Christian belief that they hold; in the support given by relatives and friends; and in the knowledge that they too are part of a larger family – the police family.

The finest tribute that the Metropolitan Police can pay will be to remember his family. That we will do.

Today relatives, friends and colleagues we pay tribute to Frank.

He gave his life in pursuit of justice; in pursuit of a better life for us all.

Frank O'Neill has not died in vain. His example, his inspiration and his sacrifice will long be remembered. Certainly evil will never triumph while we have officers of his kind.

May he rest in peace.

INDEX

255